McILVANNEY

ON FOOTBALL

HUGH McILVANNEY

MAINSTREAM
PUBLISHING

First published in Great Britain in 1994 by
MAINSTREAM PUBLISHING COMPANY (EDINBURGH) LTD
7 Albany Street
Edinburgh EH1 3UG

Reprinted 1994

ISBN 1 85158 661 X

A catalogue record for this book is available from the British Library

Typeset in Sabon by Servis Filmsetting Ltd, Manchester

Printed and bound in Great Britain by
Biddles Ltd, Guildford and King's Lynn

Contents

ISSUES

WORLD CUPS

Acknowledgments

The sources from which this book is drawn are clearly indicated in the text. Here I wish to give thanks for permission to reprint, and to express my gratitude to all the colleagues and friends whose help, understanding and tolerance enabled me to produce the pieces in the first place.

In the tolerance department, I must make special mention of Bill Campbell, Peter MacKenzie and all of their staff at Mainstream, who have coped valiantly with my paranoia over the proofs. Even more remarkable has been the unfailing kindness of the Gillespie branch of my family, Alan and Elaine, and their three marvellous children, Claire, Louise and Robbie, who put up with me during the last anxious phase before publication. Elaine must feel like adapting an old Jimmy Durante line: 'Who's Hughie? My uncle. He was (and is) mad.'

Introduction

This collection of pieces about football is one of a series on several sports to be published over the next two or three years. The title echoes that of a boxing book I put together a while back and the note of presumptuousness bothers me as much now as it did then. But this was one area in which the publishers carried the heavier vote. They point out that the title is nothing more than an acknowledgment that the book is highly subjective, strictly one reporter's experience of a game which has defied endless attempts to diminish its fascination. Anyone who suspects that such an approach to titling reflects delusions of authority on the part of the author should consider the fact that a future collection in the series will deal with horse racing. Could I delude myself about my inadequacies in the betting ring? Perhaps we'll call that one 'McIlvanney on his knees' or 'McIlvanney on the rack' or 'McIlvanney on the run – pursued by men with baseball bats'.

I admit that when it comes to arguing about football I exhibit no more reticence than is likely to be found in anybody brought up in what used to be the industrial West of Scotland. Having given the world countless outstanding players and – in Stein, Busby and Shankly, not to mention the present generation of Ferguson, Smith, Dalglish and Graham – a richer crop of remarkable managers than any tiny corner of a tiny country was ever entitled to produce, we are convinced that a basic feel for the game's true values is bred in our marrow. But kinship with giants has a dual effect. It encourages pride and humility at the same time. Having listened at length to Big Jock and Sir Matt, Bill and Alex and the rest, I am never likely to imagine that my own opinions about football mean very much.

Yet, being around such men was never a belittling experience. Almost invariably they, and all the other great players and managers of many races who are celebrated in the pages that follow, have raised my spirits and deepened my attachment to what I regard as the most beautiful and exhilarating of all team games. If this book has credentials, they exist in the range of close-quarters exposure to the best and the brightest in football that 35 years of sports reporting have afforded me. Whatever you think of the name on the cover, there are a hundred inside that need only be uttered to quicken the blood and fill the mind with dramatic images.

The one claim I will make is that, notwithstanding my eagerness to be enlightened by the masters I have been fortunate enough to call friends, as a reporter I have always seen the game through my own eyes. Not so long ago such an assertion would have seemed laughable, since just about every professional in my business could say as much and expect to be believed. In recent years, however, there has emerged a breed of football journalists who appear unable to put pen to paper or fingers to Tandy until some player or manager has interpreted the action for them. They cannot function unless fuelled by quotes. You feel that if they went blind their working efficiency would be unaffected, but if they went deaf they would not have the first idea of what happened on the park. Their method is a plague, and it's spreading.

There was a point in the preparation of this book when it was in danger of being afflicted by another kind of epidemic, a nasty outbreak of afterthoughts. Given that it spans four decades, there was a powerful temptation to put some of the pieces in the context of events that occurred after they were written. It had to be resisted but resistance was less than total. The result is that, while the bulk of the material has been left to fend for itself, there have been quite a few minor interventions in italics. I hope they inform more than they annoy.

As for the production as a whole, I know it has plenty of flaws – but the quality of the cast may save it.

Period Piece

I had been reporting major football matches for some time before I covered the European Cup final at Hampden on 18 May 1960, but the occasion was a watershed for me, as it was for so many. Here was the game as we had always known it could and should be played.

The report reprinted here was written for The Scotsman *as 'a runner', which means that the copy was transmitted to the paper's Edinburgh office by Telex in short takes during the course of the match. If the ending seems abrupt and unrounded, that is because the edition was going to press. Clearly, this piece is included for its historical interest, not its literary merit.*

Real Madrid 7 Eintracht (Frankfurt) 3

ALMOST 130,000 Scottish football enthusiasts were privileged last night to see Real Madrid display the unmatchable talents that have made them the greatest club side in the history of world football.

The fact that they were engaged in winning the European Cup for the fifth successive year seemed equally inevitable and incidental, in the midst of some of the most magnificent sporting artistry Hampden Park has ever seen.

Fittingly, the great Glasgow stadium responded with the loudest and most sustained ovation it has given to non-Scottish athletes. The strange emotionalism that overcame the huge crowd as the triumphant Madrid team circled the field at the end, carrying the trophy they have monopolised since its inception, showed that they had not simply been entertained. They had been moved by the experience of seeing a sport played to its ultimate standards. Similarly, their tributes to Eintracht, a team whose quality deserved better than the role of heroic losers, contained a reverence for something Scotland cannot equal.

Scots in the ground could not conceal an awestruck appreciation of the glories that had been paraded before them. It is one thing to see the wonders of Puskas, Di Stefano, Gento, Vidal and the rest on a television screen. It is another to see them in the flesh, to hear their urgent shouts as they wreak precise devastation on an opposing defence. Last night they flaunted all that has made them incomparable. The unflagging generalship of Di Stefano, the technical perfection and breathtaking ingenuity of Puskas, the industry of Del Sol, the deadly pace of Gento, the striking directness of Canario, and behind all that the drive of Vidal and the dominating strength of Santamaria and his defence – to list the Real team is to chronicle greatness.

Eintracht will realise that they are saluted when it is said that they never ceased to be worthy opponents for the masters – creditable challengers to the undisputed champions. Some of their players, such men as Kress, Stein, Weilbaecher and Loy, rose close to the peerless level of Madrid, and the others, if less gifted, were equally gallant. The Germans, no less than their conquerors, had contributed to the healthily frenetic excitement that caused thousands of Scots to linger around Hampden long after the cheers and embraces of the presentation ceremony.

The tense expectancy of the audience emphasised the untidy, uninspired nature of play in the early minutes. But the quality of the players steadily overcame the unfamiliar peculiarities of the ground, and the Scottish spectators settled to enjoy their national game as only foreigners can play it.

Their sympathies were clearly with the German underdogs, who were already showing more bite than many had anticipated. Only one minute had gone when a swinging shot from Meier forced Dominguez to slap the ball against his cross-bar. Then Kress and Pfaff both revealed a capacity for making progress along Real's left flank.

Del Sol restored confidence in Madrid with a hypnotic exhibition of footwork which had Loy sprawling desperately at his feet, but Kress and Pfaff again stirred hopes of a miracle when they surged clear on their right wing to whip a long cross in front of Dominguez.

Twice only anxious interceptions prevented a goal before the Germans eventually claimed full reward for those right-wing assaults in the twentieth minute. Stein accelerated along the byeline and cut the ball sharply back for Kress to leap inside Santamaria and sweep it to the net from half a dozen yards.

Madrid's urgency increased visibly after that goal, and their scientific onslaught forced the Eintracht defence to yield an equalising goal in the twenty-sixth minute. Canario beat Hoefer simply on the right, and his low cross eluded everyone but Di Stefano, who was perfectly positioned to direct the ball past Loy.

Three minutes later the centre-forward's faultless positioning and alertness were again illustrated when a swerving shot from Canario spun away from the diving body of the German goalkeeper. Di Stefano covered four or five yards before any other player moved an inch, and hooked the ball over the prostrate figure of Loy to the net.

Real's superiority was now unmistakable, and the German goal had a freakish escape when a 25-yard shot from Vidal cannoned off a defender's back, and slapped against a post before being cleared.

There was no such luck to rescue Loy one minute from the interval when he fell victim to the type of goal that has become almost the hallmark of the Puskas genius. The Hungarian inside-left, taking a pass from the fluent feet of Del Sol, jockeyed for position on the byeline and from a truly incredible angle, drove the ball surely into the net directly above the Eintracht goalkeeper's head.

Lutz, who was apparently taking little comfort from the knowledge that he was opposed to the fastest forward in the world, allowed his frustration to express itself illegally from time to time, and one such lapse brought the maximum punishment in the fifty-fourth minute. The full-back pushed Gento in a race for the ball, and Mr Jack Mowat, after a discussion with a linesman, awarded a penalty.

Puskas was called upon to take the kick, and coped with the expected competence. Six minutes later he gave more striking evidence of his craftsmanship by scoring his side's fifth and his own third goal.

Gento's speed was again the preliminary factor, for the winger outstripped Lutz to cross accurately to his inside-left. Puskas merely seemed to bow acknowledgment of his colleague's excellence as he headed the ball inside Loy's right-hand post.

The Puskas mastery once more left the huge crowd stunned in the seventieth minute, when he reached back for a straying pass from Vidal, halted the ball and pivoted swiftly to put a splendid left-foot shot high into the net from 15 yards.

Within two minutes Stein shot a fine second goal for the Germans, but the achievement merely stressed that Real were outclassing a good-class team. As if to underline the point further, Di Stefano ran through almost immediately, sending several defenders moving in an unprofitable direction, while he steered the ball along the most rewarding route of all – to the net.

A quarter of an hour from the end Vidal made one of his very few errors in misplacing a pass to his goalkeeper, and Stein jumped in to take a third goal for Eintracht.

THE BIG MAN AND OTHER GIANTS

Some of the men written about in this section have meant so much to me, professionally and personally, that they are absolutely central to my feelings about football. Four of the greatest (Stein, Busby, Shankly and Moore) are dead, but every time I see the game played well the pleasure I take in it is increased by something of what they imparted to me. Football, like everything else, comes down in the end to the quality of the people identified with it. The game can count itself lucky that it had the commitment of the calibre of men who figure in the pages ahead.

Immortality for Celtic's big man

(*The Observer*, 28 May 1967)

TODAY LISBON is almost, but not quite, back in Portuguese hands at the end of the most hysterically exuberant occupation any city has ever known.

Pockets of Celtic supporters are holding out in unlikely corners, noisily defending their own carnival atmosphere against the returning tide of normality, determined to preserve the moment, to make the party go on and on. They emerge with a sudden burst of Glasgow accents from taxis or cafés, or let their voices carry with an irresistible aggregate of decibels across hotel lounges. Always, even among the refugees who turn up at the British Embassy bereft of everything but the rumpled clothes they stand in, the talk is of that magical hour-and-a-half under the hot sun on Thursday in the breathtaking tree-fringed amphitheatre of the national stadium.

At the airport, the impression is of a Dunkirk with happiness. The discomforts of mass evacuation are tolerable when your team have just won the greatest victory yet achieved by a British football club, and completed a clean sweep of the trophies available to them that has never been equalled anywhere in the world. They even cheered Helenio Herrera and his shattered Inter when the Italians left for Milan yesterday evening. 'Inter, Inter, Inter.' The chant resounded convincingly through the departure lounge, but no one was misled. In that mood, overflowing with conquerors' magnanimity, they might have given Scot Symon a round of applause.

Typically, within a minute the same happily dishevelled groups were singing: 'Ee Aye Addio, Herrera's on the Buroo.' The suggestion that the most highly paid manager in Europe is likely to be queueing at the Labour Exchange is rather wild but the comment emphasised that even the least analytical fan had seen through the hectic excitement of a unique performance to the essential meaning of the event. *Mundo Desportivo* of Lisbon put it another way: 'It was inevitable. Sooner or later the Inter of Herrera, the Inter of *catenaccio*, of negative football, of marginal victories, had to pay for their refusal to play entertaining football.' The Portuguese rejoiced over the magnificent style in which Celtic had taken retribution on behalf of the entire game.

A few of us condemned Herrera unequivocally two years ago after

Inter had won the European Cup at their own San Siro Stadium by defending with neurotic caution to protect a luckily gained one-goal lead against a Benfica side with only nine fit men. But he continued to receive around £30,000 a year for stifling the flair, imagination, boldness and spontaneity that make football what it is. And he was still held in awe by people who felt that the statistics of his record justified the sterility of his methods. Now, however, nearly everyone appreciates the dangers of his influence. The twelfth European Cup final showed how shabbily his philosophy compares with the dynamically positive thinking of Jock Stein. Before the match Stein told me: 'Inter will play it defensively. That's their way and it's their business. But we feel we have a duty to play the game our way, and our way is to attack. Win or lose, we want to make the game worth remembering. Just to be involved in an occasion like this is a tremendous honour and we think it puts an obligation on us. We can be as hard and professional as anybody, but I mean it when I say we don't just want to win this cup. We want to win it playing good football, to make neutrals glad we've done it, glad to remember how we did it.'

The effects of such thinking, and of Stein's genius for giving it practical expression, were there for all the football world to see on Thursday. Of course, he has wonderful players, a team without a serious weakness and with tremendous strengths in vital positions. But when one had eulogised the exhilarating speed and the bewildering variety of skills that destroyed Inter – the unshakable assurance of Clark, the murderously swift overlapping of the full-backs, the creative energy of Auld in midfield, the endlessly astonishing virtuosity of Johnstone, the intelligent and ceaseless running of Chalmers – even with all this, ultimately the element that impressed most profoundly was the massive heart of this Celtic side. Nothing symbolised it more vividly than the incredible display of Gemmell. He was almost on his knees with fatigue before scoring that thunderous equaliser in the 63rd minute but somehow his courage forced him to go on dredging up the strength to continue with the exhausting runs along the left-wing that did more than any other single factor to demoralise Inter.

Gemmell has the same aggressive pride, the same contempt for any thought of defeat, that emanates from Auld. Before the game Auld cut short a discussion about the possible ill-effects of the heat and the firm ground with a blunt declaration that they would lick the Italians in any conditions. When he had been rescued from the delirious crowd and was walking back to the dressing-rooms after Celtic had overcome all the bad breaks to vindicate his confidence, Auld – naked to the waist except for an Inter shirt knotted round his neck like a scarf – suddenly stopped in his tracks and shouted to Ronnie Simpson, who was walking ahead: 'Hey, Ronnie Simpson! What are we? What are we, son?' He stood there sweating, showing his white teeth between parched lips flecked with saliva. Then he answered his own question with a belligerent roar. 'We're the greatest. That's what we are. The greatest.' Simpson came running back and they embraced for a full minute.

In the dressing-room, as the other players unashamedly sang their supporters' songs in the showers and drank champagne from the huge Cup ('Have you had a bevy out of this?'), Auld leaned forward to Sean Fallon, the trainer, and asked with mock seriousness: 'Would you say I was the best? Was I your best man?'

'They've all got Stein's heart,' said a Glasgow colleague. 'There's a bit of the big man in all of them.'

Certainly the preparation for this final and the winning of it were impregnated with Stein's personality. Whether warning the players against exposing themselves to the sun ('I don't even want you near the windows in your rooms. If there's as much as a freckle on any man's arm he's for home.') or joking with reporters beside the hotel swimming-pool in Estoril, his was the all-pervading influence.

Despite the extreme tension he must have felt, he never lost the bantering humour that keeps the morale of his expeditions unfailingly high. The impact of the Celtic invasion on the local Catholic churches was a rewarding theme for him. 'They're getting some gates since we came. The nine o'clock and ten o'clock Masses were all-ticket. They've had to get extra plates. How do they divide the takings here? Is it fifty-fifty or in favour of the home club?'

It was hard work appearing so relaxed and the effort eventually took its toll of Stein when he made a dive for the dressing-rooms a minute before the end of the game, unable to stand any more. When we reached him there, he kept muttering: 'What a performance. What a performance.' It was left to Bill Shankly, the Scottish manager of Liverpool (and the only English club manager present), to supply the summing-up quote. 'John,' Shankly said with the solemnity of a man to whom football is a religion, 'you're immortal.'

An elderly Portuguese official cornered Stein and delivered ecstatic praise of Celtic's adventurous approach. 'This attacking play, this is the real meaning of football. This is the true game.' Stein slapped him on the shoulder. 'Go on, I could listen to you all night.' Then, turning to the rest of us, 'Fancy anybody saying that about a Scottish team.'

There is good reason to hope that people will say such things about Scottish and English clubs with increasing frequency in the near future. Now that the Continental monopoly of the European Cup has been broken, British football is poised for a period of domination. Glasgow Rangers can strike the next blow when they meet Bayern Munich in the final of the European Cup for Cup Winners at Nurnberg next Wednesday. Scot Symon has rebuilt his Rangers team with patient thoroughness this season, and their thrilling draw with Celtic at Ibrox three weeks ago confirmed how far they have come. Spurred by their great rivals' achievement, they will not be easily denied.

Continental clubs can expect no respite next season when the powerful challenge from Scotland will be backed by the presence of Manchester United and Tottenham Hotspur in the two major competitions. It seems unlikely that anything short of the personal intervention of de Gaulle can prevent us from being in among the European prizes again.

Hero worshipped by his people

(*The Observer*, 15 September 1985)

THE LARCENOUS nature of death, its habit of breaking in on us when we are least prepared and stealing the irreplaceable, has seldom been more sickeningly experienced than at Ninian Park in Cardiff on Tuesday night.

Those of us who crowded sweatily into the small entrance hall of the main stand to wait for word of Jock Stein's condition will always remember the long half hour in which the understandable vagueness of reports filtering from the dressing-room area lulled us into believing that Jock was going to make it through yet another crisis. The raw dread that had been spread among us by his collapse on the touchline at the end of the Wales–Scotland World Cup match gave way to the more bearable gloom of acknowledging that the career of one of the greatest managers football has known would have to be ended by immediate retirement.

Then – off in a corner of that confused room – Mike England, the manager of Wales and a deeply concerned first-hand witness of what had been happening to Stein, was heard to say that he was still 'very, very poorly'. There was no mistaking the true meaning of those words and suddenly the sense of relief that had been infiltrating our anxieties was exposed as baseless. We felt almost guilty about having allowed ourselves to be comforted by rumours. Then, abruptly, we knew for sure that the Big Man was dead and for some of us it was indeed as if our spirits, our very lives, had been burglarised.

Of all the reactions to Stein's death, none meant more than that of the thousands of Scotland's travelling supporters who learned of it haphazardly but with eerie swiftness as they got ready to celebrate a ragged draw against Wales that should guarantee their team a passage to the World Cup finals in Mexico next summer. They are, given half an excuse, the most raucously exuberant fans in the game but as midnight neared in Cardiff on Tuesday they wandered through the streets in subdued clusters, sustaining the unforced atmosphere of mourning that pervaded the hundreds who waited silently in the darkness outside Ninian Park after the last hope of reviving the stricken man inside had been abandoned.

There is no doubt that the Scots have a highly developed capacity for the elegiac mood, especially when there is a bottle about, but what was to be encountered in South Wales last week was no cheap example of the genre. When travel-soiled units of the tartan expeditionary force interrupted their morose drinking to propose toasts to the lost leader, anybody cynical enough to see such behaviour as just another maudlin ritual doesn't know much about the way the power of Jock Stein's nature communicated itself to millions of ordinary people.

His achievements in football were monumental but they can only partially explain his impact upon and relevance to so many lives. Perhaps he was cherished simply because he was a true working-class hero – and that is a species which is disappearing almost as fast in industrial Scotland as elsewhere, if only because the values that governed its creation are being relentlessly eroded day by day. Even the common misery of unemployment has not halted the fragmentation of a sense of community that once seemed indestructible.

In an age when, if I may quote a line from my brother William's latest novel, it is as if 'every man and his family were a private company', Stein was the unpretentious embodiment of that older, better code that was until not so long ago the compensatory inheritance of all who were born of the labouring poor. No one was ever likely to mistake him for a saint, or even for a repository of bland altruism. He could look after himself and his own in the market place or anywhere else, but there was never the remotest danger that he would be contaminated by the materialism that engulfs so many of those who find prosperity through sport or other forms of entertainment.

These days it is hard to avoid having the eardrums battered by some unlikely pillar of the New Right who – having persuaded himself that a largely fortuitous ability to kick a football or volley a tennis ball or belt out a pop song or tell a few jokes more acceptably than the next man is actually evidence of his own splendid mastery of his fate – insists that the dole queues would fade away overnight if people got off their arses, got on their bikes and showed the enterprise that has carried him to what he imagines is glory. Stein's whole life was a repudiation of such garbage.

He was utterly Scottish, utterly Lanarkshire in fact, but his was the kind of loyalty to his roots that made his principles universal. His father was a miner who was a miner's son and Stein himself worked underground until turning belatedly to full-time professional football at the age of 27. During a long, incalculably rewarding friendship with him, I heard him say many memorable things and some of the most vivid were inevitably about the game he loved and the great practitioners of it, but he was most moved and most moving when he talked of that earlier phase of his working experience.

There was a dynamic, combative quality to most of his conversation (mischievous wind-up was a favourite mode and, though he did not drink alcohol, he occasionally dipped his barbs in curare) but when the subject was mining and miners a tone of wistful reverie invaded his voice. 'I went down the pit when I was 16 (at first I was working with ponies – it was still that era) and when I left 11 years later I knew that wherever I went, whatever work I did, I'd never be alongside better men. They didn't just get their own work done and go away. They all stayed around until every man had finished what he had to do and everything was cleared up. Of course, in the bad or dangerous times that was even more true. It was a place where phoneys and cheats couldn't survive for long.

'Down there for eight hours you're away from God's fresh air and sunshine and there's nothing that can compensate for that. There's nothing as dark as the darkness down a pit, the blackness that closes in on you if your lamp goes out. You'd think you would see some kind of shapes but you can see nothing, nothing but the inside of your head. I think everybody should go down the pit at least once to learn what darkness is.'

Phoneys and cheats did not flourish ·in his company during four decades of involvement with senior football. As a player he was shrewd, well organised and strong rather than outstandingly gifted, though he made a fundamental contribution to the rich streak of prize-winning enjoyed by the Celtic team he joined unexpectedly for a fee of £1,200 after modest seasons with Albion Rovers and a motley troupe of non-league men at Llanelli in South Wales. He became an influential captain of Celtic and when his playing career was ended by an injury to his right ankle that left him with a noticeable limp for the rest of his days, it was clear that he would make a manager.

His old employers were certain to be impressed by his successful introduction to the trade in charge of Dunfermline, for he gave that humble club the Scottish Cup by beating Celtic in the final tie, and after a further rehearsal period with Hibernian he went back to Parkhead as manager in 1964. It was a genuinely historic return, perhaps the most significant single happening in the entire story of Scottish football.

All of Stein's family associations, centred on the Lanarkshire villages of Blantyre and Burnbank, were vehemently Protestant but he had never hesitated for a second over first identifying himself with a club traditionally seen as carrying the banner for the Catholic minority in Glasgow (and throughout Scotland) and when he emerged as Celtic's first non-Catholic manager he became a living, eloquent rebuke to the generations of bigotry surrounding the Rangers–Celtic rivalry.

Under him, Celtic dominated the whole range of Scottish domestic competitions to a degree that stamped him, in his context, as the supreme achiever among the world's football managers. Nine League championships in a row is in itself a record no one can ever hope to equal but it was the triumphant lifting of the European Cup in Lisbon in 1967, a feat that had previously proved beyond the most powerful British clubs, that set him totally apart in the annals of the sport. That other legendary Scot Bill Shankly got it just about right when he held out a fellow miner's hand to Stein after the brilliant defeat of Inter-Milan and said in his coal-cutter voice: 'John – you're immortal.'

Celtic in Lisbon performed with irresistible verve, representing perfectly Stein's ideal of blending athletic speed and competitiveness with imagination, delicacy of touch at close quarters and exhilarating surges of virtuosity. Of course, when all Stein's technical assets had been assessed – the vast tactical awareness that owed nothing to coaching courses, the precise judgment of his own and opposing players, the encyclopaedic retention of detail, the emphasis on the positive while eradicating the foolhardy – the essence of his gifts as a manager was seen to reside in something more basic and more subtle: in his capacity to make men do for him more than they would have been able to do for themselves.

Stein's allegiance to Celtic withstood more than one attempt to coax him to switch dramatically to the manager's chair at Rangers and it was sad that when his connection at Parkhead was eventually severed in 1978 he should leave with a justified feeling of grievance about how he had ultimately been treated. By that time he had survived a warning skirmish with heart trouble and a car crash that almost killed him in the summer of 1975. Many men would have throttled down there and then but he had been a compulsive worker around football most of his life and when the manager's job at Leeds United was offered he decided, at the age of 55, to move south.

However, two months later he received the call millions of admirers believed he should have had years before and was given control of the Scotland team. He took them to the World Cup finals in Spain in 1982 (the Soviet Union kept them out of the last 12 on goal difference) and after a match last Tuesday notable for its tensions and controversies, never for its quality, he had the result required to open a way to the finals of 1986. But suddenly the strains that had been mounting mercilessly over the years, strains whose ravages the obsessive in him insisted on belittling, proved too much for a system weakened by that earlier illness and, most crucially, by the desperate car crash of 10 years ago.

The pain of his death from a heart attack dug deepest into his wife Jean and into Rae and George, the attractive, strong-minded daughter and son of whom he was so proud. But there were many others in many places who felt last week that they did not have to go down a pit to know what real darkness was.

Passing of a special man

(*The Observer*, 5 September 1976)

AN IRREPLACEABLE bit of Glasgow was chipped away last week and British sports-writing lost more than it can afford to lose. John Rafferty died on Friday at the age of 64 after a struggle against cancer that was prolonged by a characteristic refusal to let his spirit deteriorate along with his body.

All those readers who sought Rafferty's company on weekdays in the pages of *The Scotsman* and on Sundays in *The Observer* have been deprived of one of the wisest and most entertaining voices in sport, a voice whose whisper was worth more than the shouts of most other writers; one that talked plainly about complicated things, that was equally at home using the mordant wit of his native city to amuse his audience or to slaughter the overblown arguments of opponents. It was, above all, a clear voice, ambiguous only when it was meant to be, when the tongue was in the cheek.

It's gone now and his readers cannot expect to find another like it. Many of them, in Scotland especially, had come to feel that they had a personal relationship with Rafferty. That feeling was strengthened by the relaxed, conversational style he favoured in his frequent broadcasts on radio and television. He had an appearance that fitted the weight of his personality, with powerful shoulders and a large, youthful face dominated by a humorous mouth and eyes whose intelligence would have been visible through a blindfold.

He was mistaken occasionally for Jock Stein, the great manager of Celtic Football Club, and, as it happened, there was more than physical likeness to connect the two men. Like Stein, he enjoyed employing his mental sharpness in the making of mischievous fun. They were worthy adversaries at the game. You could have sold tickets for some of their amiable collisions.

Rafferty's journalism was direct and – though he had so little time for coarseness that he was never heard swearing unless he was obliged to quote someone else – its overriding concern with the people rather than the technicalities of sport gave it a natural earthiness. He was at once moral and worldly, as befitted the product of a spirited, close-knit Irish Catholic family raised in Anderston when it was a dock-side area of Glasgow. (The Archbishop of Glasgow was a visitor during the last illness and he was no less welcome because he arrived with a bottle of Courvoisier under his arm.)

Having made it through university, reading science, John Rafferty was a schoolmaster for a time and he was doing that job when he first began to make a mark as a part-time journalist. His work for newspapers was so distinguished that he came under a great deal of benevolent pressure to give up teaching and concentrate on writing. When he did that it was inevitable that he should specialise in sport, in which he had taken an active interest all his life. His reporting in other fields (coverage of the Aberfan disaster and the massacre of the Israeli athletes at Munich, for example) was often brilliant but he will be best remembered for the sustained quality of his sports writing.

There was little he did not know about football but perhaps his greatest strength was a true feeling for the hardest game of all: boxing. The Anderston club was, in its day, a major nursery of boxing in Scotland and it was as trainer to one of that club's greatest prodigies, Jackie Paterson, that Rafferty absorbed the essence of the strange, brutal poetry that runs through the experience of the professional fighter.

Paterson was a southpaw and at his zenith as the fly-weight champion of the world was one of the hardest punchers, pound for pound, that British boxing has seen. But his career was a hellish war against weight. He walked the streets at 9st 4lb and was fit enough at that weight. Yet he fought at 8st and so had to shed 18lb in an agony of thirsting and sweating, before he went into the ring.

When Paterson was killed in a drunken brawl in South Africa in 1966, dying penniless and psychologically wrecked, John Rafferty wrote a long piece in *The Observer* that was the truest and most moving account of a fighter's life ever to appear in a British newspaper. This brief extract cannot represent that article adequately, but it has the ring of truth that characterised the whole piece:–

The night before the Rinty Monaghan fight was one of such torture that it must have affected the soundest mind. Paterson had trained hard for over a month. He had wasted dreadfully. It was plane time and he was completely dried up; his body was on fire calling for water; his mind was racked and he was five-and-a-half pounds heavy. We disappeared.

He was so helpless and worried and tortured, but there was one hopeful sign. A bottle of lemonade lay near him but he had not rushed to open it. How he thirsted! Pat Collins and I got him involved in a game of gin rummy. We threw him a few cards, he won a few games. Soon he was about seven shillings in front. He felt good then; he was winning; he was the champion again.

He reached across the table and poked me in the chest. 'You think I'm yellow,' he said.

'I think nothing except that I'm losing a few bob.'

'You think I can make the weight but I haven't got the guts to try,' he persisted.

'Will you deal the cards?'

He got to his feet, pushed the table aside and grabbed my arms. 'Come downstairs and I'll show you how wrong you are. I'll show you I can't make the weight.'

Soon the fire was blazing, the training woollens were on. He wanted a scrambled egg. 'I can't work without food,' he said. In that heated basement he squeezed five and a half pounds of sweat from a shrivelled body. It was a monumental effort. He made eight stone showing us that he could not.

The kind of life John Rafferty had led made him a cool hand in awkward situations. There was a time when the two of us found ourselves in the company of a huge South African journalist who appeared to be moving towards volcanic violence.

'John, what do we do if this man goes over the edge?' I asked him. Rafferty's reply came without pause. 'It's a Gulliver job,' he said. 'Three men to a leg.'

My own relationship with that special man went far beyond the professional. I was allowed to impose myself on John and his wife, Ruby, without warning or limits and going into their flat on the south side of Glasgow was much the same as going home. He was, among other things, one of the very few people my mother trusted to save this ageing problem child from the deserved consequence of his folly. 'As long as you are with Mr Rafferty,' she would say, 'I know you are all right.'

My mother is not a bad judge. Somehow, after last Friday, I don't think I will ever be quite as all right again.

Motivation!

(*The Observer*, 18 November 1975)

IT'S NOT TOO EASY to motivate Brian Clough to talk about motivation. He is healthily suspicious of the word and the fatuous accretions that debase its use in modern football.

'I'd want to be number one in my industry for management rather than just motivation,' he said last week. 'I couldn't motivate a bee to sting you if it didn't have the equipment. I couldn't motivate a snake to bite you if it didn't have the teeth. You can only bring out of people what they are capable of giving. Two of the great myths circulating now are that Heinz's beans are the best and that I can get more out of men than they have inside them.

'If we all learnt our jobs and lived our lives on the basis that you can't get blood out of a stone we'd be a hell of a sight better off in every way. One of the worst crimes you can commit in life, not just in football but in life, is to ask people to deliver something they haven't got. That destroys them totally.'

Beyond the windows was the cold, damp murk of Nottingham, a town for which November does no favours, but inside a well-lit room at the Forest ground Clough was profligate with his warmth and brightness. His capacity to glow was not diminished by a yellow sweater that made him as vivid as a goalkeeper on a cigarette card, or by the couple of brandies he had taken as antidote to the chilly exposure of a tree planting ceremony he had just performed. At such times he has charm to burn.

This was not the Clough conveyed to an awed if admiring public by television. On the box he comes across as a man of relentless, sometimes grinding loquacity, with an ego as persistent as Ali's left jab. When he casts himself in that role what makes his audiences want to listen to him is his tendency to be right far more often than he is wrong, in short his record – that and a well-practised genius for the outrageous.

His record as a manager (following a career as an outstanding goal-scorer) has a whiff of alchemy about it. The greatest achievements of his 14-year partnership with Peter Taylor have been in the Midlands, where they took Derby from the Second Division to win the championship of the First, then did the same at Nottingham Forest, adding an unbelievable bonus there by winning the League Cup in successive years (the hat-trick is still on) and, at the end of last season, claiming the supreme prize of the European Cup.

If he had been involved with the Salem and District League he would have been incinerated as a witch or, at best, as a heretic. In that bright room at the City Ground he sounded like neither, more like someone with a deep understanding of the simple, frequently obscured essences of football, an inspired feel for how it works and, above all, a fierce zest for the game and the special habitat it has created for him.

'I was up early today,' he said, 'and I saw guys walking past my window in the rain with duffel coats on. That put me in a good frame of mind because I don't want to be walking in the rain with a duffel coat. I came in here soon after nine and met pleasant young men who wanted to be doing their job. I was out on the track with them, then came back into a warm office and then went off to plant two trees in the Meadows area of the town. Somebody had asked me to do that and what could be a more satisfying finish to the morning I've had?

'Apart from all the dogs that will be able to piss up against them, a lot of people will get pleasure from those trees. They'll help us to breathe, make our lives a little better.'

It is perhaps Clough's concern with a quality of life at a football club, as much as the tangible successes he and Taylor bring with them, that gives their teams such a powerful sense of integration. 'When all of us who are here now came together we had one thing in common – disenchantment. Some, like me, were out of work, some were in work and didn't like what they were doing, others were beginning to wonder what they were being paid for. All that has changed because we made it change. Now we are fulfilling what we think the game has to offer. It's not a crime not to want to let that go.

'When you come to terms with yourselves you realise you are not going to be Einsteins, that you are not going to be Presidents of the United States. And you look around yourself and see so few things that are right in the world. The Labour Party isn't what we'd like it to be. You've got to wonder about the credibility of Edward Kennedy as a man to be in the White House.

'Then you look at what we've got here and you're grateful that in our own little fraction of the world we've got it just about right. It may not mean much to people outside but we want to hang on to it. Our lads don't want to get off this bandwagon. We've got no habits that we particularly want to kick. We don't smoke, some of us might booze a little bit, but all in all we don't think the values around this place are too bad.'

Clough unhesitatingly gives much of the credit for establishing the technical football values to Peter Taylor. 'Peter looks for and identifies the ability to play a ball, to get a ball, to hold a ball, the ability to fit into a side. Once he is convinced individuals have such talent, I can persuade them to deliver it and I can persuade them to deliver it a second time when they are knackered.

'People get mixed up about themselves, they become bad judges of what they have to offer. I try to show them what they are really capable of and help them to give it. You tell me I often give the impression of bullying, even belittling players. I'd have to say that sometimes that's true, though it's just as true that I belittle myself, bully myself and laugh at myself. It's no secret that I'm conceited on certain aspects of life but with others I'm totally embarrassed. I try to be truthful about myself and I think the only way to get the best out of footballers, out of anyone, is to start with the truth. You point out everything that life has to offer and every single thing they might want to run away and hide from. All of us have certain areas of our lives and characters that we're uncomfortable with and we're not too happy to discuss.

'Take John Robertson. I had to overcome a barrier with him. He's a little fat lad. When you come down to it, that's a good description. He's a little fat lad. But once you've got him to accept that, you can go on to say that he is one of the best deliverers of a ball in the game today and therefore a lad who can do great things on the park. But there is no way he is going to get the most out of that fact unless he accepts the other.

'Sometimes these basic truths are told nastily, almost brutally, and sometimes they involve belittling, but that is something I'll have to work on, something I'd like to improve. I'll have to be more explicit. If you seem to be belittling people, however good your ultimate motives may be, there is a danger that they think you will have ceased to be loyal to them. I never want players to feel that about me. I want them to feel that whatever has to be faced, good or bad, they won't be facing it alone. I attack their pride initially but at the end of the day they have more pride than they ever thought existed.

'There was a big fuss because I was reported as saying that Trevor Francis was a c . . . I was trying to explain that he was a c . . . to himself, that he was a lad of great abilities who was selling himself short. There are enough mediocre people in this world to last us for the rest of mankind's history without people who have ability selling themselves short.

'There is no bigger exasperation than when you're in charge of 10 people or 10,000 and you know they are not doing themselves justice. It's a double exasperation because they have failed to realise what they have and because you have failed to teach them. That lesson is about pride, of course, but you can't teach players to be proud on the field if they are not proud when they walk off it. There must be pride in themselves first and then pride in what they do.'

Mention of the Francis incident brought to mind a story of how Clough had, in the company of pressmen, called to Peter Shilton, who is widely regarded as the finest goalkeeper in the world, and given him peremptory instructions to pour some drinks. The recalling of that tale occasioned no dismay.

'We are a small family circle and we have the best democracy here that you will find in any football club. No one is above doing something for somebody else. If on a lot of occasions I pour a glass of champagne for Peter Shilton and take it over to him, then he shouldn't mind looking after me now and again. I think it's his job to get the drinks if other people are occupied, or to put it more accurately, it's just good manners. We believe in everybody's rights and everybody's obligations here. I'm sure Peter Shilton hasn't reached the stage where he thinks he is above the standards of good manners I would ask of my own family. And let me tell you, when he poured the drinks he did it like a guy who had been at it for 20 years. He didn't spill or drop a thing.'

As he spoke that last sentence, the fresh-complexioned, mobile face yielded entirely to the mischief that is always threatening to take it over and the flat, elongated sounds of his north-east Yorkshire accent added wryness to the joke. He is more fun than the public at large is liable to appreciate. Talking of the possibility that he would sign Peter Ward from Brighton, he elaborated with mock horror on the hazards of life in the South Coast resort, where he had a fleeting experience as manager.

'They say young Ward hasn't been doing it at Brighton but people don't know what that place is like. It's the show-business bit personified. They're all there. How could you expect a lad like Ward not to be unsettled by moving from Burton-on-Trent to Brighton, from the smell of the brewery to the smell of the grease paint? He's liable to have found himself sitting on the same train as Sir Laurence Olivier.

'In the short time Peter Taylor and I were at Brighton we had two main problems. First, the players couldn't play and, second, they had been seduced by their environment into believing they were stars. That combination is bloody dynamite. We got out quick.'

An even more brief and vastly different episode saw him spend 44 days at Leeds, run into a players' revolt and leave with enough money to make him financially secure. 'Those senior players, if you were writing a play you'd have to call them the villains of the piece – fellas like Giles, Bremner, Hunter, Madeley, Lorimer – they sold themselves short. They turned out to be very sensitive about criticisms and home truths. I had thrown a few barbs at them over the years and I meant every one, but I thought the slate would be wiped clean on both sides. How could I know they would be so sensitive? They hadn't conveyed much sensitivity on the field. I thought that was something Don had erased from their lives.

'What is sure is that I'm a better manager because of what happened at Leeds. I don't have to worry about the money now. I don't have to worry about one little twerp on a board having the power to rule my life. That makes me a better manager.

'My attitude to players may have changed a bit. I'll always demand their respect just as I am prepared to respect them. Early doors it was vital to me that they liked me, too. But I became so attached to them as players that when I left Derby I found I liked them more than they liked me. So the liking business recedes with every year of cynical life that wraps itself around me inside and outside of football.

'Still, you can't help feeling something very special for them. When young Tony Woodcock was in his real dilemma this week about whether to stay with us or go to Cologne all I felt like doing was putting my arm around him. Half-an-hour earlier I had felt like strangling him but when I saw how confused he was I wanted to reach out to him as if he had been one of my own two boys or my daughter. That's not meant to be patronising, I just felt for the lad.'

At 44, Clough sees his wife Barbara and his family as the central strength of his life, offering a balance against his obsession with football. It is an extension of an earlier family experience in the Clough home in Middlesbrough.

The Cloughs are still close and two of his five brothers went with him on a recent European Cup expedition to Romania. One of them succinctly rationalised Brian's habit of carrying a squash racket with him almost everywhere he goes. 'I see you've got your dummy,' said Bill. 'You seem to need that thing the way a baby needs a dummy.'

He needs football far more. 'Alternatives? Not a clue. It's a nightmare that rises up after defeat, when I'm on the floor and the job appears more demanding than I can cope with, when I think everybody is against me, when I'm in my really stupid moments. Then I realise again that the alternative to getting out of bed is staying in bed, the alternative to eating is not eating, the alternative to breathing is not breathing, the alternative to management – well, I haven't found it yet. Sometimes I wish I could.'

Anyone who wants Brian Clough to find that alternative must have an abiding hatred of the game of football.

A *man with more than education*

(*The Observer*, 4 October 1981)

OPPONENTS OF Liverpool Football Club would be rash to assume that they have done with Bill Shankly. Once Bill's ashes have been scattered on the pitch at Anfield any visiting forward who is setting himself to score an important goal is liable to find suddenly that he has something in his eye.

Certainly Shanks would want us to believe in the possibility. Even after the results were in the paper, showing a scoreline against his men, he always refused to give defeat houseroom. Maybe we should follow his example and regard his death as just an ugly rumour.

To those who knew him well his loss is about as sore as any could be. But there is some easing of the grief in the knowledge that few men ever had such a capacity for warming and delighting their fellows without being physically in their company. For many of us he really will always be there.

Most of the thousand and one anecdotes, the tales of his doings and his utterances, are distorted and diminished in the telling but he communicated such a strong sense of himself that enough of what was unique and marvellous about him is bound to survive. Nearly everyone connected with British football has tried at one time or another to impersonate the accent and the mannerisms he brought out of the South Ayrshire coalfield as a teenager and guarded against even the tiniest erosion through half a century in England. Few of the impersonators get within touching distance of the reality but nobody minds. The Shankly legend is the living, genuine article and the smallest fragment of it can spread laughter in any group of football people.

Clearly, however, he needed far more than earthy, utterly original wit to make the impact he did. His unshakable attachment to the ordinary supporters of football ('I'm a people's man – only the people matter') was a big help but his real strength was, perhaps, drawn from something even more unusual. With his drill-sergeant's hairstyle, his boxer's stance and his staccato, hard-man's delivery he did not fit everybody's idea of a romantic. But that's what he was, an out-and-out, 22-carat example of the species. His secret was that he sensed deep down that the only practical approach to sport is the romantic one. How else could a manager persuade grown men that they could glory in a boy's game? Shankly did that and more.

Looking into the faces of some of his outstanding former players in the last few days, men like Ian St John and Ronnie Yeats and Kevin Keegan, we could see how much they felt they owed to the Boss. He gave them more than a share in trophies, nothing less than a wonderful dream. He fed it into their spirits by many means; by humour, dedicated example and that romanticism that insisted on talking defeats away as if they were fleeting embarrassments that a malevolent and dishonest fate had inflicted on his teams without regard to their true worth. His performances in that line were like those of a witch doctor, full of blind faith and incantations. They worked so well that his players never allowed defeat to become a habit.

Of course, he had learned plenty about the nuts and bolts of the game in his long career as a player with Carlisle, Preston (where he developed a bottomless admiration for Tommy – never Tom – Finney) and Scotland, and his management years at Carlisle, Grimsby, Workington, Huddersfield (where he had a brief, memorable alliance with the young Denis Law) and from 1959 at Liverpool.

His Liverpool won the Second Division championship in 1962 by eight points and by the time he retired prematurely in 1974 they had taken the League title three times, the FA Cup twice and the UEFA Cup once. It is no diminution of the splendid manager who succeeded him, Bob Paisley, to say that Shankly left behind a foundation that contributed hugely to the subsequent domination of Europe by the club.

He also left behind a great deal of himself and the pathos of his self-precipitated conversion into a peripheral, haunting and sometimes embittered figure at Anfield was painful to his friends. But he was never reduced in the eyes of those who knew him best. No manager gave more to the spirit of a city or the folklore of a game than he did.

'Me havin' no education,' I once heard him say, 'I had to use my brains.' He used his heart, too. It was as big as a town.

Everybody's favourites again

(*The Observer*, 14 February 1982)

THOSE WHO BLUFF and swank their way through careers in football (and they show a marked reluctance to become an endangered species) should turn a corner and keep walking if they see Bob Paisley up ahead.

The mere presence of the Liverpool manager has a shrivelling effect on mountebanks, however personable. His own authority about the game has grown like a tree during more than 40 years at Anfield, and if the acquired wisdom is passed on too obliquely for some tastes, often through muttered, unfinished asides in the idiom and accent of the coalfields of north-eastern England, its substance is unmistakable to anyone who listens carefully enough. It has been even more tangible lately to the footballers who have faced his Liverpool teams on the field, where a resurgence closely identified with the inspired introduction of fresh talent has produced some of the most thrilling aggression seen in the British game for several seasons.

After faltering miserably, at least by their standards, in the last weeks of 1981 and inviting premature condolences over what many took to be a long-term decline, they have found so much conviction since the turn of the year that when they went to Stamford Bridge in the FA Cup yesterday they were the bookmakers' favourites for that competition and for the First Division Championship, the League Cup and the European Cup as well.

In the 11 matches before the Chelsea tie they took nine victories, moved to within grappling distance of the League leadership, won through to next month's League Cup final at Wembley and scored 30 goals while losing only four. By the middle of last week Bob Paisley was, in short, back in the old routine. And he was, needless to say, reacting in the old unextravagant way.

None of the mountainous successes he has achieved since inheriting the great club from the great Bill Shankly, not even an extraordinary treble in the European Cup, has disturbed the solidity of Paisley's nature. His feeling for the game is too deep for him ever to be immune to its romance, but he likes to steady the pulses of those around him with talk of practicalities. He insists that the champagne and caviare will come within reach only if you get the bread and butter values right. So at Anfield his voice is often the most downbeat on the premises.

It was certainly like that in his office on Wednesday morning as he looked back on the second leg of the League Cup semi-final with Ipswich, a match in which his men scored twice to take their aggregate lead to 4–0 and then lost two goals to finish with a comfortably gained place in the final but an unsatisfactory draw on the night. When charged with slackening concentration the players could plead extenuating circumstances but Paisley wasn't likely to be deeply moved by their case.

'After Kenny Dalglish scored our fourth goal there was a testimonial atmosphere about the whole thing and I detest that,' he said. 'I know the supporters are entitled to be happy when things are going well and we want that. But the players can't allow the complacency to creep on to the field. Quite a few of our fellas did. "Brucie's goin' to Wembley," the crowd were singin'. Brucie had gone to the bloody pictures at the end of the game.'

That specific criticism of his Zimbabwean goalkeeper, Bruce Grobbelaar, for some aberrations late in the evening should not obscure Paisley's firm belief that experience will add sensible restraint and positional soundness to Grobbelaar's boldness, speed of reflex and spectacular agility. The manager acknowledges that he had not legislated for the suddenness of Ray Clemence's departure to Tottenham Hotspur, that he had hoped to groom his young goalkeeper for a more gradual succession. But he thinks the abruptness of the change need not prove too costly and it may well be that the replacement of Thompson in the back four with the more positive marking of Lawrenson will be a substantial help to Grobbelaar.

If some of us have yet to be converted to the faith concerning the Zimbabwean, there are other young men in this new Liverpool team who are already entirely convincing and one in particular, the Irish midfield player, Ronnie Whelan, who is liable to make the most guarded observers reach for tributes of the heaviest metal. The tendency to babble eulogies is instantly diminished the moment you enter that large, plain office at Anfield, with the wallpaper that might have come from a suburban living-room, and sit opposite Bob Paisley. He is clad as usual in a cardigan that didn't come from Dior and offering an expression that endorses the message on a picture above his head. It shows a litter of pigs scrambling for nourishment and the text says: 'It isn't easy to stay on top.'

Still, even a man who has seen as much as he has does not deny that Whelan is the kind of 20-year-old footballer who stirs dreams in a 62-year-old manager. 'All things being equal, if he avoids injury he can be a great player. I've felt that from the moment I saw him but I had to keep my reactions a little bit low key. We got him from Home Farm, the boys' club in Dublin, and I think the lads who come to you from that sort of background in the game are the best type. You get England schoolboys and their heads are away before they arrive at the club. I think the failure rate is about 96 per cent. A lot of them get away with physique at school but they're found out when the others catch up physically.'

He remembers that when he was a schoolboy he went to represent the North against the South in Dewsbury. All the players were to assemble at a grammar school and after coming off the train he asked directions of a chap wearing a bowler hat and carrying a rolled umbrella. 'I sirred him all the way to the school, taking him to be a teacher. I didn't know where to look when we went out to play and lo and behold he was the left back in the South team. Built like that, he was bound to frighten everybody to death while he was a schoolboy but he probably never did anything later on.'

Whelan's credentials are of a different stamp. 'He's so skilful, he can take the ball any way you like,' said Paisley. 'Even a player like Frans Thijssen always takes it with the inside of the right foot. I'd like to have played against him. I think I'd have had a shout. But it's different with someone like young Ronnie or Kenny Dalglish who can take it however it comes, either side without restriction.

'Another of Whelan's strengths is his heading. He's got the heading ability of a centre-back. Even George Best didn't have that. He's a tremendous mover around the field and he's got good vision. He can relieve the pressure on himself when he wants to. Altogether, he's got so much going for him that if he escapes the bad injuries and keeps his mind on the job, I'd say he's bound to go all the way. He's the son of a professional player – an international for the Republic of Ireland, in fact, like young Ronnie – and I've had his father in for a talk about just how much is at stake with a boy who's as talented as this one. He's got high hopes all right.'

Those hopes are considerably strengthened by the quality of encouragement Whelan is guaranteed at Liverpool. Bob Paisley is marvellously supported by Joe Fagan, his veteran assistant manager, and Ronnie Moran, who has the vital responsibility of steering men like Whelan and the lately established goal-scorer Rush through the reserves to the first team. Just as the current boss tended to be a confidant for the players in Bill Shankly's time, so Fagan and Moran are sympathetic listeners now. 'If I say anything it's taken as an order or a criticism,' says Paisley. 'If something a player says gets to me it's an issue. It's a great help they can talk to Joe or Ronnie without thinking it's that serious.'

When the hard intervention does become necessary, he can make a job of it. 'I've learned from everything I've done during all the years I've been around the game. I put things across to players that I know they are going to run up against some time. There are people who can talk me under the table about football, but if they had to explain what they were talking about *they* would be under it. I might get beat with a big word or two but when it comes to getting things to work it's different.

'I'm not as soft a touch as people think. I never was on the field but some seem to think I am here.'

Any rival manager who has such delusions should be confined in a cork-walled room. Paisley never allows the word transitional to be applied to his teams – he sees it as the kind of word people hide behind and he hates hiding in football – but he admits that for a long time, and even to some extent in last year's European Cup final, he was 'foxin' around' with inappropriate players in some positions and unfit or off-form men in others. The fluent, purposeful aggression of the last month is, he declares, the way he has always wanted to play. He looks forward to putting it on show at Wembley in the League Cup final against Spurs. 'Yes, goin' to Wembley and that. It's nice. It's the only exercise I get, walkin' out there.'

Marauder of North End

(*The Observer*, 17 April 1983)

ONCE THE CASE has been made for Stanley Matthews and George Best, there is hardly another winger in the last 50 years of British football who belongs in the same parish as Tom Finney.

That assessment implies no insult to a dozen memorable talents from Cliff Jones and Jimmy Johnstone to Bobby Mitchell and Cliff Bastin. It is simply a fact that no one – not even Best (who was, for two or three seasons, probably the most comprehensively brilliant footballer these islands have produced) – could equal Finney in combining ball skill, imagination and demoralising pace with the capacity to infiltrate from the edge of a game and score vital goals.

He hit 30 in 76 full internationals for England and only a couple were from centre forward. Seven more were struck in his 17 Inter-League appearances and, overall, he scored 247 goals in 565 matches in first-class football. For any forward these would be wonderful figures. For someone who was, until the age of 35, a marauder from the periphery, they are monumental.

When the scale of his achievements as a scoring winger is mentioned to Finney, the reaction is characteristically objective and practical. He reflects quietly that perhaps he shouldn't have been a winger at all. 'If I had my career to play over again, I'd be a centre-forward,' he said last week. 'With the freedom of movement and the variety of openings I'd have found playing there, I'm sure I could have done more damage, scored more goals, than I did from the wing. Mind you, apart from the odd bad memory of days when I contributed less for Preston or England than I wanted to give, I've got no serious regrets about my years in the game.

'In a true sense fellas of my generation had the best of it. I can't believe that English football will ever again be as exciting or as full of outstanding performers as it was when we were in our prime. There was one more great period, after the men I was brought up with had gone, something you could look back on as a sort of golden era. That was when Greaves and Law, Bobby Charlton and Best, the tremendous Tottenham team that did the League and Cup double and a lot of other class players were around. But real quality has become scarcer and scarcer since the late 1960s.

'Of course, terrific footballers still emerge. Kenny Dalglish is a marvel and would have been recognised as special regardless of when he played, but I don't think I'm being prejudiced when I say that if he'd come through in my time his brilliance wouldn't have been nearly as isolated as it is now.'

The thread of understatement running through that last comment is not there for sardonic effect. Finney is always concerned with being an entirely fair witness and his utterances are not blurred by nostalgia, whether he is recalling dramas he helped to shape 30 years ago or seeking to relate his experiences to what is happening in football today. Lunching with him on Thursday, at a pleasant restaurant outside Preston, imparted a genuine sense of privilege which even the recollection of all the horrors he inflicted on so many Scotland teams could not diminish. No star of the past ever had more right to distorting vanities or ever showed less trace of them.

He is 61 now, and the hair that was conspicuously thick, fair and crinkly in the photographs of three or four decades ago, is receding. But the face is unmistakable, and the body remains trim. That is no surprise, for this is a man whose retirement at 38 was considered premature by many of those best placed to judge. No one was less surprised by Finney's longevity as a footballer than Bill Shankly, who believed that one of his duties in life was to tell the world that Tommy (always Tommy) Finney was one of the supreme geniuses of the game Bill regarded as too important to be described as a matter of life and death.

When the teenage Finney made himself a regular member of North End's first team in 1940, the rasping Ayrshire voice of Shankly was transmitting brusque counsel from the right-half position. Their relationship became warm enough to survive even Sunday tea in the Shankly's little terrace house in Deepdale Road, where Finney's young wife Elsie, who has never been in the least passionate about football, found her sanity threatened by Bill's inevitable insistence on dissecting the previous day's action relentlessly from the moment his guests came through the door.

Long afterwards, when Shankly had made himself a legend as manager of Liverpool and Finney travelled to Anfield now and again to report matches for the *News of the World*, the hard miner's arm would be thrown round the younger man and all within earshot would be bombarded with eulogies. A colleague of mine once had the temerity to ask Merseyside's favourite Scotsman (such as St John, Dalglish and Souness wouldn't hesitate to grant him that status) if Finney would have been strong enough for the modern game. Shankly spun on the doubter with the familiar Cagneyesque hitching of the shoulders. 'Tommy Finney, son?' he said, letting the syllables curdle with disbelief. 'Tommy Finney was grisly strong. Tommy could run for a week. I'd have played him in his overcoat. There would have been four men marking him when we were kickin' in.

'When I told people in Scotland that England were coming up with a winger who was even better than Stanley Matthews, they laughed at me. But they weren't bloody laughing when big Geordie Young was running all over Hampden Park lookin' for Tommy Finney.'

Many a Scottish defender was embarrassed in that way, especially at Hampden, where Finney was never on the losing side. Typically, he is quick to point out that the results didn't favour England as consistently at Wembley. He suggests rationally that the wide open spaces of the old Glasgow ground suited the English style of play better than it did the Scots, whose close-passing game was, he thinks, more comfortable on Wembley's slower, truer turf.

There is nothing forced about his concern for Preston North End, the club that has never had a serious rival for his allegiance since he was lifted over a turnstile as a five-year-old to be enthralled by the virtuosity of Alex James. He was just a year into his apprenticeship as a plumber when he was offered £2.50 a week to join the Preston ground staff, but his father encouraged him to go on working at his trade for six shillings a week and sign initially as an amateur.

Considering that Tom's mother had died when he was four, leaving six children, and that his father's second marriage had produced two more, it was a major sacrifice to forego the two-and-a-half pounds a week and the son is still grateful. So are the other members of the close-knit Finney clan who are among the 80-odd people earning a living from the family plumbing firm started by Tom and his brother Joe, who died tragically young.

For the man whose name is above the door, the successful business, which he still opens up every weekday at 7.30 a.m., has meant security and freedom from any temptation to contrive an involvement with football after he stopped tormenting defenders. His only formal connection with the sport now is as honorary president of Preston North End.

There were two points in his career when the link could have been broken but two chairmen of the club prevented a parting that might have led to civil disorder in that corner of Lancashire. The first brief crisis came after Preston were relegated to the Second Division in 1949. Finney feared that the descent might make it too easy for the England selectors to overlook him but he was persuaded to dismiss thoughts of a transfer, new players were bought to strengthen the team, and within two seasons North End were back in the First Division.

The pressure to move was more dramatic in 1952 when, at a banquet following England's 1–1 draw with Italy in Florence, he was approached by the president of the Sicilian club, Palermo, and promised £10,000 to sign, plus wages of £130 a month, huge bonuses, a villa on the Mediterranean and a car. It is not hard to calculate the impact of such guarantees on a player who was still receiving only £20 a week in season, £17 a week in the summer, and bonuses of £2 for a win and £1 for a draw when he retired eight years later.

The injustices of the maximum wage system, especially as applied to the footballer of extraordinary ability, will never cease to rankle with him and, in someone in whom bitterness is an alien currency, the memory of how meanly England rewarded service to the national colours is painfully fresh. His 76 internationals were paid at rates ranging from £20 to £50 a match in an age when vast grounds were filled to overflowing. Equally significant was the rule that, on trains, players should travel in the same class as they did with their clubs, which meant that only those from Arsenal and maybe one other heavy battalion were allowed to go first. After helping to beat Scotland at Hampden one year, Wilf Mannion had to stand in the corridor throughout the wearying journey home.

In the context of all this exploitation, the Sicilian proposition seemed to be an offer he could not refuse. But Nat Buck, the local builder who was chairman of Preston then, simplified the issue. 'What's 10,000 quid to thee, Tom?' he asked without a smile. 'Nay, lad, tha'll play for us or tha'll play for nobody!'

The way he performed for them through 20 years at the highest level is one of the abiding wonders of British sport. As has been said of Paul Scofield in the theatre, he was the player's player. But he was the audience's too, able to exhilarate them without engaging in self-indulgent displays of his prodigious technique. When Finney dazzled, he did it with a deadly sense of relevance.

He was naturally left-sided but made himself two-footed in his teens, in the same painstaking practice sessions that developed his intricate control and sharpened his speed off the mark sufficiently to bring him respect as a decent sprinter during his wartime years in the Army, when he spent enough time in the front line to make nippiness an asset. One of his basic strengths on the field was the economy with which he collected the most awkward ball. 'You didn't have to pass to Tom,' Tommy Docherty declares. 'You could drive the ball at him and he took it as if you had rolled it underhand.'

His feinting, swerving dribbles bewildered defenders and once he was past them they were usually spectators. 'I liked to give them the impression of running flat out when in fact I had another gear left. They would think they were going to get to me and suddenly I'd be away, out of reach. I always preferred to go on their outside, get to the byeline and steer the ball back low for somebody coming in. When you got that simple move to work smoothly there wasn't a lot the opposition could do.'

Since he was unostentatiously fearless, violence didn't provide a way out for the persecuted full-back. Usually Finney ignored the threatening mutterings in his ear but sometimes he permitted himself a response. 'How the hell did you ever get all those caps?' one defender asked with a show of contempt. 'Mainly by playing against silly buggers like you,' was the reply. It's the kind of answer that works well in his Lancashire accent.

A pedant scrutinising Finney's superb playing equipment for a weakness might claim that his heading didn't amount to much. But if that was a handicap it bothered him hardly at all, as was emphasised when Preston switched him to centre-forward at 35 and he was so devastating that he scored 28 goals in a single season. Tommy Thompson, the Geordie who in those days formed a partnership with him that is still celebrated at Deepdale, has his joiner's shop in the yard of Finney's plumbing business. Tom Finney never found it hard to make or keep friends.

He has stayed close to his roots, in contrast with the nomadic, perhaps lonely life of Stanley Matthews, who figured with him for so long in one of the most exaggerated rivalries ever nurtured on the sports pages of this country. Finney did not enjoy the outside-left position that Matthews's towering presence frequently obliged him to occupy. But he would gladly have played anywhere for England.

The success he enjoyed when given a brief taste of being inside-right to Matthews, and the pleasure he took from it, convinced him that they could have established an exceptional alliance. 'What is there to say about Stan's qualities that hasn't been said before? At his best, he was unstoppable. His control was so ridiculously good that he could take the ball right up to a defender until you were sure the fella just had to reach out and snatch it away. But Stan was like a mongoose. When the defender lunged, he wasn't there. And he had a fierce killer instinct. Once he had the better of an opponent – that poor man would suffer desperately all afternoon. There was no mercy. Stan was marvellous and he was unique.'

The definition is no less applicable to Finney. George Eastham senior, father of the player whose court case precipitated the demolition of the maximum wage 20 years ago, was one of many given proof of that. In 1963, the older Eastham was managing Distillery in Northern Ireland, and preparing them for the preliminary round of the European Cup against Benfica. He decided that his friend Tom Finney, who had been retired about three years, could integrate and inspire his young hopefuls to make a show.

Some prolonged pestering, and a desire to have a belated experience of the European Cup, eventually coaxed the veteran into saying that he would turn out in the first leg at Windsor Park. Whatever happened in that match there would be no question of playing in the return. Eastham gladly agreed, and the great Germano was among the Benfica players astonished to find such a famous face in the otherwise anonymous ranks of Distillery. Footballers from Portugal had good cause to know Finney, who had been one of the principal assassins when England slaughtered the national team 10–0 in Lisbon.

He did a fair job in Belfast and Distillery (who were to be taken apart 5–0 in the second leg) were lifted far above their normal standards to claim a 3–3 draw. Tom Finney had made a mark on another great competition. He was 41 years old.

Greaves gets by on his own spirit

(*The Observer*, 7 October 1984)

JUST SITTING WITH Jimmy Greaves, talking and drinking tea from a paper cup at a bare canteen table on a weekday morning, does more to rekindle the old deep enthusiasm for football than half a dozen afternoons spent watching the swirl of incoherent energy that is the predominant language of the First Division in 1984.

Perhaps it is unfair to ask contemporary players to stand comparison with one of the most gifted forwards who ever kicked a ball. But those of us who saw him in his prime cannot be expected to understate the privilege. Nor can we be relied upon to absorb quietly the accusation that our memories of his career in the first-class game, which began in the Fifties and ended prematurely at the start of the Seventies, are flatteringly blurred by distançe. When we say that British football is unlikely ever again to know the riches brought to it by Greaves and the other great players who shared some of his finest seasons (a host of superior talents that is merely hinted at by the mention of names such as Best, Charlton, Law, Mackay, Jones, White, Blanchflower, Wilson, Moore, Baxter, Cooke, Bremner, Giles) we are dealing in reality, not nostalgia.

Of course, brilliant footballers still emerge in these islands. Bryan Robson is one conspicuous example and another, Liam Brady, is scheduled to be the subject of the piece that will take this space next week. But – especially now that Souness has joined Brady in Italy – they are rare enough in our landscape to be considered an endangered species. The simple pleasure of evoking vivid images of a time when such poverty was unimaginable is sufficient reason for appreciating a conversation with Jimmy Greaves. But it is not just the recollection of that compact, beautifully balanced figure spurting lethally towards the goals which were always the focus of his genius that makes his company a warming experience.

Greaves has been a hero twice in his life, first for the millions who thrilled to his inspired performances on the field as the deadliest scorer in living memory and much later, in a far more private and more desperate context, as a man who descended deep into the squalid miseries of alcoholism and then fought his way free of the addiction and back to the loving family life his behaviour had almost destroyed. The basics of the story are well known but, as a reporter who first had professional contact

with Greaves over 20 years ago, I found its extraordinariness intensified
by his own telling of it.

What is so impressive is not simply the scale of the battle he has won
but how much of the engaging, mischievously droll Greaves of the early
days has survived the struggle. Genuinely reformed alcoholics are likely
to be cleansed of self-deception and he certainly has that advantage. But
whereas some find themselves replacing one obsession with another, his
concentration on resisting the enemy he can never regard as beaten – only
as held at bay – is managed without a trace of the fanatical.

The deep regret he feels about the suffering that spread out from him
like poisoned shrapnel during the years he lost to drink is not
compounded by guilt. He thinks it is pointless to be guilty because you
have been devastated by a terrible sickness. There is a brief glimpse of
evangelical zeal when he condemns the inadequacies of our society's
attempts to learn and do more about the disease of alcoholism, a
widespread indifference he sees as particularly shameful when compared
with the urgency of the campaign against smoking. He argues the case
eloquently and then suddenly the seriousness lifts from his face and his
voice and he adds a characteristic postscript. 'One of the reasons may be
that half the medical profession are alcoholics themselves,' he says.

Laughter comes as readily to him now as it always did when he was
playing, back when Alf Ramsey, a manager unconvinced of Greaves's
relevance to England's challenge for the World Cup of 1966, would hear
that familiar East London voice sing out from the back of the team bus:
'What's it all about, Alfie?'

Greaves is amused by communications he receives from people who
credit him with a bleak, blanket disapproval of drinking. Such attitudes
are alien to someone who accepts without difficulty that while drink was
a disaster for him it can be a pleasant adjunct to the lives of those who can
control it. 'I get calls from various organisations who assume that I'm
anti-booze. I'm not. We've got a cabinet full of the stuff at home. People
who come round our house moan about the measures I give them because
I pour as I used to pour for myself. They're pissed out of their brains after
one drink.'

As he sipped his canteen tea in the breakfast hour after one of his
regular, twice-weekly appearances on TV-am, he conjured up a dozen
frightening images to show that his drinking was a world apart from that
of the man who hangs one on now and again. There was the occasion
when his wife, Irene – who was driven to divorce him but with whom he is
now happily reunited – had poured all the spirits down the sink and he
pursued the empty bottles to the dustbin, where he was oblivious to being
drenched as he tried to catch a few raindrops that would give him 'a little
bit of flavour' from the dregs.

The day before our meeting the latest of the three grandchildren his two daughters have given him had been christened James. 'All our family and friends were there and as I looked around I realised again just what Irene had achieved in keeping that life together. She is the heart and soul of the whole situation. What I did could have destroyed the family totally and I'm a lucky man to have been let back through the door.'

Perhaps he would have encountered his personal demon if he had been a bricklayer or a clerk but there is no doubt that the abrupt, engulfing sense of anti-climax that often assails the great sportsman when he retires contributed to the horrors that mounted between 1971 and 1978. He had retired prematurely at the age of 31 in the first of those years after a career whose excitements are only partially conveyed by the statistics of his record: the 124 First Division goals for Chelsea and 220 for Tottenham Hotspur, nine in ten games during a brief unsatisfactory alliance with AC Milan, 44 in 57 matches for England.

By 1971 he was with West Ham and seeking to apply his high skills in midfield but an ebbing of confidence made him think of quitting and Ron Greenwood, whose own work as manager was being invaded by uncertainties, offered less opposition to the idea than Greaves thinks he should have done. 'I needed a good talking to from somebody in the game, somebody who could have convinced me that I still had a lot left to give, but Ron Greenwood wasn't the man to provide that. Suddenly it was all over. I was an ex-footballer.'

His interests in a packaging business in Romford, a travel agency in the City, a couple of sports shops, might have been an effective substitute for another kind of personality but for him the removal of the need to maintain fitness steered him towards the bar. The almost daily but undestructive drinking he had done as a player rapidly degenerated into addiction. There were two years of not knowing he had a major problem, one year of knowing but not troubling to do anything about it, two more of battling and eventually conquering it.

As his family temporarily disintegrated and his businesses declined ('We finished skint but owing nobody') he endured the recurring agonies of drying out. 'The last few times were in the local mental hospital and that's not exactly the Ritz. There are a lot of people caring for you but you're on your own. Afterwards, when you've stopped drinking as I did on 28 February 1978 you must make sure you remember how it was when you were at your lowest. It's easy to submerge the memory when you feel good again. Over those two years I would kick it for a couple of months, feel fine and think I could have another drink. To a degree George Best might be still going through that phase. I think Bestie might still get off it completely although I'm sure he's wrong to get involved with something like the restaurant business. I don't want to be around any of that wining and dining stuff and if my television work obliges me to speak at a lunch or a dinner I can't get away quickly enough when I've done my turn.

'If reluctance to be there when the drink is flowing occasionally upsets people, that's the way it's got to be. It's a lesson you don't learn overnight. You tend to sit in the crowd and drink tonic water but that isn't the answer. It's a horrible mistake to exaggerate your own strength. No way am I a strong person. All that talk about doing it my way is a lot of crap. You have to survive on the terms life and your own nature impose on you. Those people who think you are anti-social because you don't want to be around the big drinking scene aren't going to visit me in Warley Hospital if I'm lying there violently ill, with the DTs, shaking and sweating as I dry out.'

Soon the humour intervenes again to lighten his talk and, as is not unusual with him, it comes through an unlikely door. He has been speaking seriously against the sort of implant of aversion drugs that he underwent twice long before George Best had his highly publicised skirmish with the treatment. 'It doesn't stop you thinking alcoholic and that's what you've got to get rid of before you can be cured. You can be off the drink for months and yet, subconsciously, be planning a collision with the stuff somewhere up ahead. The implant, which has a time span attached to its effect, encourages that thinking. I don't believe in it.'

Then his eyes (an elusive mixture of green and brown in a face whose lines, like the grey in his moustache and retreating hair, confirm that he has packed too many extremes into his 44 years) begin to twinkle as he recalls the embarrassment the first of his own implants caused him while he was playing non-league football for Barnet at Yeovil. 'I went into this sliding tackle and suddenly I was aware that these little yellow pellets were popping out of a slit high up on the outside of my right thigh and scattering all over the pitch. I was petrified in case somebody would notice and wonder what the hell was going on. Then later when I was asked about the gash in my leg I couldn't very well say that a surgeon in Tottenham Court Road had done it.'

Maybe he should have kept sliding tackles out of his repertoire. They did not loom large when he was the game's most dreaded infiltrator of the opposition's penalty box. He has a charming resentment of being seen purely as a goal-scorer. 'I feel robbed in a way by that reputation. I feel I was a better player than some people gave me credit for. A lot of them, including other players, thought I was idling about for 80-odd minutes and somehow managing to make myself a hero by scoring an exceptional goal. It was crazy version of what I was doing. To be a goal-scorer you have to work very hard. I used to be running up and down and across the field endlessly and because the ball didn't come to me I was accused of doing nothing. They only remembered the goals. I'd say at Spurs, "Hey, what about that great pass I gave to Jonesy?" But that didn't count. It was as if it wasn't allowed.

'To an extent I regret giving myself to just one aspect of the game. I had the equipment to play in the middle of the field and I should have forced people to accept that after I'd had 12 or 14 years up front. Of course, in another sense I recognise the tribute paid to me by remembering me as a scorer. You need a lot of conviction, moral and physical, to do that job. I used moral conviction to get in there and miss the buggers. If I'd scored every goal I should have scored and missed, and missed every one I did score, my record would have been the best in history by far.'

It's difficult to reconcile that modest assessment with the pictures that fill the mind from two decades ago. He was a much slighter figure then than the soft middle-aged man who sat at the table last week (around ten and a half stone against a height of about five feet eight inches) but where it mattered he was, as Bill Shankly said of Tom Finney, 'grisly strong.' When he looks at his naked body nowadays he reckons it is just grisly. 'Horrendous' is his favourite term and a glance at the hard fitness of his two young sons, who are both aspiring footballers with Cambridge United, does not take the wince off his face. But even when he is in the self-mocking role he willingly occupies for his various regular appearances on television – a medium in which he hopes to be promoted soon from the level of 'perennial studio guest' – he cannot avoid recalling for many of us the incredible skills that were already the everyday coinage of his football before he left school in Hainault, Essex, at 15.

Apart from the overwhelming, obsessive hunger for goals that he identifies as the first essential in a scorer, he had other indispensable attributes in the killing pace that leaves defenders irrevocably stranded and technique of the highest calibre. He had an innate subtlety in the timing of his runs into space and his striking of the ball was so refined with either foot that Nicklaus with a full set of golf clubs could not have produced a wider variety of effects or more consistency of precision. And Greaves was working with a moving ball.

'To be an outstanding finisher,' he says, 'you must be able to hit the ball at any angle from any position, even if you are falling over. Right now I can visualise Georgie doing that, just pinging one away as he tumbled. Second-rate finishers want to line everything up like a golf shot.'

In addition to Best, he has a natural admiration for the scoring abilities of such as Puskas, Muller, Law, Roger Hunt, Ray Crawford and Brian Clough. The short backlift of Puskas makes him almost lyrical, as does the memory of the service he received from Haynes in the England team and from a handful of great allies at Tottenham. The greatest of these, he says categorically (adding his voice to a chorus of praise that runs throughout British football), was Dave Mackay. It is ironic that Mackay should have been in the Scotland team that a Greaves hat-trick helped to slaughter 9–3 in 1961.

Greaves actually knocked in another goal that would have made the massacre even more hideously historic but it was disallowed. He claims he is still sore about that decision, which is as believable as the declaration that the most satisfying goal of his life was a screaming 35-yard volley – for Barnet against Grantham.

All of us whose lives have been brightened by Jimmy Greaves will want him to take laughs wherever he can find them. He has already had as much pain as any man should be asked to handle.

The happiest of exiles

(*The Observer*, 14 October 1984)

THE FOOTBALLER who leaves Britain to swell his earnings in a foreign league is traditionally more tourist than emigrant, a man so reluctant to immerse himself in the ways of the adopted country that he might be expected to take the field with a return ticket tucked into his sock.

But there have always been a few stronger spirits that were bred to stay and the most impressive of these to emerge in recent years belongs to Liam Brady. When he left Arsenal for Italy as a 24-year-old in 1980 Brady was surrendering a secure eminence in the English game to bet on his belief that he should and could prove his worth and develop his talent in a wider, more demanding context.

In the short term he was, of course, guaranteed a small mountain of lire. But the attraction of that had to be set against Arsenal's offer of the most seductive contract ever laid before any player in the club's history and the substantial risk that his Italian experiences would make a bleak contrast with the exhilaration of a 1978–79 season in which he had collected not only an FA Cup winner's medal but, more importantly, the Player of the Year Award of the Professional Footballers' Association.

'People are bound to scoff when I say I didn't come here just for the money,' he says. 'But, truthfully, there was a hell of a lot more to it. I really was concerned with reaching for my limits. I didn't come to snatch the cash and run. Football is my main means of expressing what's in me and I wanted to find out how much was there.'

Anyone who is sceptical about that declaration should consider how he coped with the shock of being sold by his first Italian club, Juventus, after figuring significantly in the winning of two successive Championships. The pleasant Dublin voice still betrays remembered pain when he talks of that episode but what he says has an objective honesty that sets him apart from all but a tiny minority in his business.

He reflects quietly that Gianni Agnelli, whose family's Fiat millions finance Juventus, apparently decided that he would gain more enjoyment from his stake in the club if he replaced the Irishman, Brady, with the more flamboyantly brilliant Frenchman, Michel Platini. 'I was sickened at the time. After what I'd helped the team to do over those two seasons I couldn't believe what was happening to me and neither could the other players at the club. But when I look back on it now I see that Mr Agnelli, from his point of view, was right. How can you argue against bringing in someone like Platini?

'When you are a foreigner in a team here you are only one of two and therefore under far closer scrutiny every week, far more threat of being replaced than an Italian player is. In my position it might have been natural for me to hope Platini would fail but once I had seen him play I held up my hands. He's tremendous. I just had to admire him. I do to this day. He's number one in my book.'

The rejection by Juventus would have reduced many to the depth of disenchantment that leads to repatriation but quitting isn't a Brady habit. He moved on to Sampdoria of Genoa and after two satisfying and distinguished seasons there he has entered his fifth year in Italy with Internazionale of Milan. His market value has increased steadily, from about £400,000 when he joined Juventus to around £700,000 when he moved to Sampdoria, up to the £1.2 million or thereabouts that he cost Inter. But neither these sums nor his genuine popularity with the big crowds he entertains can adequately convey how much this happy exile has accomplished.

The measure of his achievement is the extent to which he has attuned himself to the nuances of Italy's football, its language and its day-to-day life – his mature commitment to the environment he has embraced, whether he is in front of the roaring thousands at San Siro, in the elegantly spacious home whose garden wall is lapped by Lake Como or out on the streets of Milan, where the Inter supporters are liable to treat him with proprietorial familiarity.

The warmth of his upbringing among the Brady clan of North Dublin and the strength of his relationship with a wife who is as intelligent as she is attractive are powerfully benevolent influences but other footballers have had similar advantages and ended up adrift in the wreckage of their careers. The balance and stability of Brady's personality is as much a natural gift as the creative subtlety and accurate vigour of a left foot that has few equals in contemporary football. And the one blessing has always vitally complemented the other.

He has never lacked competitive fire, and occasionally in the past physical maltreatment on the field has caused him to erupt, but in general his abilities have been consistently and profitably harnessed to a controlled temperament. Above all, he gives the impression of having learned from just about everything that ever happened to him, since the day when he was expelled as a 15-year-old from St Aidan's Christian Brothers School because he went to Wales to captain Ireland's schoolboys instead of turning out for St Aidan's in a Gaelic match.

His resentment of narrow-mindedness, whether of the nationalistic, religious or any other kind, hardened then and has not softened since. 'I'm proud of being Irish, proud of my origins. But hypocrisy and bigotry depress me. I'm not mad Irish, not stage Irish. What happens in my country, the crazy, destructive attitudes that separate people from each other, would make you despair.'

At the more simple and manageable level of sport, there was never any doubt that Brady's boyhood obsession with football, and his precocious brilliance as a performer, would take him to England. Two of his four older brothers, Ray and Pat, crossed the water to play for Millwall and Queen's Park Rangers and Ray made it to the Republic of Ireland team that Liam would eventually captain. There had to be a long gap between those honours for the Brady family because Liam is nine years younger than his brother Frank, who is the one closest to him in age. The father, who was a docker, is now 74 and relating to a son 40-odd years younger than himself could never be easy but that son appreciates the support he received when it was most needed.

As a prodigy who was first brought to Highbury for trials at 13 he could hardly avoid a few traumas on his progression to greatness as a professional but there was always enough advice and encouragement to reinforce his own considerable will. Of all the coaches and players who have helped his development, easily the most influential have been John Giles, with the Republic team, and Alan Ball at Arsenal. Both had an immense educational and inspirational effect and during two days I spent with him in Milan last weekend the lessons learned from them were equally identifiable from a press box seat at San Siro or a chair at his hospitable table by the lakeside. Sunday's match with the leaders of the Italian first division, Verona, ended in a goalless draw but, despite its physical and psychological tightness, it was neither dull nor sterile and the 72,000 spectators had little cause for disgruntlement.

Karl-Heinz Rummenigge came from Germany during the summer to join Brady at Inter and the Irishman is as impressed with Rummenigge's form as with his rapidly increasing fluency in Italian. The German might have had a big say in what happened against Verona if his partner at the front, Altobelli, had not been uncharacteristically inept. Brady did his best to feed both, finding them amid crowding defenders with the finest passes struck in the entire match, but the combination of Altobelli's off-day and the extreme conservatism of some of his other Inter team-mates ('They are terrified of making a mistake at home, far more likely to show something in an away game') he was unable to lift his side beyond the point where they were obliged to be content, almost relieved to take a draw.

Later, away from the clamour of the stadium and back in the coolness of his apartments, he was in no mood to congratulate himself over his performance. His principal consolation was that he had been persistently miserly in his reluctance to lose possession. 'I really hate to give the ball away. When I watch videos of the matches I dread every moment like that and I know exactly when each of them is coming up. Here it is essential to apply the principles of patience I absorbed under John Giles. If you cannot attack suddenly you must attack gradually. I don't accept that that approach makes the game less entertaining. The public don't necessarily want a lot of hectic, brainless action in the box. They like to see quality, thinking players on the field, and at the end of the day the thinkers are the deadliest men. It is partly because there is more emphasis on that sort of build-up, less on fierce battling for the ball in midfield, that you will see exceptional players lasting well into their thirties in Italian football.

'The long careers of these men are a tribute to their own talents, of course, but they also indicate that the league here is not as hard on your legs and you don't get as many knocks. In Italy we only have 30 league games and one domestic cup competition. Even if you have a good run in Europe you will play only 50-odd games.

'In England, with 42 league matches and two domestic cups, European competition can easily bring you a total of 20 more in the season. And over there you can be playing three games in five days at bank holiday time, whereas here we are nearly always given the week between one Sunday and another to recover from knocks.

'As a midfield man, you don't have nearly as much risk of injury in Italy. You are given room to play. Hard tackling in midfield is rare. In England they try to play the ball from one area to another as quickly as possible and you find it bouncing around in midfield with players competing for it as it is hopping about. It's in those 50–50 challenges that you are liable to get hurt. Here the fouling is more cynical but you are certainly a lot less likely to get injured. Maradona will know a huge difference compared with Spain. He will be marked man for man every game but he won't be battered as he was with Barcelona.

'It's obvious that class midfield men like Ray Wilkins and Graeme Souness should do well here, and although it is a very different story for the men up front, I reckon young Mark Hateley has a real chance.'

Of the famous English forward who played alongside him at Sampdoria, Trevor Francis, Brady says that he was terrific when fit to play but sadly kept out of action by too many injuries. 'While Trevor was on the field you couldn't have asked for anyone better but it was depressing to find out how often he was unfit to be there.'

One of the advantages Brady shares as an expatriate with Francis is that his wife has taken wholeheartedly to the life in Italy. With their delightfully lively 21-month-old daughter Ella, Sarah and Liam Brady present a convincing picture of contentment on the outskirts of Como. He has a two-year contract with Inter – at annual wages on the right side of a quarter of a million pounds – and the club have an option of retaining him for one additional season. Even at the end of three years he would be only 31 and have every prospect of surviving several more in the English First Division. But for the moment he is concentrating on his weekly assignment with Inter (and the extra European commitments that will soon pit him against Glasgow Rangers in the UEFA Cup) and his international career with Ireland, which may eventually take him past the record number of caps gained by his hero, John Giles.

When he assesses how he is playing nowadays that unfailing honesty comes through again. 'At the age of 22 or 23, before my last year with Arsenal, I probably brought more passion to the game. I wasn't frightened of anything on the field, every decision was a positive one. I still think I'm a very positive player but perhaps not quite to the degree that I was. Now I calculate the choices more carefully and I am aware of that change in myself. But I am sure that it is balanced by the fact that I am a wiser footballer than I ever was before.'

Since Liam Brady never was in danger of being mistaken for a dummy, those who take him on these days had better have their wits about them.

Accentuating the wonder of Liverpool

(*The Observer*, 14 February 1988)

THERE ARE quite a few men attached to microphones and notebooks up and down the country who will tell you that Kenny Dalglish reacts to interviewers as if they are trying to mug him, that he tends to meet their inquiries with the verbal equivalent of Mace.

Such assertions often carry the seeds of their own justification, for it is obviously hard to remain amiable towards people who accuse you of being habitually awkward. But these days Dalglish contents himself with insisting that he has too much respect for the obligations that go with being manager of Liverpool Football Club ever to allow himself a cavalier attitude to public relations.

He is adamant that all legitimate requests for a talk with him are reasonably dealt with (and almost always granted) and says that those who object to his way of operating are mainly resentful of his refusal to 'mark their cards' about transfer negotiations or other aspects of the inside workings of Anfield. Readily admitting that he will always be pedantic about the confidentiality of his club's business, he adds that if a player, reporter or anyone else takes liberties with the code the response isn't guaranteed to be gentle.

Ordinary followers of football can be forgiven for deciding that there is not too much of a problem here. Considering the irresistibly convincing statements made on Dalglish's behalf by the teams he has sent out to obliterate any trace of challenge in the First Division this season, very little hinges on whether or not he feels like pouring his heart out to journalists and broadcasters.

And that last point is sharpened by the fact that the image of Kenny Dalglish unburdening himself of his inner thoughts and feelings to interrogators from the media is so improbably out of character as to be mildly hilarious. The day he becomes a gusher of controversial quotes, stones will be queueing up to give blood transfusions.

In fact, his lifelong adherence to a conversational style that might be defined as Glasgow Laconic, and its limiting effect on after-match press conferences in particular, has almost certainly done far more than the odd harsh exchange with a journalist to make him loom as something of a bogeyman in newspaper and television sports departments. He is never likely to be seen in that light by this reporter who, as someone born within

20 miles or so of Dalglish's roots, perhaps has a better chance than most of understanding not only his incorrigibly West of Scotland diction but the wary drollness of his nature.

By the time Dalglish joined Liverpool from Celtic, Bill Shankly's historic managership was over but the new hero on Merseyside was, naturally enough, presented almost ceremonially to the great Ayrshireman. Shankly, true to his legend, offered curt and unforgettably practical advice: 'Don't overeat and never lose your accent.'

Talking with Dalglish for a couple of hours on a recent evening, it was easy to accept that Bill's counsel was never really necessary. With his thirty-seventh birthday due next month, the strains of maintaining the fitness that entitles him to go on drawing wages as a player-manager (even if his prospects of forcing a way into his current first team are already remote and rapidly diminishing) have drained away most of the ruddy glow that used to make his face look like the well-scrubbed centrepiece of an old-fashioned soap advertisement. It is sculpted into more blatantly concave surfaces now, the curved nose is more of a prow than before, and when we met there was a ragged stubble on the strong jaw to emphasise that the fellow across the table had long since stopped being a wonder-boy, though he shows no signs whatsoever of ceasing to be a wonder.

The accent was, of course, never in any more danger of being lost than was the eagerness to employ its guttural cadences in the delivery of mordant one-liners or pseudo-innocent rejoinders.

After he visited Buckingham Palace to receive his MBE, a friend who kidded him about being the first man from his working-class district of Glasgow to be tricked out in the full regalia of morning suit, with top hat and tails, was told: 'When you're gaun to somebody else's hoose, you've got to try to look dacent.'

Describing the other night how the chairman of Liverpool, John Smith, and the club secretary, Peter Robinson, telephoned his home prior to calling on him to offer the manager's job, Dalglish said: 'They phoned to ask if they could come to the house and I said aye that was all right, then they told me what it was about and I said they could still come.'

They must be extremely glad they went. Dalglish's appointment dated from the morning after the most hideous experience in Liverpool's history, the carnage precipitated by hooliganism at Heysel Stadium in Brussels during the European Cup final with Juventus on 29 May, 1985. Nothing could begin to erase the horror of that disaster but the club was fortunate in finding itself with a manager whose youth and freshness of spirit were always likely to be invaluable in the process of emerging from the shock of Heysel.

The transition from prodigious footballer to overwhelmingly success-ful manager has been effected so swiftly and smoothly that the football world has not fully absorbed how astonishing it is. My own reaction to his accomplishments as a manager is one of fairly straightforward awe. His gifts as a goal-scoring player for Celtic, Liverpool and Scotland were immense. Denied the crucial asset of exceptional pace, he compensated so gloriously with subtlety of mind and technique, with supreme awareness of everything around him on the field, with imagination and touch, quiet, deep courage and a dozen other splendid qualities that fellow professionals discussed him in reverential terms. Graeme Souness declared that Dalglish 'would win more games for you than Diego Maradona' and if that claim will definitely be disputed the Argentine would have to go some to emulate Dalglish as a manager.

Having taken the double of League championship and FA Cup in his first season (while still able to inflict substantial damage with the boots on), he had to settle for runner-up position in the First Division in his second season, and now in his third has made a procession of the League and could well be on course for another double with one of the most comprehensively talented squads English football has ever seen.

Admittedly, the old Merseyside rivals Everton may ruin the romantic script at Goodison today, since Cup ties between such competitive neighbours are never sure to be governed by the rational dictates of form. But the odds must be on a Liverpool victory and there can be no betting about Dalglish's right to have his deeds set alongside those of the remarkable managers he played for: Jock Stein, Bob Paisley and Joe Fagan.

From the day he took Steve McMahon from Aston Villa for £375,000 in early September 1985, he has consistently recruited players who could not only qualify quickly for the first team but, more often than not, bring to that already powerful unit new dimensions of excellence. Look at this list and judge whether he knows what he is doing: Barry Venison (£200,000 from Sunderland), John Aldridge (£750,000 from Oxford United), Nigel Spackman (£400,000 from Chelsea), John Barnes (£900,000 from Watford), Peter Beardsley (£1.9 million from Newcastle), Ray Houghton (£800,000 from Oxford United). Even with the £3.2 million collected from Italy for Ian Rush, and a series of rebates up to and including the £500,000 paid by Spurs last week for Paul Walsh, Dalglish must be identified as a hefty spender but you won't hear complaints from the Kop – or from such as Barnes and McMahon, whose careers have been marvellously revitalised by his faith in them.

And it is the young manager's belief in their ability as footballers that counts for far more than any other factor when the buying of players is discussed at Anfield. He is at pains to acknowledge all the educational influences he has been exposed to since he started earning a living in the game and is especially unstinting in his praise of Bob Paisley's worth as a consultant over the years and the present indispensability of his closest

aides, Ronnie Moran and Roy Evans. But Kenny Dalglish's is the decisive
voice and listening to it at length leaves no doubt that it is the voice of a
true football man, one whose enlightened philosophy may yet lift his
players to even more glittering performances on the field.

'The people who come to watch us play, who love the team and regard
it as part of their lives, would never appreciate Liverpool having a huge
balance in the bank,' he says. 'They want every asset we possess to be
wearing a red shirt and that's what I want, too.'

Ferguson is defiant under siege

(*The Observer*, 1 October 1989)

THERE IS no sense of the bunker about Alex Ferguson's pleasant, spacious house out in the tranquil greenery of Cheshire. But being there for several hours of conversation with the Manchester United manager confirmed anew just how severely professional sport can put a strong man's spirit under siege.

Talking nearly a week after a 5-1 humiliation by Manchester City shovelled salt into the widening wound created by lack of success during the two-and-three-quarter years he has been running Britain's most famous football team, Ferguson seemed awed by the depth of his own feelings. 'Believe me, what I have felt in the last week you wouldn't think should happen in football,' he said. 'Every time somebody looks at me I feel I have betrayed that man. After such a result, you feel as if you have to sneak round corners, feel as if you are some kind of criminal. But that's only because you care, care about the people who support you. At Manchester United you become one of them, you think like a supporter, suffer like a supporter. They have been waiting 22 years for a League championship. I've been waiting less than three but in terms of frustration it seems like 22 already.

'There's been a lot of speculation in certain papers over the last few days about my position at Old Trafford, some of it going as far as to link Howard Kendall with my job. At the very least it's been unsettling and at its worst it's been really mischievous. But I mean to be here, making a success of things, three years from now. I know I have the courage to deal with all the sniping but you worry about the effects on your family.'

That is a natural concern in spite of the capacity his wife, Cathy, has shown in the past for preventing their home life with their three sons (one of their 17-year-old twins is on United's books) from being pervaded by the distorted perspectives of football. Through his days as a rumbustious centre-forward who troubled defences and referees almost equally (in his best season he scored 45 goals in 51 matches for Dunfermline) and on through the eight-year spell of quite incredible achievement as manager of Aberdeen, she never allowed herself to become mere comforter to the celebrity bread-winner. 'You'd come in after a bad result and wait for a bit of sympathy and you'd get slaughtered,' Ferguson remembers with a self-deprecating smile. 'Cathy would say, "What a bloody day I've had with these weans. You'll need to do something about it". It was absolutely right, of course, because she was preserving a mother's priorities. Soon after we came down to Manchester, Cathy had a lot of trouble with her health but thank goodness, for her and all of us who rely on her, she's over that now. She's herself again.'

Ferguson is himself, too, which means that talk about sneaking round corners should never be taken literally. In Govan, the Clydeside area of Glasgow in which he was born 47 years ago, they would give long odds against that ever being his response to a problem. Wide-eyed combativeness fits more readily than timidity on his open features but, though his temper is legendary, last week's charge by a former Aberdeen player that at Pittodrie he was just a bully who got lucky is too ludicrous to warrant rebuttal. Enabling a provincial club to elbow Rangers and Celtic off centre-stage in Scottish football for most of a decade – winning three League championships, four Scottish Cups, one League Cup and the European Cup Winners' Cup – had less to do with luck than with inspired deployment of his playing strength, and the contagious drive that made key men hang on his every word. What he did with Aberdeen amounted to nothing less than one of the most remarkable feats of management in the history of the British game.

So why has he struggled so painfully with Manchester United since going there in November 1986? Why have United had to settle for finishing eleventh, second and eleventh again in the First Division during his tenure? Why have they not gone beyond the quarter-finals of the FA Cup or claimed any worthwhile prize? Why do some people consider him grossly flattered by the recently signed renewal of his contract for three more years at £100,000 a year?

He says he has never for a moment lost faith in the genuineness of his abilities but freely acknowledges making his share of mistakes at Old Trafford, adding that it could not be otherwise, given the scale and range of the manager's responsibilities there. As recently as that calamity at Maine Road eight days ago, he may, he concedes, have erred by failing to incorporate the tidy effectiveness of Phelan in his back four. But, having been pressured yet again by the injuries that are a nightmare constant in his life, he took the risk of liberating Phelan's penetrative skills in pursuit of the victory he thinks United should seek every time they play.

He identifies penetration from the midfield as one of his basic creeds, along with commitment to good passers of the ball and the spread and balance of quality that permit a team to do damage on both sides of the park. While reiterating his dread of sounding like a whiner, he points out how mercilessly injuries have undermined such aspirations. The chronic ankle problem that forced Moses (a player he regards as vastly underrated) out of football last summer and the ruptured Achilles tendon that has deprived him of his £1.5 million signing Webb, probably for the rest of the season, are just dramatic examples of a pattern so widespread and persistent some around Old Trafford have been muttering about a curse.

A few in the corridors of that unique institution, where great figures from the past remain forever part of the family, are more inclined to curse Ferguson. Some of the harshest critics are long-standing friends of mine but I find little virtue in their case, particularly when it shows signs of hardening into a naked desire to see an instant change of manager if Michael Knighton – the puzzling millionaire currently trying to consummate a complicated buy-out – does indeed take over from the present chairman, Martin Edwards, by the end of the year.

Inevitably, much of the criticism focuses on a comparison of the men Ferguson has acquired for an expenditure of around £12 million with those he has let go for fees totalling rather less than £4 million, a long list of leavers that includes such as Moran, Albiston, Strachan, Whiteside and McGrath. On the controversial disposal of McGrath and Strachan, he says that McGrath had richer natural talent than any other player he has ever worked with but was too often blighted by injury (no one has to be told that the Irishman's off-field activities could be spectacularly self-destructive) and that at 32 Strachan's wonderful productivity has declined as age takes away the pace to go beyond opponents on the outside.

There is only a month or so of difference in the ages of Strachan and Bryan Robson but Ferguson emphasises that Robson's great strength and the nature of his game make him another case altogether. Like many of us, he sees Robson as a heroic influence, one whose God-given gift of timing, unflashy but comprehensive skills and inspiring character could continue to make him a force far into his thirties.

He imagines the England captain, transformed into a classic sweeper, directing the new vibrant United he still believes he is building. He quotes the ages of recent costly recruits – Pallister (24), Ince (21), Phelan (26), Webb (26), Wallace (25) – as promise of a bright future and angrily dismisses suggestions that he has turned his back on outstanding in-house youngsters like Beardsmore, Sharpe and Martin. 'We have a well-structured youth policy that is at the heart of our operation but young talent must be introduced carefully, in stages, not sucked dry prematurely by over-exposure,' he argues.

'There were signs of what we could be when we beat Millwall 5-1. There was the look of goals about everything we did and that's how Manchester United should be. It was sickening to be hit with the same scoreline a week later but we can take positive lessons from that disaster, starting with Tuesday's Littlewoods Cup match against Portsmouth.

'I certainly don't regret for a moment asking Martin Edwards to go into the red to buy big in the summer. I said: "We have to go for broke, we have to show that we want to win the League, that we are not going to accept Liverpool's dominance".'

So far the words are bolder than the deeds. But that discrepancy does not usually last long with Alex Ferguson. I want to be counted among those who hope he is given plenty of time at Old Trafford to perform to his pedigree.

After Manchester United won the FA Cup at Wembley on 14 May 1994, I was able to point out, quoting from the earlier interview, just how fully faith in Alex Ferguson had been justified.

Finally, it all came together for Ferguson

(*The Times*, 15 May 1994)

FOR A long time at Wembley yesterday, it seemed that Manchester United were intent on refusing the embrace of history. But, though this victory was shaped by two penalties within six minutes in the second half, it would be unfair to suggest that they waited for their destiny to force itself upon them. They had, in fact, taken control before they took the lead and, by the end, there was more than a semblance of majesty about their bearing.

After a first half that saw them falter and slither so abjectly in the North London drizzle that equality at the interval was grossly flattering, they at last began to play like men who believed in their right to join Tottenham, Arsenal and Liverpool as the only teams this century to complete the championship and FA Cup double. Now they share Spurs' record of having won the Cup eight times.

Chelsea – whose last major trophy in English football was secured in this competition, though not on this ground, 24 years ago – were entitled to feel cruelly abused by the scoreline. Through half the match, they were its dominant force, denying the favourites time and space with intelligent industry and a rich, combative spirit that gave them numbers behind the ball whenever required and thrusting runners at the first glimpse of an opening. They paid for all that galloping after half-time but it was thrilling while it lasted.

The chant of 'Easy' from the red majority in the stadium at the final whistle was accurate only in relation to the last 20 minutes, which United turned into a stroll towards a coronation.

And even then Chelsea kept striving for a goal to preserve their self-respect. But Schmeichel's leaping, sprawling form was always in the way. The London team were weary by then and their two defeats of United in the Premier League this season were a distant, irrelevant memory. Chelsea must have known when Cantona stroked the second of his two almost identical penalties beyond Kharine's left side in the 67th minute that their cause was lost.

The decision to award that penalty was dubious and they scarcely deserved the torture that came as Alex Ferguson's men belatedly relaxed into the imaginative fluency that has been their natural language through most of the past two years. United's failure in the first three-quarters of an hour to maintain pressure along the flanks (Giggs's tendency to drift inside had been a limiting factor) prevented them from pressing the Chelsea defenders back and creating space in which Cantona could operate effectively. But now they cured themselves of that fault and the Frenchman's skills and ingenuity were able to flourish.

It was never quite possible to see 4-0, the biggest winning margin since United beat Brighton by the same score in a replay 11 years ago, as a legitimate product of their supremacy. Always there was the balancing recollection of what had happened before the interval. As they reeled before Chelsea's superior creativity in that period, United may have drawn confidence from the awareness of just how much of a winner their manager has been over the years. His record is far more remarkable than is generally acknowledged.

While with Aberdeen he accomplished the extraordinary feat of elbowing Rangers and Celtic off centre stage in Scottish football for most of a decade, winning three League Championships, four Scottish Cups, one League Cup and the European Cup Winners' Cup. With Manchester United, he has won two successive Championships (ending a drought of 26 years), two FA Cups, the League Cup and, again, the Cup Winners' Cup.

Maybe this Wembley occasion was some way short of being the stuff of legend, but it represents another substantial brick in the edifice of achievement associated with the Govan man's name. Of course, it will take the capturing of the European Cup to leave him feeling anything like contented. 'We want to do ourselves justice after last year's experience in the European Cup,' he said last night with a quiet intensity that left no doubt about the depth of his ambition. But for fellow Scots, he has already performed a major service by obliterating the claim that nobody could be a successful manager in England without coming up through the ranks of the English game.

When United hired him in November 1986, they were recruiting a true football man and one with a bottomless appetite for work and un-quenchable drive. Yet there was a time, nearly three years after his arrival, when many were ready to pronounce his managership doomed.

On a day at the end of September 1989, I sat in his home in Cheshire, less than a week after his team had been beaten 5-1 by Manchester City, and heard him say: 'Believe me, what I have felt in the last week you wouldn't think should happen in football. Every time somebody looks at me, I feel I have betrayed that man. After such a result, you feel as if you have to sneak round corners, feel as if you are some kind of criminal ... But I mean to be here making a success of things three years from now.'

He is there nearly five years on. And it might be fair to say he has made a success of things.

An amiable assassin

(31 December 1989)

JOHNNY HAYNES is living proof that the Scots are a forgiving people.

He it was who passed the knife with which Jimmy Greaves lacerated Scotland's sporting pride at Wembley on 15 April, 1961. And, not content with employing some of the deadliest distributing skills football has ever seen to help Greaves to a hat-trick, he scored two himself and emerged as the most merciless of all the assassins who contributed so eagerly to that historic 9–3 slaughter.

Yet where is this same Haynes today? Happily settled in Edinburgh, that's where. For nearly five years now he has been a well-known man about the old town, familiar in its football circles and warmly welcomed in its most fashionable hostelries. Glasgow sceptics say Edinburgh has exacted a terrible price for taking a once predatory enemy to its bosom. He has, you see, repaid the hospitality by becoming a Hearts supporter and that, they reckon along the banks of the Clyde, represents a worse bargain than Faust struck with the devil.

Having dismissed such provocative mutterings as West of Scotland mischief-making, the contented immigrant acknowledges that he had misgivings when a late flowering of romance with a lady he first met a long time ago made it natural for him to move to her homeland. 'I was a bit worried about coming up here,' he admitted over a drink in a hotel barely a hundred yards from the flat he shares with Avril in Edinburgh's West End. 'But I've got some very good friends and I really feel at home now. I suppose it makes a difference that the Scots are so fanatical about football. They do like a good footballer.'

They do and, since Haynes was a great one, they can live with the fact that Wembley, 1961, was just one of many cruelties he inflicted on them. He gave early warning of how much of an aggravation he meant to be when, in the first British schoolboy international ever televised, he scored twice in an 8–2 drubbing of Scotland.

The crispness, length and imaginative penetration of his passes from midfield (mainly right-footed, in spite of a career-long identification with the inside-left position) provided the foundation of his greatness as a creative player. But that gift for precision, in control and delivery, brought him plenty of goals for Fulham and England and few memories give him more pleasure than the hat-trick with which he crowned a brilliant performance in England's 5–0 defeat of the USSR at Wembley in 1958.

His father (Haynes remained very close to his parents until they died within a couple of years of each other in the mid 1970s) was enough of a footballer to recognise formidable precocity in his only child, who stood out even in a North London milieu in which talent for the game was never scarce. It may have been that encouraging, highly agreeable home environment, as much as his own freewheeling inclination to play the field, that kept him away from matrimony until he had the first of two unsuccessful experiences of it in his late thirties.

The relationship that has shaped his life so surprisingly and satisfyingly of late began when he retired from football after five years of success-filled twilight with Durban City in South Africa and decided he could at last indulge a long-suppressed urge to ski. He headed northward towards the snows of Austria and, by chance, a significant reunion with Avril.

She was running a restaurant in Perth at the time and now does a catering service for an Edinburgh company, which is why the man who made history when he became the first British footballer to be paid £100 a week is to be found humping loads of edible produce at the city's markets in the cold hours around dawn. 'Avril is a ferocious worker and I could get worried about how hard she's got me working,' he says, letting a slow smile spread across a face that hasn't altered drastically under hair too abundant to let its greyness concern him. 'But the truth is I enjoy keeping active and, anyway, I usually finish at half-ten or eleven in the morning.'

Some of his spare time is spent keeping in shape at the gymnasium and sauna attached to the block of flats in which he lives. He makes less use than he did initially of all the superb golf country around him and squash has been made 'more of a hassle than it's worth' by the right knee that was all but wrecked in a horrible car smash on Blackpool front at the height of his career. Ligament damage to that knee so restricted him afterwards that he never added to the 56 appearances he had already made for England – 22 as captain – and, since he was only 27, it surely cost him a score or two of caps.

Haynes is an intelligent, articulate and sociable man and talking with him in his 55th year gives the sense of being permitted a glimpse into an interesting life, one happily freed from financial pressures by the sale of a shrewdly acquired stake in betting shops.

Of course, some of us cannot resist drawing from him an invigorating stream of reminiscence of an era when a wonderful game was more wonderful than it is now, when it had more to do with grace and refined skills and application of probing, ingenious minds – and more to do with fun. Many may think that the fun sometimes went over the top at Fulham, that unique Thames-side repository of the bizarre where Haynes played out his prime. There is, for instance, his story of the occasion when he was locked out of the treatment room because a greyhound was on the table, having heat applied to its muscles in preparation for a coup. There is, too, his eye-witness account of the episode that parted Vic Buckingham, a famously theatrical manager of Fulham, and Bobby Keetch, the one-time centre-half and darling of the debs whose zest and humour have been delighting Haynes even longer than they have been brightening my existence.

'I was watching from a window of the snooker room when Vic took Bobby out onto a strip of asphalt where we used to play five-a-sides,' Haynes recalls. 'Vic suddenly launches into a Fred Astaire tap-dancing routine. Then he turns to Bobby and says, "Now you do that – it's marvellous for developing balance." Keetchie, who had been watching with a pained expression, said: "You must be f-----g joking." That was it, he was on his way with a free transfer.'

Haynes points out that all the comedy did not prevent the Fulham of his generation from staying in the First Division for 10 years when many thought they didn't belong there, or from going to two Cup semi-finals.

Of his role as standard-bearer when the maximum wage was shattered in 1961, he says: 'Tommy Trinder, our chairman, started the talk of £100 a week as a publicity stunt and when Jimmy Hill had led the troops to victory Trinder was lumbered. I had the pen and paper out before he could blink. But what people don't appreciate is that I never got another rise. I was a £100 man till I finished.'

Suggestions that he was intolerant of lesser players bring a quiet correction from him. 'More often I got the needle with myself. I was a bit of a perfectionist and if I didn't hit a 40- or 50-yard ball absolutely right I got annoyed.'

Yes, John, but think of the relief those rare aberrations brought to a lot of suffering souls who are now your neighbours.

Ireland's honest hustler

(*The Observer*, 25 February 1990)

JACK CHARLTON delights in making the highly successful playing strategies of the Republic of Ireland the worst kept secret in world football.

'I want the managers of other countries to know how we play,' he says cheerfully, 'because there is bugger-all they can do about it. And the more they try to cater for what we are doing, the more likely they are to interfere with their basic approach and misuse their strengths. That gives us a real chance of putting them in trouble.'

Putting more fancied opponents in trouble has been the hallmark of Charlton's four years in charge of the Republic's national team. He has transformed the football fortunes of a nation long blessed with a steady flow of outstanding talents but blighted by a persistent inability to integrate its gifted players into a unit powerful enough to challenge effectively in the game's greatest competitions.

By 1988 his guidance had given the Irish their first experience of the finals of a major international tournament and their honourable showing in the European Championship (not least the 1–0 defeat of England in Stuttgart) confirmed the wisdom of asking a man who is unmistakably and unalterably Geordie to be a guardian of Celtic pride. Now, as he and his intensely motivated squad prepare for this summer's World Cup finals in Italy, Ireland happily accords him not only the sporting equivalent of canonisation but a celebrity's earning capacity which – while it scarcely soars to the crazy heights mentioned in the tabloid papers (one credited him with pulling in £5,000 a day) – certainly ensures that Britain's best-known field-and-stream enthusiast won't have to worry about where his next fly or cartridge is coming from.

Anyone who resents the money Charlton is making from a busy schedule of public engagements and commercial activities has a peculiar idea of economic justice. His habit of working without the insurance of a formal contract means that he is forever betting on his ability to do a good job and when he does a magnificent one, as with the Republic, he surely deserves a decent return on the wager.

Leaving aside such moral rights, it happens to be true that, by bringing a previously unheard-of succession of sell-out crowds to Lansdowne Road in Dublin and claiming the significant revenue that comes to

finalists in the European Championship and the World Cup, Charlton
has quite simply dumped millions into the lap of the Football Association
of Ireland. When the Italian campaign is over and bonuses are being
awarded, there should in fairness be at least £100,000 for Charlton and
several times that amount to be shared among the players, regardless of
how they perform in June.

Of course, how much will be in the brown envelopes at the finish must
be a secondary issue as the Republic's footballers get ready to make a
little history, and for Charlton himself at 54 it is still always the battle,
more than the booty, that excites. Spending a night with him last week, at
his attractive home among a group of converted farm buildings in the
wind-scoured countryside a dozen miles north-west of Newcastle, gave
pleasant reminders of that and other constants in his nature.

More than anything, 24 hours in his company strengthened a
conclusion already drawn – that the warm affinity this Englishman has
developed with the Irish and the remarkable potency he has generated in
their football are not due to anything as superficial as style or theory,
though he has his own versions of both in abundance. What he has
accomplished as Ireland manager (like his achievements in the chair at
Middlesbrough and Sheffield Wednesday and his earlier trophy-rich
years as a player with Don Revie's Leeds United and Alf Ramsey's World
Cup-winning England) grows naturally out of his character, from the
peculiar strengths of a personality that is resolute and generous, earthily
straightforward and disconcertingly original, sometimes to the point of
perversity.

He insists, justifiably enough, that there is nothing remotely perverse
about the playing method he has inculcated in the Republic team and that
it only appears somewhat original because all but a tiny minority of
current national squads have a remarkable sameness about how they
operate on the field.

'Nearly all the countries in the 1986 World Cup were like peas in a pod
and most of the matches were boring as hell,' he told me over coffee in his
kitchen, thrusting the long, weather-reddened face forward and letting
the light-blue eyes present the familiar invitation to argument. Since the
main purpose of the visit was to hear in advance a communiqué on how
he means to cause a nonconformist stir in the 1990 competition (and since
he and his wife Pat were being extremely hospitable), it was both polite
and judicious to concentrate on listening.

He identifies Holland as thrilling exceptions to the general dullness
and, whereas he is bullish about securing a result against England in
Cagliari, he believes both he and Bobby Robson may struggle to take
profit from their first-phase encounters with the Dutch. 'They are the
only nation who can claim maybe as many as four world-class players,'
he said. 'Most other teams are separated from one another by the quality

of a brilliant individual who can do damage from midfield. The huge majority of foreign sides (the home countries are predictable in a different way) give you standard problems, using sweepers and pushing their full-backs up to become key servers of the ball in attack and adopting an overall policy of building in tight little areas until they feel sufficiently comfortable to commit men forward. Only Holland habitually use the entire length and width of the field. They are always just as happy to send a pass 50 yards as 10. It's a lot harder to get to them to apply the hustling tactics that are crucial to our method.'

Such admiration will not prevent Charlton from putting his men out against Holland in Palermo on 21 June in an aggressively optimistic frame of mind. They will be buoyed by the memory of how close they went to ejecting the Dutch from the Europeans in 1988 before being killed off by a late goal and, even more, by the constantly deepening conviction that their manager's simple, coherent deployment of their assets can and does make them desperately difficult opposition for the most gifted teams. 'We are working to the same principles now as we did the first day I took over,' he acknowledges breezily. 'Ours is basically a hustling game. We play the ball in behind people, aiming to turn them all the time. We prefer to play the game in the other team's half of the field. If we get the ball behind full-backs, into the holes, one of our fellas will try to reach it first and if he does we'll support him wide and support him deep, creating productive triangles. Once we're in those hurtful positions there's nothing cut and dried – our fellas can be as imaginative as they like.

'The idea is to go towards the corner flags first, which draws the sweeper out, and move the ball in from there to the goal-scoring areas. When I was playing, the only time I was totally uncomfortable was when the ball disappeared over my head towards the corner flag and I had to turn and chase. If it was lifted over me towards the goal that wasn't so bad because, as I'm always drumming into Packy Bonner in our team, the goalkeeper should be living every minute of action and alert enough to come out and mop up like a sweeper. But it's a defender's nightmare if he gets to the ball first and all he can see is his own corner flag and he is being hustled from behind, forced to play with his head down.

'I don't take kindly to losing the ball in places where it can harm us. Whenever things get tight in the midfield build-up, you stop passing the ball to people and get it behind their defenders so that we are facing the right way and they aren't.

'Ronnie Whelan is a superbly skilful player, our captain on merit, but he's got to watch that he doesn't overdo his Liverpool habit of passing to people when the risk of losing possession is too serious. It's different if we give it away in those attacking spaces behind their defence. Then we just have to chase and pressure to get it back. Another fundamental is that in coping with crosses or set-pieces we expect the small men to mark and the big men to attack the ball. We count it a disgrace if an opponent gets a free header.'

His principal worry these days concerns the simultaneous ageing of his group of centre-backs and the bad injury that has recently troubled one of them, Mick McCarthy, whose driving enthusiasm makes Charlton more than willing to ignore outside criticism of his technical shortcomings. 'McCarthy, Moran, O'Leary and McGrath are all getting on a bit and, though the Republic has traditionally been well-off for centre-backs, young contenders don't seem to be coming through. But I'm confident we'll manage a strong partnership there for this World Cup.'

And, with Morris and Staunton likely to be at full-back, Houghton, Whelan, Townsend and Sheedy the probables across the middle and Cascarino and Aldridge up front, he is exuberant about the rest of his armament. Nevertheless, at the risk of confusing those who see him as the dourest of pragmatists, he admits that he would love to have Chris Waddle at his disposal. 'All the passing movements in the world are no substitute for a player who can beat the man in front of him and do damage once in behind the defence – and Chris really can do damage in the corners.'

However, equipped as he is, the Republic's manager boldly asserts that 'if we can get through our very awkward first group we might be lifted so high we can go all the way and win the bloody thing.' One guarantee is that rivals will not have to resort to thumbscrews or Sodium Pentathol to learn what Jack Charlton has in store for them. Are more heavyweights about to discover they can do bugger-all about it?

Pele . . . a talent beyond compare

(World Cup magazine, Spring, 1990)

IF ALL THE QUALITIES that make football irresistible to countless millions have ever been embodied in one supreme player, that man is Pele.

The history of the game brims with great performances and unforgettable talents. But none of the others – not even the imperial Alfredo Di Stefano or the electrifying George Best – could pervade the field with quite the divine sense of superiority that radiated naturally from Pele at the height of his powers.

His relationship with the ball was different from that achieved by anyone else. Other great footballers concentrate on mastering the ball and using it like a tool. For him it often seemed to be a living ally, dancing between and around his sprinting feet as if it chose to be there. He appeared able to run at maximum speed without concerning himself with an ordinary mortal's problems of control. The impression given by his explosive, dribbling surges was of the ball somehow galloping with him, matching every adjustment of his stride while it mischievously frustrated the most determined attempts to dispossess him.

There seemed to be scarcely anything he could not do with a ball but the mesmeric trickery invariably had deadly motive. He saw or sensed everything that mattered on the field, being one of the many Brazilian virtuosos whose sophisticated understanding of the game's subtleties totally refutes the silly notion that their country's best teams operate on untutored instinct and raw flair. Though a shade less than 5ft 8ins tall, he was a sturdily built and immensely forceful player, amazingly athletic and resilient. His passing was varied, precise and imaginative and his finishing with either foot, or with the headers his soaring leaps afforded him, was violently decisive. It brought nearly 1,300 goals in his career.

Even such a catalogue of his capacities cannot convey anything like the true impact of Pele in his prime. Permeating all these gifts, and heightening their effect, there was the magic of his spirit, the way he was able to blend ferocious competitiveness with real joy in the beauties of football.

Anyone who thinks that last line is fanciful should consider his quest in the World Cup finals of 1970 for a goal so exceptional that it would be seen as unique, unrepeatable, Pele's goal. When Czechoslovakia's goalkeeper, Viktor, took advantage of an apparently unthreatening moment to move off his line, Pele frightened the wits out of him by trying to score from the Brazilian segment of the centre circle. Raising his right leg in a prodigious backlift and swinging it through with the flowing, effortless rhythm of a perfect golf shot, he sent the ball in a fast arc towards goal. Viktor's contorted features revealed the extent of his painful embarrassment as he stumbled back under the ball and then spun helplessly to watch it swoop less than a yard outside a post.

Later, against Uruguay in the semi-final, he twice almost scored that unique goal, once after inflicting a miraculous dummy on the goalkeeper, Mazurkiewicz, once directly returning a mis-hit goal-kick from poor Mazurkiewicz with an incredible volley. Yet these wonderful images from a hot afternoon at the Jalisco Stadium in Guadalajara make a less lasting statement about Pele's contribution to the most satisfying World Cup finals I have ever seen than his response to the freakish, blunder-assisted goal with which Uruguay took the lead.

The footballers of the tiny neighbouring nation have induced paranoia in the Brazilians ever since they deprived the hosts of the World Cup in 1950 with a shatteringly unexpected victory before 200,000 in Maracana. And when Felix, Brazil's suspect goalkeeper in 1970, allowed Cubilla's slackly struck cross-shot to beat him the neurosis looked like ending the favourites' challenge. Several of their stars were on the verge of despair, none more obviously than Gerson, who held his head as if to staunch a wound.

Pele ran calmly through the demoralised ranks and retrieved the ball to bring it back for the kick-off. All the way he was talking soothingly to those around him. He was the greatest footballer in the game, playing in the greatest team, and he had an iron resolve to make certain that these realities overwhelmed Uruguay that day and the Italians in the final.

Pele is about to turn 50 but enthusiasm for football still burns in him like a happy fire. When I met him recently in London he glowed with well-being and the deep, immediately recognisable voice (which can come out like a vehement growl even when he is in his usual amiable mood) was as animated about the prospect of thrilling deeds in Italy this summer as when vividly evoking the climaxes of the most dazzling career the sport has known.

He was due to travel from his Piccadilly hotel out to Wembley with a film crew and I joined him in a minibus for a journey that heavy traffic and eccentric navigation by the driver extended into an hour-and-a-half of conversation. His English is not expansive but lengthy sojourns in the US have helped to make it functional and now and then succinctly eloquent.

He began with a simple claim that thousands of players with a fraction of his ability could never make, mainly because they have never had his innate comprehension of the difference between vanity and pride: 'People may say that technically Pele was not so good or that he missed some goals he should have scored. But never in my 25 years as a player could anyone say Pele does not run in the field. If you have a talent – if you are born to do something – you must be in good condition to do it well. We all know men who are very good players but are never in good condition. I could not be like that. You have a responsibility to the others in your team and to the public because the public pay you.'

FIFA have had the wit to put him on contract as 'an ambassador of fair play', a role he fits in spite of having been not at all gentle on the park. 'Always I play very strong, very rough maybe,' he said. 'But I never start to play anyone unfair. Sometimes when a guy has the intention to hurt me then I start to be hard with him – then I would have to pay attention.'

When he talks of being rough he is referring to the intense but legitimate physical vigour that was basic to his work, but those of us who saw quite a bit of him know that when he was provoked and had to 'pay attention' he could be more than abrasive. However, of the three dismissals he chooses to recall, two were for having too much to say and the other was a case of mistaken identity that led to one of the most outlandish episodes in the annals of refereeing.

It happened in Bogota, Colombia, in 1969. Santos fielded three forwards, himself, Lima and Edu, who were – he recalls with a smile – 'about the same size, had much the same style . . . and were all black'. He says it was Edu who got into trouble but, though Pele was 'away from the problem' and protested as much to the referee, he was ordered off. Then when in the dressing-room taking off his boots he was suddenly told he had better lace them up again in a hurry and get back on the field.

His ejection had so enraged many in the huge Colombian crowd that they started setting fire to cushions and tossing them on to the pitch and to avoid a full-scale riot it was decided that Pele must return and the referee must go. The threatened official's place was taken by one of the linesmen and Pele completed the match. It was the referee, in fact, who was ordered off.

In the context of a quarter-century of serious playing that was well under way before he emerged as a 17-year-old prodigy in the 1958 World Cup, his disciplinary record was acceptable considering the severity of the treatment alarmed opponents often gave him. 'Always there would be one or two men coming at me and another man spare, waiting for me,' he remembered, 'and of course the tackling would not always be fair.' It was the cleanness as well as the high skills of Bobby Moore's play that made him respect the former England captain as much as any defender he encountered. 'The Latin player is unfair more than the Europeans,' he said, adding that macho vanity accounted for the difference.

Pele was the victim of a couple of nasty fouls in the commercial world earlier in life but these days his prosperity has a widespread base, which it no doubt needs in view of the economic ills afflicting Brazil. He spends

about four months of his year in New York, with which he established
strong links in the Seventies while seeing out the glorious twilight of his
career with the Cosmos in the North American Soccer League, an
organisation that even his power as a football evangelist could not save.
In New York he has lucrative employment in public relations with the
Warner Corporation, keeps an apartment at the coveted enclave of
Sutton Place in Manhattan and a house on the best part of Long Island.

For one month of the year he is in Europe – mainly to fulfil the FIFA
contract, which runs until 1994 – and for the remaining seven he is back in
Brazil, attending to a clutch of businesses that include a radio station, a
film company, an import-export concern and a small construction firm.
He also does commentating for the nation's biggest TV network.

His homes in his own country are a house on an island near Santos in
the south and a farm in the same region, outside Sao Paulo. Sea fishing is a
favoured relaxation but he plays aggressive tennis to keep in shape and
when he has time he puts the boots on and practises with his old club,
Santos. 'It is fun when there is no strain about playing the game, no
responsibility,' he said. 'When you get the ball there is no pressure and
everything goes well. I play in the reserve team at practice and sometimes
I tease the first-team players.' I would pay to watch those training
sessions.

When Pele himself watches his performances of the past on film these
days, his reactions can be charmingly objective. 'It is the quickness of
mind that I think is most important. Sometimes I see Pele on film and I am
surprised at the speed of his decisions. Also I see that in the air my head
was good. People did not always appreciate the heading. My physical
condition was OK and, although many remember me for my goals, more
often I helped others to score. I gave many more assists. Obviously I now
see things I should have done much better. But maybe this is because I am
a perfectionist.'

Asked to apply perfectionist criteria to the two World Cup-winning
teams he starred in (injury curtailed his involvement in 1962), he does not
hesitate to identify clear distinctions between 1958 and 1970. The men of
'70 were, he says, more thoroughly integrated and balanced as a unit, they
were more truly a team. 'But in 1958 there were greater individuals. Look
at the names. Garrincha and Didi, Nilton and Djalma Santos, Vava,
Zagalo, Zito. Could you have more great players in one team?' If you add
Pele, perhaps not.

It is intriguing to know that Pele, the game's ultimate hero, had a
childhood hero of his own in the small, light-framed Zizinho, an inside
forward whose superb touch and bewildering dribbling made him one of
the glories of the national team who suffered that historic disappointment
in 1950. But if it was natural for Pele to draw inspiration from such
an attacker, what is more surprising is his enthusiasm for playing

goalkeeper. In emergencies he was called upon to serve in that position for Santos four times and between the end of the '50s and 1962 he was the official stand-in for Gilmar in the Brazilian team.

On the subject of the present Brazil squad he is quite optimistic, convinced that they have shown notable improvement under the management of Sebastiao Lazaroni. The limited time available to Lazaroni for ironing out the difficulties inseparable from converting Brazil to the use of a libero makes Pele wonder if they will be able to do themselves full justice in Italy. But he sees the manager as a creative influence – broad-minded, conscious of the need to heed the psychological condition of the team, always ready to talk with the players.

Those who will do the playing are mainly young but he recognises them as impressively talented and he thinks Branco, an attacking left-back with a forceful personality, good technique and a thunderous shot, could be the sensation of the tournament.

Of the other contenders in the finals, he believes Italy, West Germany and Holland will be major threats and has seen enough of Yugoslavia to rate them dangerous outsiders. 'The champions, Argentina, have a problem because it is always difficult when you depend as much on one man as they do on Maradona. If he is in good shape, they will do well. When Maradona is fit he is the best player in the world.'

While looking forward to this World Cup in Italy (which he is sure will be worthy of one of the heartlands of the game) Pele has particular interest in the 1994 staging in the virgin setting of the USA. He says the granting of the tournament to America gives a special satisfaction to him and the rest of the band of legendary players who tried to spread the faith there more than a decade ago. But he is not certain that the World Cup will be properly used to give soccer real roots in the US. 'There is a danger that it will be just a big party,' he warns. 'The Americans love to have big parties and they are very good at it. But how much of the interest in football will last after the World Cup? That is what matters.'

Before we parted, I had to ask him for his personal list of the greatest matches he was involved in. Memories of magical occasions came pouring out: Brazil in Sweden in 1958, Santos against Milan at San Siro, Brazil's epic victory over England in Guadalajara in 1970, Santos beating the formidable Czech national side in Chile in a collision described by witnesses as the 'match of the century'.

But there seemed to be one jewel of a memory that outshone all the others. It was of the World Club Championship decider in Lisbon in 1962 when Benfica, who had beaten Real Madrid 5–3 in one of the finest European Cup finals, were overwhelmed 5–2 by Santos. 'I scored two goals,' Pele recalled, his eyes lit up by the pictures in his head, 'and for one goal I came with a dribble from the midfield. It was fantastic.'

Suddenly we had reached Wembley and were through the tunnel and on the edge of the pitch, where the nets were up for an England international that night, and Pele was shouting to his film crew: 'A ball! Get me a ball!' He had been on the bench at Wembley three or four times, he explained, but had never been fit enough to play. Now he wanted to score a goal at the old stadium.

And he did, in slacks and leather jacket and street shoes, twice dribbling from the halfway line on the empty field to the six-yard box before blasting the ball at the net with the exuberance of a schoolboy. It was fantastic. Nearly everything about him is.

The Emperor's exit could be glorious

(World Cup magazine, Spring, 1990)

TOWERING ABILITY AS a player and notable achievements as a manager represent only part of Franz Beckenbauer's value to football. His contribution to the game has been further enriched by his lively sense of the wider world beyond its boundaries.

After two decades of memorable exploits on the field and six years in charge of the West German national team, he cuts an attractive, cosmopolitan figure. Some will say that with his talent and good looks, and the substantial wealth they have brought him, it was natural enough that he should develop a sophisticated view of life. But there is much more to Beckenbauer than an unfailingly stylish presence.

In my own meetings with him he has shown an appealing graciousness, a warm, unforced courtesy that suggests he was never in danger of being dazzled by all the adulation he has encountered on the long upward journey from his beginnings in Giesing, a working-class district of Munich. It has obviously been no strain for the Kaiser to keep the common touch.

However, few are likely to confuse his civility with softness, least of all the critics who have been sniping at him persistently ever since he was given the West Germany job without having worked for the coach's licence that is demanded of anyone entering management in the Bundesliga. That qualification was 'presented' to him last year in recognition of his services but there is still plenty of resentment around.

Much of the harshest comment about his appointment has come from former international team-mates such as Paul Breitner (whose willingness to be a vociferous dissident, like his critical attitude towards Beckenbauer, stretches back to his playing days) and Jupp Heynckes, who took Bayern Munich to the semi-finals of the European Cup this year. Heynckes reacted sourly when asked how he would feel about taking a secondary role with the national squad: 'Me, assistant to Beckenbauer? That would be as if, in a handicraft business, a master craftsman had to work under an apprentice.'

An outsider is bound to think of Beckenbauer as a pretty remarkable apprentice. His record total of 103 caps for his country was gained under the regime of Helmut Schoen and he had such a close relationship with that wise and warm-hearted manager that it must have nourished his own considerable tactical flair. They shared a splendid run that included narrow and controversial defeat by England in the World Cup final of 1966 and victory over Holland in the final of 1974, with success in the European Championship of 1972 sandwiched between. I have frequently heard Schoen happily acknowledge that once Beckenbauer became captain (which was to be the case in 50 internationals) he as manager felt blessed with the best embodiment of his policies he could possibly have on the field.

At club level, too, the most celebrated attacking sweeper in the history of the game had a career with Bayern Munich that was liable to be educative, bringing as it did winners' medals in three European Cups, one Cup Winners' Cup and one World Club Championship. Even the three subsequent years he spent with the New York Cosmos in the North American Soccer League, where the promotional excesses owed more to showbusiness than sport, could not be entirely wasted when they set him alongside men of the calibre of Pele and the captain of Brazil's glorious team of 1970, Carlos Alberto.

Of course, Beckenbauer's handling of the national team has made the jibes of Heynckes look foolish. If reaching the World Cup final in Mexico in 1986 with an essentially moderate squad did not suggest he was a sorcerer, it showed him to be something better than an apprentice. The form of his team in the European Championship two years ago – when they were favourites as the host nation but lost in the semi-finals – was undoubtedly disappointing. He had, however, said beforehand that the 1988 tournament was arriving too early in the rebuilding process he had begun after Mexico. Now he faces the last competition of his managership with quiet but unmistakable optimism.

Win or lose, Beckenbauer is resolved to hand over immediately after this World Cup to an old ally from his time as a player, Berti Vogts. He is then expected to become a marketing executive with the governing body of the West German game, the Deutscher Fussball-Bund, although he told me recently there was still a possibility that he would go into club management and that perhaps it would be in an Arab country. There must also be a good chance that he will be wooed by the Americans, given that they would presumably be delighted to have a football giant like Beckenbauer (who has strong associations with the US and speaks reasonable English) in control of their national team when they stage the 1994 World Cup finals.

But such issues won't intrude much on his thoughts these days. A cosmopolitan sophisticate he may be, so much so that he makes his home in the Austrian ski resort of Kitzbuhel, but no one should underestimate his intensely focused commitment to improving a German record in the World Cup that is already phenomenal. In our conversation he was at pains to emphasise how crucial his race's capacity for single-mindedness has been in enabling them to qualify for the finals of every World Cup they have entered, to win the Cup twice, be runners-up three times and beaten semi-finalists on three occasions.

'It is part of the German mentality to produce a special degree of concentration for the big events,' he said. 'Technically we may not be in the same class as Brazil or other southern countries. But in a vital moment in a World Cup or the European Championship the German players can really concentrate.'

Clenching the mind on priorities was a conspicuous quality in his own play and it can still assert itself at the age of 45, even in the unlikely setting of a press conference. In dealing with the most hostile of the German football reporters – whose hounding methods can make the worst that Bobby Robson endures seem benign – he is inclined to turn his gaze contemptuously away from any question he considers cheaply offensive or insultingly banal, letting his disdain slap against the questioner's face like iced water.

When approached with less loaded inquiries, he is frank and informative and the message that comes across now is that he believes the men currently at his disposal have respectable prospects of putting West Germany in the same category as Brazil and Italy by claiming a third World Cup. As recently as 1988 he felt he was severely handicapped by the lack of a true leader in his team, someone who could accept the kind of responsibility he undertook for Helmut Schoen. Today he is satisfied he has two men equipped to provide leadership.

One is his captain, the driving, combative midfielder Lothar Matthaus, and the other is the oldest man in his pool, the 32-year-old sweeper from Bayern Munich, Klaus Augenthaler, who returned to favour with the national team after an extraordinary variety of candidates for his position had been tried and found wanting. 'Moving to Italy to join Inter Milan has helped a lot with Lothar's personality,' Beckenbauer told me. 'He is ready to be a real leader now and is the right man to be captain. But Augenthaler is a powerful personality too, and can inspire others. So, I don't have the worries in that respect that I had two years ago.'

It is characteristic of Beckenbauer that he should also praise the contribution made to the morale of the team by an entirely different type of individual, one he describes as 'a very charming man'. This is Pierre Littbarski, whose effectiveness as a dribbler and dangerous shooting can alarm the best of defences when he is attacking from midfield. 'He is very important to us on and off the field,' said the manager. 'He makes jokes and keeps spirits high. Everybody likes him.'

Such an assessment will far outweigh the fact that Littbarski passed his 30th birthday in April of this year. There will, in any case, be no shortage of youth in the midfield from which Beckenbauer expects so much. Two of its principal elements are likely to be Thomas Hassler, who will turn 24 just before the World Cup finals start, and Andreas Moller, who will be even younger at 22.

Hassler's brilliance with Cologne prompted Beckenbauer and the 18 Bundesliga club captains to vote him Player of the Year and in April he was transferred to Juventus for £5.5 million. He is quick, perceptive and highly skilled and, since Moller is also impressively creative, both could be profound influences. Further midfield depth will be offered by Hans Dorfner of Bayern Munich and that other young Bayern star Olaf Thon, provided that Thon recovers swiftly enough from the blunting effects of a recent ankle operation.

Looking at his resources, it was hard to argue with Beckenbauer when he said: 'We have some very good players, particularly in the midfield. We will be different this time from the Germany of '86 in Mexico. In Mexico we were mainly defensive. In Italy the emphasis will be more on attacking. We should be a goal-scoring team. At the front Rudi Voller will be our most experienced striker. I am very happy about his form with Roma as I am about how Jurgen Klinsmann is playing with Inter Milan. Klinsmann has learned a lot in Italy.' In addition to Voller's accomplished technique and appetite for scoring and the tall, blond Klinsmann's exciting pace and penetrative strength, West Germany can, as Beckenbauer stressed to me, call on the threat of Karlheinz Riedle, who will soon leave Werder Bremen to join Lazio for another vast fee. Riedle is especially strong in the air. With a heavily manned midfield geared to aggression and a proven cutting edge at the front, Beckenbauer's promise of goals should not be an empty one.

Among men who may be ruled out of contention for a place by physical problems, one of the most worrying cases is Stuttgart's Guido Buchwald. Whenever I have seen that 29-year-old he has been a formidable component of the German defence, marking intelligently and tackling decisively, but he is another who had to have an ankle operation and time is running out for him. If, as seems probable, Bodo Illgner of Cologne remains the first-choice goalkeeper, he would surely regret being deprived of Buchwald.

But Illgner, like his manager, will be reassured by the presence on the left side of the defence of Andreas Brehme. Opponents will not be so happy, since Brehme mixes stout defending with spirited attacking thrusts and, in common with Augenthaler, is a fierce blaster of the ball. 'Brehme is a key man for us,' says Beckenbauer unequivocally. 'And his club form is very good.'

There is extra significance in the fact that Brehme's club is Inter Milan and that Matthaus and Klinsmann are among his team-mates there. Two other members of the West German squad, Voller and Thomas Berthold, play their football with Roma but the Italian connections of Brehme, Matthaus and Klinsmann are doubly relevant because the Germans will be based in Milan for their three group matches in the first phase of the finals. If they win their group they will stay in Milan and should they prosper in the second phase their quarter-final, too, will be in that northern city. They could, therefore, have five successive matches in which the clamour of their own travelling supporters will be swollen by local enthusiasm for the Inter heroes.

The United Arab Emirates appear doomed to be abused victims in West Germany's initial group and, although Colombia are somewhat enigmatic and Yugoslavia positively threatening, Beckenbauer's men look certain to progress. When asked to identify the outstanding contenders for the championship he takes a moment to pay a special tribute to the transformation Jack Charlton has wrought in the Republic of Ireland: 'What they did in the 1988 European Championship after years as a third-class power in the game was wonderful, a miracle, and they could have an excellent World Cup.' But he goes on to deliver ratings that are as orthodox as they are rational.

Yugoslavia could be the surprise of the competition, he suggests, although with authorities like himself and Pele touting them they can no longer be all that much of a surprise. England and Spain may do well, he feels, but he plainly attaches more weight at this stage to the challenges of Italy, Brazil, Argentina 'and, of course, Holland'. Then he smiles as he adds quietly: 'And maybe Germany.'

Knowing what we do of West Germany's World Cup tradition and their present developing strengths, that 'maybe' from Franz Beckenbauer is sufficient to make some of us reach for the betting money.

The long trial of John Barnes

(The Observer, 14 October 1990)

THE LONGEST TRIAL of talent football has seen goes into another session at Wembley on Wednesday evening, with the familiar throng of jurors reassembling to argue about whether John Barnes's form for England is an offence demanding banishment from the national team.

Though many of the accusations levelled at the country's most gifted forward may be riddled with presumptuousness or prejudice, there is obviously a case to be answered. That much is established by relating the number of caps he has earned (59) to the generally bland impact he has made on the international game, a comparison rendered all the more disturbing by the match-winning brilliance he so regularly displays for Liverpool.

Barnes, who will be 27 in three weeks, has already swept beyond the total of England honours achieved by legendary figures such as Stanley Matthews (54), Johnny Haynes (56) and Jimmy Greaves (57). Yet, unlike them, he has still to prove that the qualities which enrapture League grounds can dazzle on the bigger stage.

The gulf between his club and international standards did narrow encouragingly against Hungary at Wembley last month, when he responded to the positional licence calculatingly granted to him by Graham Taylor, a manager new to England but well known to Barnes from the days of his prodigious youth at Watford. But the match was a friendly and Wednesday's meeting with Poland, which counts towards qualification for the European Championship of 1992, will be a far sterner and more valid test.

As he goes out into what has lately become an unwelcoming arena, his hamperful of caps will mean less than the extent of his self-belief. That resource, he insists quietly, is just about bottomless. 'No one could persuade me that I'm not a good player,' he says. 'If Kenny Dalglish or Franz Beckenbauer came to me and tried to tell me that, I would know they were wrong. If I have two or three bad games in a row, I get myself going again by saying, "No matter what happens, I know I am a good player".'

Many who have seen his talent at the flood will go further and put him with the great players. Being great for England is the problem and it is inevitable that attempts to explain why he has not yet cracked it should involve speculation about the extra pressures inseparable from being the first black footballer to break through as an undeniable star in Britain. Other blacks have been notably successful in our domestic game and two, Des Walker and Paul Parker, are almost certain to represent England against Poland. But Walker and Parker are defenders and the attention they attract is both less glamorous and less hazardous than the glare focused on Barnes.

After talking to him at length, however, the impression gained was that the isolating effect of his status is not as significant as the specific nature of his black experience and the innate coolness of the temperament exposed to that experience. There is a conspicuous absence of anger in John Barnes and even hints of fire are extremely rare. Strength there is, without question, but it is almost always conveyed at a low emotional temperature. Rage is alien to him.

How much of this he was born with and how much was contributed by an upbringing that was not only middle-class but distinctly insular is hard to tell. His Jamaican childhood was not shaped by the streets of Kingston (though he saw something of them) but negotiated from within the army base where his father was serving as an officer. John was 12 when Ken Barnes, who recently retired with the rank of colonel in the Jamaican Defence Force, moved to London as military attaché. Home for the only son then was a flat in Baker Street. By the time his parents were returning to the West Indies, the teenage Barnes had been received into the surrogate family of Watford FC.

Army camps and football clubs can be rigorous environments but they are bastions of separate, insulated values and it is probably not surprising that someone so long enclosed in them should find it natural to make a clear distinction between racial abuse on the football field and 'in life'.

'I am a footballer trying to do a job for Liverpool and my team-mates and my football would suffer if I were to take the racial stuff seriously,' he said. 'If I get angry with the crowd and start ranting and raving, or wanting to knock people out, because I am being called a black so-and-so, it can only harm my performance and that of my team. You have to laugh at the racists, treat them with contempt. Letting them get to you is as self-destructive as letting the kickers get to you, because the result is the same – reduced performance.

'My reaction would be entirely different in the street. I would feel much more strongly if my girlfriend or my two sons or my mum and dad were insulted. An angry reaction is fine in life but in football it lessens you. Maybe when I retire I'll become more involved in these issues – perhaps not a black activist but more directly concerned.

'For the present, as a footballer, the best thing I can give black people is proof that their kids can get on. No matter what I achieve I am not going to change the attitude of the majority of the population to black people. I said to some of our players, "Having me next door to you would be no problem because I'm me, John Barnes. But if some fella from Toxteth came to live next door you know you wouldn't be too happy." So instead of kidding myself I can do a lot to change white attitudes to blacks – though everybody has to keep working on that – I want to help to change blacks' attitudes to themselves. England isn't such a bigoted country that black kids can't get on.'

He is too intelligent to overlook the likelihood that many will see such reasoning as the luxury of a man in privileged circumstances. 'Some say I'm letting my people down, call me an Uncle Tom, tell me I'm not for the black cause. They say I'm too ready to make jokes about colour prejudice, that I hide behind a laugh. I believe the way I handle my life is the right way but when black people throw things back at me I feel plenty of pain and strain below the surface.'

One place where he never found pain and strain, he will assure you, is in his relationship with his parents and two sisters. He was profoundly hurt during an already traumatic World Cup in Italy by a tabloid story based on half-baked psychological theorising around the fact that his mother was not always inclined to spare the rod. 'Every boy is naughty and when you are getting beaten by your mum you wish at the time that all sorts of wicked things would happen to her. It is only when you look back that you realise how much your mum and dad loved you and how much they did for you. There was never a single moment when I did not feel loved and secure. My parents did a brilliant job. They prepared me for life and for football, too.'

His strong awareness of how football differs from the wider world does not prevent him from recognising that the essence of a man's personality can be expressed through the game. 'And I'm not just talking about so-called personality players like myself and Paul Gascoigne. You've seen Vinny Jones on the field and he's just like that in life as well, I can tell you. I don't have to say anything about Bruce [Grobbelaar], do I?

'You can probably tell I'd be soft as a manager. I'd field 16 players for my team because I couldn't disappoint anybody. Kenny Dalglish doesn't worry like that but then he could be naughty at times as a player.'

These days, in his sixth season as Liverpool manager, Dalglish is a fiercely competitive participant in the practice games which predominate in a club training schedule that has little respect for physical slog. 'At Watford I had more of the fitness you need for cross-country runs,' said Barnes, 'but I wasn't as fit as I am now for 90 minutes of football.'

Of Dalglish as a team-mate at practice, Barnes says: 'He was such a great player himself that he expects you to see a chance to pass the ball through the legs of two opponents and off another's shins into the stride of one of your men. "Didn't you see that was on?" he'll ask, deadpan.'

What the famous Scot wants to pass to Barnes now is a new contract which, if signed, would pre-empt an apparent urge to depart when the old agreement expires at the end of this season. A long-standing desire to try European football discourages immediate acceptance of Liverpool's attractive terms and if the right offer comes in from the Continent he seems likely to go. A number of such approaches would surely have materialised if Barnes had shown his true worth in Italia '90. Instead, miserable form and injury trouble made the World Cup a personal agony. 'A major disappointment but only a temporary one' is how he describes it but the big European clubs may see it differently.

Of course, they cannot be disenchanted enough as far as Dalglish and the Liverpool supporters are concerned. There was evidence of that feeling in the kind of looks the narrow-waisted, wide-shouldered figure (5ft 11ins and about 12st 10lb) drew on a short walk through the city centre, and in the Adelphi Hotel a porter took him by the arm to say: 'Don't leave us, John, don't ever leave us.'

But he has a measured response to fan adulation. 'There's special loyalty among Liverpool supporters but the main reason for that is the club's success. If you can't be loyal supporting Liverpool, where could you be loyal? Most fans don't want you to belong to yourself, they want you to belong to them, to be used for their purposes. Because there were some complications and doubts before I came here, when I did arrive a lot of people wanted me to fall flat on my face. Luckily, things went well from the start but it could have been the other way. Liverpool will continue if I go. I may have a special place with the supporters now but they will soon find someone else to fill it.'

The fickleness of the public, as exhibited at recent England matches, where the racist factor has been manifest, must bother him more than he admits. But the nonchalance that is genuinely basic to him is clearly a help. When his white girlfriend and mother of his children, Suzy Bicknell, moved their family base back from Merseyside to Hemel Hempstead to be among familiar faces, he leased a 'grotty flat' above a dentist's and though it has all kinds of modern appliances he has not yet exerted himself to acquire a sofa or armchairs. He uses two bean bags. 'I'm easy-going,' he smiles, adding that the only two bookings he has drawn in eight years were for nothing worse than shirt-pulling.

But criticism of his football can harden his tone. He is unpersuaded that with England crucial deficiencies in his positional sense are laid bare. He does not accept that once deprived of the reassuring context Liverpool provide for his swift and powerful dribbles, precise crosses and deadly finishing, he too readily becomes a lost spirit, lacking the imaginative alertness and understanding of the game's fluid geometry to make himself consistently relevant.

Creative attackers like himself and Chris Waddle have, he is convinced, been wrongly used. 'In the England team for too long the norm has been that when you get possession you have a cross, a shot, get a goal or lose the ball within 10 seconds. That's all right for specialist goal-scorers like Gary Lineker but the players expected to create need to keep the ball longer.

'I also want flexibility to move around the pitch. That means asking for more, not less, responsibility. But it is the responsibility of finding the best way of helping the team to attack – whether on the left, the right or through the middle. In international football your marker is inside your shorts and won't care if he doesn't touch the ball so long as he stops you. If I can wander intelligently it puts him in two minds and gives me the half-a-yard I need to cause problems.'

He was considerably stimulated by Graham Taylor's accommodation of these requirements against Hungary. 'Particularly in the first half, in terms of movement, passing, angles, getting people free, creating things, that was the best England have played in a long while. I was happy with the licence I was given.'

If Barnes is happy again on Wednesday, Taylor will be delighted, particularly if his former protégé is exploiting what the manager praises as a unique capacity to impart instant lift to his centres while swinging his left leg across his body at the gallop. 'It comes naturally,' says the player. 'I can't kick the ball straight. I've always got to swing across it, so that everything I hit has a curl. I simply couldn't blast free-kicks straight in as Stuart Pearce does. I can't help bending them, which is handy for putting the ball round the wall.'

No lover of football would want John Barnes to stop doing what comes naturally. A few million of us hope that he will do more of it for England.

The Best years of our lives

(*The Observer* Magazine, 18 October 1992)

GEORGE BEST had come in along the goal line from the corner-flag in a blur of intricate deception. Having briskly embarrassed three or four challengers, he drove the ball high into the net with a fierce simplicity that made spectators wonder if the acuteness of the angle had been an optical illusion.

'What was the time of that goal?' asked a young reporter in the Manchester United press box. 'Never mind the time, son,' said an older voice beside him. 'Just write down the date.'

The date was in the '60s, and by 1974 Best had walked out of first-class football at the age of 27 and headed into another life shaped by a painful and continuing struggle with alcoholism. Yet when I accompanied him to a Tottenham Hotspur–Manchester United match recently, he stirred more excitement in the main lounge at White Hart Lane afterwards than any contemporary player other than Paul Gascoigne could have expected to generate. 'I never do this, but I'll do it with him,' one middle-aged Spurs supporter said as he joined the polite scramble for autographs. 'That,' he told his son, 'is the best player that ever lived.'

The assertion is a shade excessive. Pele, the Brazilian phenomenon who had a stunning impact on the World Cup finals of 1958 as a 17-year-old and was the orchestrator of the best team I ever saw when his country won the Cup again in 1970, has irresistible claims to being considered the supreme footballer of all time. Diego Maradona would be a popular nomination as the principal challenger and another, very different Argentine of an earlier generation, Alfredo Di Stefano, would have his advocates, as would the elegant, swift and cerebral Dutchman Johan Cruyff. But Best could run Pele as close as any of them. Where the Brazilian was superior (leaving aside his extraordinary longevity as a player) was in his far broader awareness of the imperatives of team play and in the humility with which he deployed vast abilities, his refusal to do anything complicated where something simple would cause more damage.

Yet even Best's extravagances were a joy, so long as you weren't Denis Law making a killer run, only to find that the ball had not arrived because Georgie had opted to beat the defender twice. He was most likely to inflict such humiliation on desperadoes who had threatened to break his leg.

With feet as sensitive as a pick-pocket's hands, his control of the ball under the most violent pressure was hypnotic. The bewildering repertoire of feints and swerves, sudden stops and demoralising spurts, exploited a freakish elasticity of limb and torso, tremendous physical strength and resilience for so slight a figure and balance that would have made Isaac Newton decide he might as well have eaten the apple. It was Paddy Crerand (whose service from midfield was so valued that Best says the Glaswegian's was the first name he looked for on the Manchester United team-sheet) who declared that the Irishman gave opponents twisted blood. He was an excellent header of the ball and a courageous, effective challenger when the opposition had it, and he reacted to scoring chances with a deadliness that made goalkeepers dread him.

That was an attribute emphasised by Alex Ferguson, the present United manager, when he talked to me about the stupidity of likening his impressive young winger, Ryan Giggs, to Best. 'He'll never be a Best,' said Ferguson. 'Nobody will. George was unique, the greatest talent our football ever produced – easily! Look at the scoring record: 137 goals in 361 League games, a total of 179 goals for United in 466 matches played. That's phenomenal for a man who did not get the share of gift goals that come to specialist strikers, who nearly always had to beat men to score. . . Here at Old Trafford they reckon Bestie had double-jointed ankles. Seriously, it was a physical thing, an extreme flexibility there. You remember how he could do those 180-degree turns without going through a half-circle, simply by swivelling on his ankles. As well as devastating defenders, that helped him to avoid injuries because he was never really stationary for opponents to hurt him. He was always riding or spinning away from things.'

Best, of course, was always capable of hurting himself, with help from the girls who were constantly willing to accompany him all the way through long boozy evenings and sexually hectic nights. Apart from the lithe grace of his body, his attractiveness had much to do with colouring, with the vivid blue eyes set wide in a dark, mischievous face framed by luxuriant black hair. 'If I had been born ugly,' he once said to me, 'you would never have heard of Pele.' In fact, he was never remotely as vain as the joke makes him out to be.

The warmth felt towards him by so many old players is not merely a tribute to a man who embodied a beautiful fulfilment of the dreams they all started out with. It is a recognition of the extent to which, for all his pride in his gifts and his certainty that they were unique, he remained essentially unspoilt. My own memories of many hours spent in his company contain nothing but proof of how unaffected he was by finding himself the first British footballer to be treated like a pop star.

One fresh image is of a night when, after a European Cup match at Old Trafford, a bunch of us gathered in the Brown Bull, a pub near the

Granada television studios. No one had given much thought to dinner but, by the time the after-hours session was under way, hunger was a problem. At least it was until Best went round taking fish and chip orders from everyone in the bar, then disappeared. He returned half-an-hour later, not merely with all the orders accurately filled but with plates, knives and forks for everybody. The waiter seemed less like a superstar than the appealing boy who had worked small miracles with a tennis ball on the streets of the Cregagh housing estate in East Belfast.

For those who witnessed Best's brief zenith in the '60s, the effect went beyond the realisation that we were seeing the world's most popular game played better than all but two or three men in its long history have ever played it. Sport at its finest is often poignant, if only because it is almost a caricature of the ephemerality of human achievements, and Best's performances were doubly affecting for some of us because they coincided with an uneasy suspicion that football was already in the process of separating itself from its roots. It would be dishonest to claim that we foresaw the pace and extent of the separation that was to occur over the ensuing 20 years. How could we? The true working-class foundations of the game were still incarnated and articulated all around us by managers like Bill Shankly, Bill Nicholson, Matt Busby, Jock Stein and, regardless of what happened to his accent, Alf Ramsey. English football still contained dozens of highly gifted players (that would have been an insulting description of Bobby Charlton, Bobby Moore, Denis Law, Jimmy Greaves, Ray Wilson, John Giles and Gordon Banks) and they, like the managers, were bonded by shared background with the mass of ordinary supporters on the terraces.

From the vantage point of such an era no one could accurately predict the hurtling decline in standards and the cynical distortion of priorities that have brought us to the lamentable mediocrity of the Premier League, a competition in which an unreconstructed hod-carrier called Vinny Jones not only qualifies for first-team wages but is enough of a roughneck celebrity to promote a video that purports to be a macho-man's guide to dirty tricks. Plenty of hod-carriers made it in football in the past but they had to learn to play first. The elevation of the plainest of the Joneses is, however, a lot less remarkable than it would have seemed two decades ago.

In the intervening years a shameless emphasis on speed and muscle, on making the field claustrophobic with clattering bodies, has established his kind of negative physicality as a viable commodity. Well over £2 million has been spent on his transfers between clubs.

The self-proclaimed hard case happens to be linked by the laying on of hands (an unapostolic grabbing of the testicles, actually) to the one player constantly put forward as comparable with any seen in English football before the current blight descended. Paul Gascoigne would undoubtedly have been recognised as an immense talent in any period. His feet are wonderfully deft, whether dribbling or passing the ball; he has the alertness and the imagination to see and exploit openings of which others have no inkling; he shoots with dramatic power and accuracy; and in the application of his skills he has more balls than a bully like Jones could ever hope to crush.

But Gascoigne's qualities have to be weighed against an immaturity that has effortlessly survived his twenty-fifth birthday. However, even if the likeable man-boy from the North East did not have these problems the messianic status accorded him would be an alarming confirmation of the scarcity of exceptional performers in our national sport. If the midfields of England were peopled, as they once were simultaneously, by Charlton, Giles, Martin Peters, Colin Bell, Billy Bremner, Alan Ball, Alan Hudson, Paddy Crerand, Charlie Cooke and a few others nearly as distinguished, a Gascoigne would still be outstanding but he could not possibly have been singled out for the idolatry that was lavished on him before he moved to Italy. And mention of Best, of course, introduces another dimension altogether.

Many will dismiss such speculation as an offensive lurch into nostalgia. But the real offence is perpetrated by those who try to persuade us everything in football is as good as it ever was, for that is an attempt to cheapen an experience that enriched millions of lives. What they are telling us is that the excitement and sense of aesthetic pleasure stirred in us by the football of that other time might, if we were unprejudiced, be just as readily created by the banalities encountered on an average day in the Premier League. It is a kind of mad sporting structuralism, the equivalent of suggesting that you can get as much from McGonagall as you can from Yeats.

Of course, English football has not become an absolute wasteland. There are still skilled and entertaining players, matches that offer more than clamorous vigour, and apologists believe the fact that these are painfully rare must be set against evidence of a worldwide drop in standards. Italia '90 provided much the poorest World Cup finals most of us who attended have ever seen.

But blaming global conditions for the technical impoverishment of England's domestic game is about as valid as making the same excuse for the state of the nation's economy. Diagnosis must start with the twisted values on and off the field.

The Premier League itself is an unsightly symptom. Having instantly reneged on the original concept of reducing the number of clubs to raise the quality of play, the founders blithely trampled on the interests of their traditional public by selling television rights to a satellite company. Nothing they have done since – least of all their internecine squabbling over the spoils – has obscured the truth that their overwhelming priority is profit. Long after Thatcherism has been discredited, they appear happy to inhabit its mores.

As the corporate entertainment boxes multiply in grandstands, and the cost of following football climbs almost as dramatically as the unemployment figures, the regular fans feel betrayed, left out on the edge of the sport their commitment built. They have good reason to fear that their game is being taken away from them. Rogan Taylor, a former chairman of the Football Supporters' Association who now works at the Centre for Football Research at Leicester University, defined the fear when he said that the current packaging was apparently designed to appeal to some imagined Home Counties family in which the husband would say to his wife on a Saturday morning: 'Well, darling, is it to be the golf club today – or is it the Arsenal?'

In such a time of poverty on the field, and threat from the indifference of the legislators, people who have grown up with football as a vital adjunct to their lives can hardly avoid a yearning for happier days. The longing does not have to reach back as far as the prime of George Best and his contemporaries.

Long after he had made his disenchanted exit, Liverpool produced a team worth cherishing, constructed around Hansen, Souness, Dalglish and Rush. A later version, with Barnes, Beardsley and Whelan prominent, was rather memorable, too, and Brian Clough's Nottingham Forest did their bit to sustain the morale of the discerning. But as we lament what has gone from our football, perhaps forever, it is inevitable that Best, the greatest player ever bred in these islands, should be the most potent symbol of the loss.

Within the legend, a life has to be lived. Since the Brown Bull days, Best has owned the odd bar and night club and helped to pay for dozens of others, he has known a lot more bad times than good and the grey that is taking over his beard is not the only sign of what the world (often at his invitation) has done to him.

When we went to that Spurs–Manchester United game two or three weeks back, the rendezvous, predictably, was in a pub. But it was one in which his celebrity brought no hazards. His home is in a street off the King's Road, Chelsea, and the pub, tucked around a quiet corner a few hundred yards away, is used by locals who regard him as one of them.

Having tried drying out in clinics, attending meetings of Alcoholics Anonymous and taking alcohol-deterrent drugs, both orally and by having them implanted in his body, he has convinced himself that the best compromise he can manage in his efforts to cope with his drink problem is an attempt to shorten the binges and lengthen the periods when the craving is under control.

'I'd be sitting in AA meetings longing for them to end, so I could get to a bar,' he admits. 'When I was supposed to be swallowing those tablets

that make you allergic to alcohol – I was married to Angela, the mother of
my son, at the time – I was sometimes hiding them behind my teeth and
getting rid of them later. And even when I had the implants, I was saying
to myself: when the effect of these pellets wears off, I'll have a good drink.
So those therapies didn't have much chance of working. Now I have a
drink when I feel like it and concentrate on preventing things getting out
of hand. The better times are getting longer and longer, whereas a few
years ago they were getting shorter and shorter.' The fear that this is
another of the convenient rationalisations in which alcoholics become
expert is at least partially allayed by some corroboration from Mary
Shatila, who has been with him for five-and-half years in a relationship
that has been the strongest mooring he has ever had since childhood.
After all the years of frantic bedding, of lurching hazily from one brief
embrace to the next, after the Miss Worlds and the actresses and a
marriage that began drunkenly in Las Vegas and was too ill-starred to be
saved by the birth 11 years ago of his son, Calum, he finds himself at 46
with an attractive, caring woman who has the intelligence, the tolerance
and, perhaps most crucially, the stamina to go on trying to reduce the
hurtful chaos into which he has habitually plunged himself.

Mary Shatila has been matured by deep sadness in her own life. When
her marriage in Lebanon broke up she brought her daughter, Layla, back
to England but in 1988 her husband snatched the child away and Mary
has not seen her since.

She and Best both talk frequently of the children who are separated
from them by thousands of miles, one in Beirut, the other in California.
Best went to America in 1975 and stayed until 1981, combining his
football-playing commitments in Los Angeles, Fort Lauderdale and San
Jose with spells on this side of the Atlantic with Fulham and Hibernian, in
Edinburgh. But the talent, not unnaturally, was suffering premature
erosion, and the drinking became cataclysmic. When he returned to
Britain he was met with a tax bill for £16,000. He offered £10,000
immediately and the rest in six months but was told that was not
acceptable. The result was a marathon wrangle which, he estimates, cost
him 10 times the original debt, and made him bankrupt. It was a tunnel
without the smallest glimmer of light until he was introduced recently to
Bryan Fugler, a solicitor who acts for Tottenham Hotspur. Fugler quickly
made sense of the tax muddle and reached an agreement with the revenue
men. With the help of £72,000 raised by a testimonial match and dinner in
Belfast, Best was able at last to lift a shadow that had darkened his spirits
for more than a decade. ('The people of Belfast have sorted my whole life
out,' he says emotionally.)

He is no longer a bankrupt and last June he was able to open a bank
account for the first time since he was in the US. The account will not be
threatened, as it once would have been, by betting fever. Though he

claims he was never really a heavy hitter, that £50 was a big wager, there was a steady volume of activity. And two or three spectacular wins (like the night when he and a business partner were £17,000 down in a Manchester casino and then held the dice for an hour and 40 minutes and finished up cashing chips worth £26,000, or the £22 Yankee on the horses that brought Best more than £12,000) merely ensured that he stayed keen enough to be a long-term loser. 'These days if I lose a fiver on a horse, I want to go into the toilet and throw up,' he told me. Quality paper crosswords have more interest for him now than the racing pages.

His name is still a passport to lucrative employment. He works regularly as an analyst on LBC Radio's coverage of the Premier League, has been in demand lately for appearances on Sky Television and makes occasional sorties to the Middle East, where expatriates pay him handsomely for some coaching and a bit of chat about the great years. He can still turn out in celebrity matches but his right leg, ravaged by cartilage trouble and the thrombosis that gave him a major fright in the '70s, cannot withstand much strain. Strain of another kind is involved in his speaking engagements on the sporting dinner circuit. Though he is highly intelligent and the possessor of nuggets of knowledge on an unlikely range of subjects (like many drinkers, he is liable to be reading when others are sleeping), being publicly articulate has never been easy for him. The lifetime of headlines notwithstanding, he is shy. When he was a boy at Manchester United and travelled to the ground by bus, he had to make a change at a point that put him on the route driven by Matt Busby each morning, and the Boss was always eager to give him a lift. But Best, embarrassed by the need to make conversation, used to hide until the car went past. So rising to make a speech is an ordeal. 'Going out to perform in front of a hundred thousand in a stadium never worried me, because I was doing something nobody could do better, but standing in front of an audience of two or three hundred to say a few words could frighten me to death.' However, in pursuit of solvency, he has overcome his nervousness, helped recently by the formation of a double-act with Denis Law.

As the negotiator of his fees and organiser of his schedule, Mary has her share of difficulties. An obvious one is her man's reputation for failing to keep appointments. She insists there has been a substantial improvement of late but her armoury of excuses has to be in constant readiness. Of a booking he should have skipped, the infamous appearance on *Wogan* in 1990, she says (perhaps with more love than logic) his descent from controlled behaviour to lolling, swearing drunkenness in the studio was so abrupt that she wonders if someone doctored his pre-show drinks as a malicious joke. A persistent commercial handicap is the widespread assumption that Best's contracts are still handled by Bill McMurdo, the Scottish agent with whom he became associated after his return from the

States. In fact, Best has been bitterly estranged from McMurdo for years.

Best believes he has mellowed sufficiently to be disciplined by a diary well filled with entries that will earn money. In keeping with a long-established habit, he reacts to any disfiguring increase in weight by going to a health farm. There was a time when his first move on arrival was to set up an escape committee, but when I went to see him at Henlow Grange in Bedfordshire he and Mary were leaving their VIP room only to exercise or take the treatments. Admittedly, she made herself busier than he did but his visits to the gym were rather more serious. Back in a tracksuit, and with four days of abstinence already removing the smudged look from his features, he evoked moving echoes of his youth. He was always a voracious trainer, proudly torturing himself to keep pace with less indulgent team-mates. 'I knew I had to be fit to avoid being battered by some of the guys who were after me on a Saturday. I wouldn't have stayed out of hospital very long if I'd been stumbling around with a hangover.'

He has been through so many awful scenes, sometimes as the befuddled, brawling offender, often as the malevolently chosen victim, that a capacity for gallows humour was a necessary protection. Sober after an evening at the cinema, he slipped into a pub near Piccadilly Circus that was run by an elderly couple he knew would let him use the telephone to order a Chinese takeaway. As he was making the call, the mirror in front of him suddenly accommodated the nightmare vision of a drunken customer, a man he had never seen before, raising a heavy pint mug above his head. When the glass crashed into Best's skull ('I can still see the whole thing in detailed slow-motion'), the wound was so terrible that bar towels had to be stuffed into it. At the hospital, a doctor told him a brain scan was indicated. 'Don't bother with that,' said Best, 'I'm Irish.'

After failing to appear in court on a drunk-driving charge in 1984, he was violently arrested at his home by a posse of police formidable enough to round up the Dalton Gang. When he eventually went to Southwark Crown Court to appeal against a prison sentence imposed earlier at Bow Street, his counsel somehow reasoned that it would be of assistance if Jeff Powell of the *Daily Mail* and I turned up as character witnesses. In the court canteen, I told George that having us on his side might make him the first man to be hanged for a driving offence. But such feeble efforts at cheering him up were soon stifled by the realisation that he was probably going to jail (he did, for two months), and before long everybody was staring into the bottom of the coffee cup, with nothing to say. Then he glanced across at me with a smile. 'Well, I suppose that's the knighthood fucked,' he said.

He thinks he can specify the day when his career at the top reached a similar condition. It was in January 1974, on a Saturday when Manchester United were at home to Plymouth Argyle in the FA Cup.

Best, following the most prolonged of several defections from the club, had been persuaded into one more comeback by Tommy Docherty, the latest hopeful to step through the revolving door that appeared to have been fitted to the manager's office at Old Trafford. Having fought to regain a respectable percentage of his former fitness, the great footballer was beginning to feel the penetrative surge returning to his play, and he was sure the limited resistance of Plymouth would give him the chance to put on a show. Then he missed a morning's training in midweek. He went in and punished himself the same afternoon and, when Docherty made no complaint, assumed the lapse had been forgiven. But shortly before the kick-off (it had to be then, because Best never arrived early) he was called into the referee's room and told by Docherty that he would not be playing. He tried to remonstrate but Docherty was adamant.

'When he and Paddy Crerand left me, I sat in that room and cried my eyes out,' Best recalled at Henlow Grange. 'Then after the match I went up into the empty stands and sat on my own for about an hour. I knew I had ceased to be a part of Manchester United and it was a desperate feeling.'

Considering that he was attached to United before he was properly into his adolescence, that the club was his world through the most exciting an fulfilling years of his life, the reaction was inevitable. Equally natural, perhaps, is his vehement assertion that disenchantment was entirely responsible for the shortening of his career. 'It had nothing to do with women and booze, car crashes or court cases. It was purely and simply football. Losing wasn't in my vocabulary. I had been conditioned from boyhood to win, to go out and dominate the opposition. When the wonderful players I had been brought up with – Charlton, Law, Crerand, Stiles – went into decline, United made no real attempt to buy the best replacements available. I was left struggling among fellas who should not have been allowed through the door at Old Trafford. I was doing it on my own and I was just a kid. It sickened me to the heart that we ended up being just about the worst team in the First Division and went on to drop into the Second.'

His conviction must be respected but the case is an over-simplification. Had his life and his personality not been in such confusion, he might have withstood those miseries on the field and refused to let the mediocrities who had invaded Manchester United drive him away from the most important means of expression he would ever know. His rationalisation of his departure at 27 is no more convincing than the argument of those who tell us that disillusionment with football provides a total explanation of his alcoholism.

There is no doubt that great sportsmen are immensely vulnerable when their gifts, and the drama they create, begin to fade, when the rest of their lives may loom like a dreary anti-climax. But alcoholism is a complicated disease, one not readily susceptible to simplistic cause-and-effect analysis. Recent research suggests that there may well be a relationship between heredity and alcoholism and, whatever other factors have been at work in the case of George Best, there could be significance in the sad fact that his mother died an alcoholic.

Best loved his mother, just as he loves his father, Dickie, a spirited, engaging little man who was an iron turner in the Harland and Wolff shipyard. They gave him a warm, carefree childhood. It was a Protestant upbringing but that was in the '40s and '50s and, though there were plenty of Catholics on the Cregagh council estate, he was not troubled by sectarian bitterness. His lack of bigotry shows in consistent advocacy of a united Ireland on the football field. He is proud of his origins and has a dream of having a house that would enable him to be near his father.

There is another dream, one that comes to him repeatedly in his sleep. 'The theme is always basically the same,' he says. 'I am the age I am now but I have been brought back to play for Manchester United, along with some of the players from my own time and others of the present day. Sir Matt's in charge and he's put me in the previous week and I've played well. But I've been away for a while – well, I have, haven't I? – and I am worried about whether he will pick me. Bryan Robson of the current squad is often involved, and big Steve Bruce and young Giggs. And Paddy and Denis are nearly always there.'

If George Best concentrates hard in his dream, he will see quite a few of us on the sidelines, straining to catch a glimpse of a footballer whose like we may never look upon again.

Heroic symbol of a golden age

(*The Observer*, 28 February 1993)

AMID THE COARSENING of spirit that has been manifest in this country over the past couple of decades, there is a measure of reassurance in finding so much of the nation so deeply affected by the death of Bobby Moore.

It is impossible to doubt the spontaneity of grief felt by millions whose intimacy with the man was no greater than could be developed through watching him from the terraces of a football ground or on a television screen. Wherever people gathered onWednesday, there was a pervasive sense of loss, an unforced emotion that suggested many had been taken unawares by the depth of their feelings.

Their reaction seems to spring from a number of identifiable sources. By being not only the captain but the unmistakable leader of the England team who in 1966 brought the World Cup to the islands that like to be considered the home of football, the incomparable central defender made himself an abiding presence in countless lives. The timing of that achievement helped to give it a lasting resonance. Much of what passed for glamour and creativity in the '60s was sham but the decade was a genuinely distinguished period for football in England, with Moore, George Best and Bobby Charlton at the apex of a broadly based pyramid of exceptional talent.

Viewed from the vantage point of the present grey era in the game, that was something of a golden age and the blond, upright, regally composed figure who orchestrated the defeat of West Germany at Wembley on a July afternoon nearly 27 years ago was naturally freeze-framed in the mind's eye as its golden symbol. That he should become the first of the glory boys of that distant summer to die was sure to make the jolt all the more sickening when he was claimed by cancer of the liver and colon at the age of 51.

Yet the impact of his death, and the remarkably widespread ache of deprivation left by it, cannot possibly be explained in terms of accumulated nostalgia. Even the length and sustained distinction of his professional career (his total of 108 international caps remains a record for an English outfield player) do not take us halfway to an explanation. The encouraging truth may be that Moore's place in the hearts of such a large percentage of the population confirms the survival among us of the capacity to recognise and applaud heroic style.

To say the manner of what he did on the field counted for nearly as much as the substance is meaningless, because the manner and the substance were inextricable. His bearing, the aura of imperious authority that almost defied any honest reporter to avoid the word majestic, grew directly out of his profound understanding of the job he had to do and an unshakable belief that no one anywhere was better at it. His nerve under siege was awe-inspiring. It was never simply a matter of being unfrightenable, whether confronted by physical risk or mountainous responsibility. The impression was of a nature so comfortable with challenge that it needed crisis to show its true strength. Of the supreme sports performers I have seen in action, perhaps only Muhammad Ali was a more conspicuous example of grace under pressure.

Ron Greenwood – who, as an intelligent and principled manager of West Ham, was Moore's mentor during many of the 16 years he spent with that club – said of him: 'Bobby is not a bread-and-butter player. He is made for the biggest occasion. The more extreme the challenge, the more commanding he will be. He should play at Wembley every week.'

Or at Maracana in Rio or San Siro in Milan or Jalisco Stadium in Guadalajara, Mexico, where in the 1970 World Cup the opposition of a Brazilian team who must rank with the most formidable of the century brought out the incredible best of Bobby Moore. He had flown in behind the rest of the squad after being held in Colombia on a wild charge of having stolen a bracelet in Bogota. It was an accusation that eventually came to nothing (the most convincing theories about its origins concern a younger England player and a prank that went wrong) but the ordeal of arrest and interrogation might have been expected to wreck his ability to concentrate on the World Cup.

Instead, to those of us observing at close quarters he seemed effortlessly single-minded, still the rock of dependability so treasured by his manager, Sir Alf Ramsey, that the architect of triumph in 1966 described the Bogota episode as 'the worst experience I've had in football'. And against Brazil, in an unforgettable contest that his side scarcely deserved to lose 1–0, the captain deployed the full, extraordinary arsenal of his gifts.

At the end of the match, we were given a moment as pure and moving as sport can offer when Pele, the most accomplished player in the history of football, and Moore, the adversary the Brazilian admired more than any other, exchanged shirts and smiles and affectionate slaps on the cheek. Even now, few of us who were there can look at photographs taken at the time without being warmed by the obvious sincerity of their mutual respect – by that and the sheer happiness they found in recognising that, for them at least, the clichés about brotherhood in sport had meaning.

They were linked by a quality of spirit as much as by talent, for at the centre of their greatness as footballers pride and humility coexisted without strain. Both cherished the virtues of simplicity, refusing to do anything complicated if something apparently ordinary would have more effect. They left the swaggering to lesser men.

When connoisseurs of Moore's game are listing his assets, they are obliged to start with his almost supernatural aptitude for divining the intentions of opponents, his capacity to identify a threat before even its perpetrators were fully aware of what they were doing. 'There should be a law against him,' Jock Stein, a giant among managers, once told me with mock bitterness. 'He knows what's happening 20 minutes before anybody else.' That inspired reading of play and the crucial interventions it produced were testimony to more than heightened alertness, sharp intelligence and an instantly rational interpretation of danger signals. The extra dimension of effectiveness is best attributed to a kind of intuition, the mysterious 'feel' for the ebb and flow of action that only a tiny élite of team-game players possess. In Moore's case its value was multiplied by the diamond nerve, which allowed him to act on his judgments with utter decisiveness, however intimidating the implications.

As he patrolled his extensive area of influence, straight-backed, handsome, head up and eyes sweeping the field like a radar scanner, he was everybody's ideal of the thinking footballer. But if attackers decided they were outgunned tactically, it was inadvisable for them to seek a physical duel. Moore was six feet tall with a playing weight of slightly under 13 stone, and in his prime he went out as fit and hard as a prize-fighter. He was (as Pele stressed) a clean player by nature, and contemptuous of provocation, but if real liberties were taken he had no taste for turning the other cheek.

Being raised as an only child, by loving parents who 'gave me everything they could', never threatened to be a softening experience for him, perhaps because the raising was done in Barking, a borough that lies a few miles beyond London's East End and is inevitably pollinated by it. From the start, strength of will was crucial to his success in football. As a schoolboy he was outstanding but not a prodigy. Rising through district teams at the primary and secondary stages (he passed the 11-plus and attended Tom Hood Technical School, Leyton, until he was 16), he played for London but never internationally at that level.

What impressed knowledgeable judges as he went straight from school to join West Ham as a ground-staff boy, and moved quickly into the England youth team, was the authority of his presence. If he was in a team it tended to revolve around him and he nourished the confidence of the other players as if by a kind of solar energy. But he had basic deficiencies. His rather stiff-legged action would never generate more than modest pace and he betrayed further inadequacy in jumping and heading the ball.

Then there were the limitations of his left foot, which throughout his career he was inclined to use only under duress, often preferring to simulate its effect by playing the ball off the outside of his right foot.

Instead of being weighed down by such shortcomings, Moore made his determined response to them a launching pad from which he would reach the ultimate heights of his sport. He was one of the great trainers and practisers of all time, never too proud to work hour after repetitive hour on honing the most simple techniques. 'The greatest satisfaction I take from football is the sense of doing something well,' he told me back in 1975 when the spell with Fulham that was the last phase of his playing career took him to the FA Cup final. (Strangely, that final saw Fulham lose to West Ham, the club he had recently left and with whom he had won FA Cup and European Cup Winners' Cup medals.) 'When some players are told in training to kick the ball from one point to another they think the whole thing is so ridiculously easy that they can't concentrate and they kick it all over the place. That really annoys me. If I've got to play the ball from here to there 10 times, then I want to do it right 10 times.' One result was the excellence of his passing.

Operating through most of his senior years as free man in defence, charged with scenting trouble and smothering it at birth, his comparative frailty in the air was seldom damaging (the frequency with which he positioned himself perfectly to collect the ball on his chest was freakish). His tackling was precisely timed and uncompromising and his brilliantly early and economical distribution constantly transferred pressure from his own to the opponents' goal area. His extremely rare blunders could be theatrically explicit but that merely emphasised the outrageously high standards he encouraged us to take for granted.

Just about everything he did, important or trivial, was characterised by efficiency and neatness. The staff at West Ham used to marvel at how the kit he handed in did not arrive in a dishevelled bundle, as it did from most other players, but folded as meticulously as anything on a shop counter. 'I find it strange that people should be surprised by efficiency,' he told me. 'We all know footballers who couldn't check through an airport on their own. They've got to have their tickets and passports handled for them and be shepherded through when it's time to go. I find that incredible.'

His most influential attributes as a player were firmly related to the confident rationalism that underpinned all his attitudes. It did not take long to assert itself when we talked about his play. 'OK, if speed is only a matter of taking yourself physically from A to B, then I'm not fast. But isn't it important to know earlier than the next man that it's necessary to go from to A to B? Isn't speed of thought as vital as how fast you can move your legs? Of course, pace is a good thing to have, especially when it helps you to recover after you've been skinned. But I like to think I compensate for my slowness by seeing situations quickly, by anticipating and reacting before others realise what is happening.'

As understatements go, that one should have been auctioned as a collectors' item. Somehow the drive, leadership and perceptiveness that made him such a potent force on the field did not translate into a worthwhile career in football coaching or management and his business ventures were equally disappointing. Undoubtedly, greater effort should have been made to give him a more prominent role in English football than the radio commentating he had done for some years and which, with typical courage and lack of fuss, he insisted on continuing to within a week of his death. But maybe management was always going to be a less obvious metier than performing had been for someone whose inspiring effect was rooted in example and whose personality had a core of carefully guarded privacy.

'Ask me about Bobby Moore the footballer and I'll talk to you for a week but ask me about the private side of Bobby's nature and I'm liable to dry up after a minute,' Ron Greenwood admitted to me. 'That's not because he's uninteresting, cold or unfriendly, but because the inner part of his personality remains a mystery to me and, I'm sure, to the great majority of those who come in contact with him.'

Of course, the reserve inherent in a player-manager relationship can leave its residue. However, even as someone who had the privilege (one of the most valued to come out of my professional life) of being on relaxed and friendly terms with Bobby Moore over nearly three decades – of savouring, many times in many places, the quiet strength of his individuality, the dry humour, his gracious, unaffected courtesy – I can testify to a feeling that no matter how much of himself he opened up there might still be an inner door or two left closed.

In recent years, having stayed close to the children of his first marriage while finding happiness with his second wife, Stephanie, he was wonderfully engaging company, especially when good wine was flowing. But, if anyone with interrogative tendencies joined in, he was always liable to rediscover his old habit of answering questions with questions of his own. Once, when I taxed him about the device, his blue eyes flickered with mischief for a moment, the eyelids drooped and the composed, lightly freckled face yielded slowly to a smile. 'Well,' he said, 'you've got to try to learn something as you go through life.'

Bobby Moore's life was tragically short but he learned quite a lot in the time he had, like how to be so much of a man that he turned into a hero.

Boss with his eye back on the ball

(*The Observer*, 28 March 1993)

IF IT IS POSSIBLE to specialise in diversity, Terry Venables has always done so. No other leading figure in British football has matched a width of interests ranging from shared authorship of fiction to a high-level stake in the licensed trade, from an early, unprofitable dabble in selling menswear to his recent emergence as the entrepreneur who runs and partially owns Tottenham Hotspur.

But when Venables talked last week of the reviving fortunes of Spurs, both the business and the football team, he was full of conviction about the rewards to be gained from single-minded concentration of vigour and talent. At the age of 50, he seems to have decided that, when you have serious targets, a sniper's bullet is more effective than a blast from a scatter-gun. 'Sometimes I have been good at diversifying and sometimes I haven't,' he said. 'But, if you want to be successful, the basic principle must be to identify what you are really good at and concentrate on it wholeheartedly. That's definitely the advice I'd give my grandson. A lack of focus in applying abilities is deadly, whether in business, football or anywhere else.'

Genuine as that philosophical adjustment may be, it was never likely that his own unnatural energy would settle for only one channel of expression. He was obviously going to keep several balls in the air. The only question was whether one of them would be a football. Fortunately for the game, the answer has turned out to be a vehement affirmative.

Unable to specialise, Venables has at least compartmentalised, dividing his work days into mornings devoted (with no tolerance of distraction) to coaching at the Spurs training ground in North London and afternoons spent amid the paperwork and commercial pressure that come with his primary role in the club's life. Throughout last season, which was his first as chief executive and had to be sweatily concerned with dragging the old institution out of financial crisis, he found an increasingly painful void where his active involvement with the players had been.

He was thoroughly delighted when Doug Livermore made it a condition of taking charge of the first team that his boss should be alongside him in a tracksuit. With Livermore's assistant, Ray Clemence, completing a triumvirate, they have seen their Premier League season steadily improve and their FA Cup challenge flourish. Beaten only once in their last 11 matches, Spurs are now sixth in the table (highest of London's representatives). And by battling their way through to a Cup semi-final with Arsenal at Wembley next Sunday, they have promised a rousing echo of the minor epic of 1991 that preceded Tottenham's record-breaking eighth victory in the Cup Final.

Venables takes pains to insist that his influence on the preparation of the team is ultimately subordinate to that of Livermore and Clemence. But few will fail to see a link between Spurs' current surge and his renewed commitment to holding outdoor seminars on imaginative football. There is nothing remotely spurious, or even exaggerated, about his reputation for possessing one of the liveliest and most inventive minds in the game. When he talks tactics, the message is laden with specifics and blessedly devoid of jargon. Around the time he was ending an 11-year drought for Barcelona by winning the Spanish championship in 1985, I spent two or three enthralling hours with him over a drink in a hotel near the Nou Camp. Listening to him that day was an enlightening pleasure to be compared with a long session in the company of Jock Stein, and that's as good as football talk gets.

It would have been both ridiculous and sad if such a man had been lost to the game, as he says might have happened when his relationship with the former Spurs chairman, Irving Scholar, was at what seemed its nadir (more spectacular depths of bitterness would be plumbed later by the publication of Scholar's book, *Behind Closed Doors*). However, it is now history that he formed an alliance with the computers tycoon Alan Sugar to buy control of Tottenham (Venables owns 24 per cent, Sugar 47 per cent). After a period of considerable strain from the cost of the borrowing associated with an investment of £3.5 million, he reports that the relocation of his debts and the lowering of interest rates have combined to leave him well placed to benefit from the immense improvement he and Sugar have wrought in their club's financial health.

Football's benefits have been equally striking. In his business suit, Venables brings an informed, professional voice to the councils of the Premier League. In his tracksuit, he is helping to shape a predominantly youthful Spurs squad that (he cautiously admits) could 'cause a few problems in the championship next season'.

He believes the Premier League suffers from a tendency to be preoccupied with political games rather than the ball game at the heart of its existence. 'You can feel like an outsider because you are a football person,' he told me. 'Until football people are welcome and are not made to feel they are invading somebody else's territory, the League won't do as well as it should. I know financial considerations are vital and all the talk of greed in relation to the television deals is bollocks. Without money, you are not going to survive. You won't be able to develop and keep good players, you won't be able to implement the Taylor Report or do any of the other things that are urgently needed. But if you get the football right, the money will come in.'

His football ideals are enshrined in vivid memories of how the Dutch national squad of Cruyff and Neeskens and Van Hanegem performed in the '70s and how the Tottenham Double team achieved devastating brilliance a decade earlier. His favourite player is Dave Mackay, as much for his unquenchable spirit as his superb technique. 'When I was playing with Spurs we used to go through torture sessions in the gym, all exhausting intensity and battering physical contact, real sweatbox stuff. Dave would come in with bloodshot eyes, because he wasn't an early bedder, but when the first team had finished he would go through another hour of the same with the reserves. Some man.'

He is encouraged to find some of Mackay's legacy of commitment in the present generation of Spurs men. 'We are getting more players really keen to wear the Tottenham shirt, who feel like Tottenham people. Gazza had that kind of special identification with the club before he left and Neil Ruddock is one of several who show it now.'

Criticism for selling Ruddock at £300,000 and buying him back for £750,000 is irrelevant, since the Ruddock who returned was much more the finished article, influential enough to transform Spurs' central defence and spread confidence throughout the team. 'He is strong and can be hard but he is a good footballer, too,' said Venables. 'He can pass the ball short or long, has the composure to bring it down on his chest, and he also knows that when he smells danger he has to get that ball a distance away.' The enthusiasm for mixing pragmatism with flair would sit comfortably with Mackay and those Dutchmen.

Of course, Venables is as excited as everybody else about the promise of 19-year-old Nick Barmby, who strikes many as a classic incarnation of an old-time inside-forward. 'He's got to go on from here but right now he is as accomplished as you could possibly ask him to be. He has settled in so quickly, looking part of the first team and winning the respect of senior players. Apart from his skills, there is a cunning to what he does, a craftiness. He draws other people into the game, he is quick enough because he thinks fast and gets there early, and he can finish. He's got great qualifications.'

So has Terry Venables, and it is good to know that once again they are fully at the disposal of English football.

Soon after this piece was written, both Terry Venables and Neil Ruddock left Tottenham Hotspur, amid much public acrimony. Venables became manager of England, a job for which his talents made him a logical choice.

All Venables has to do now is keep delivering

(*The Sunday Times*, 22 May 1994)

ROUGHING UP a couple of guests outside the entrance to the big party will not sweeten England's memories of how they lost their own invitation in earlier muggings.

As an outlet for frustration, booting the ball into Greece's net beats kicking the furniture, but not by much. Even if Tuesday's cruising victory over one World Cup qualifier is followed today by a good win against another, Norway, the overall effect will be to sharpen the feeling of deprivation that is sure to come over football followers in this country when television brings the greatest event in sport into their homes halfway through next month.

If the Norwegians (who could be said to have reached the US finals at England's expense) are seen off in style at Wembley, we can expect an epidemic of 'if only' reactions. Such a response is understandable. It is also harmless unless it is tainted with suggestions that the absence of the English from America amounts to a serious injustice, the denial of a natural right. Unfortunately, that kind of self-delusion was in the air on Tuesday when some listeners made far too much of the loose-tongued tributes paid to the winners by the Greek manager, Alketas Panagoulias. At a time when he might have been better employed concentrating on the shortcomings of the team under his leadership – who will be stronger in the World Cup than they were last week, but not strong enough to be more than bit-players – Panagoulias was quoted as rating England superior to Holland and as good as Argentina. That was nice of him, but his compliment means as little as the home-grown smugness that produced the headline: 'You'll miss us!'. Perhaps the 1994 World Cup would have been enriched by an English presence but the competition will miss David Platt and his men a lot less than they will miss it.

There is obvious justification for believing that the failure to earn a place in the finals can be traced mainly to the inadequacies of Graham Taylor as a manager, though he might have been able to paper over the weaknesses of his approach had Gascoigne been fit and motivated throughout the qualifying campaign and the unique qualities of Shearer been consistently at his disposal. What is undeniable now is the need to admit that dismissal was no more or less than the team's form deserved. Nothing is to be gained by affecting the attitudes of a wronged giant. It is hard to go on claiming that status when the record shows that England have been bundled out at the preliminary stage in three of the past six world championships. And further back, remember, Alf Ramsey's squad were spared the strains of a qualifying series in both 1966 and 1970.

All of which indicates that in this initial phase of Terry Venables's tenure it might be healthy to remind ourselves, as a few of us did at the time of Taylor's removal, that England are not among the genuine superpowers of football. They are somewhere slightly above mid-table in its league of nations. That honourable ranking does not discourage optimism, or indeed a bit of swagger about what the pioneers of the game are still capable of doing to latecomers who have overtaken them. But it should increase appreciation of the intelligence and common sense with which Venables smothers frequent attempts to coax him into over-praising the encouraging start his regime has made.

Time and again at recent press conferences, he has been invited to reach for superlatives. However, even if he did not know how effortlessly certain sub-editors interchange words like terrific and turnip, his highly developed sense of the realities and priorities of football would never allow him to echo the cheerleaders' exaggerations. Whatever pressures may continue to be exerted on him by his financial entanglements, when Venables refocuses on his true vocation he is an assured and thoroughly convincing figure. Where lesser coaches might deal in generalisations clothed in cult jargon, he has the clarity of mind and the confidence to be constantly specific. That insistence on talking in practicalities, as much as his reputation for imaginative and original tactics and strategies, commands the respect of players and substantially improves the chances of a two-way relationship.

Thus when Venables encountered recurring hints, mainly from journalists, that Shearer was unhappy with his role in the system the manager has introduced to England's play, there was an instant but strictly informal addressing of the issue. The word was that the magnificently gifted Blackburn striker did not relish being so often the isolated tip of what has been called a Christmas tree formation, obliged to battle alone until supporting players arrive in the penalty box from deeper positions. It was suggested, too, that Shearer's profound, almost obsessional commitment to scoring goals caused him to be resentful when all his arduous foraging, all the unselfish running that drags defenders away from the areas they are meant to police, provided others with the glory of applying the killer blows.

If such thoughts were in fact harboured by a key member of the squad, they could not be permitted to fester. So, sitting down with the centre-forward at breakfast in the England camp early last week, Venables asked him how he felt their first shared international against Denmark had gone. 'Terrific' was the answer, a reassuring one from somebody the manager recognises as 'an honest boy, one I'd count on to express his feelings directly'. When Shearer went on to say he had got a great deal of the ball in the first half against the Danes and then found the action in the second half was going on around him, Venables was anxious to counter the possible suspicion that the experience was associated with the new system. It could, he pointed out, happen to any player in any match and was certainly not unknown to the most distinguished men in Shearer's position. He recalled that Klinsmann, operating in the advanced role for Germany against Italy recently, with Hassler and Moller coming from behind, had scarcely touched the ball in the first half, 'then in the second he had so much possession that it was almost a case of "Can't you give it to someone else?"'

The idea that England are currently working with just one man up front is, Venables told me last week, largely a misconception. 'Platt and Beardsley are essentially functioning as forwards,' he said. 'Shearer is not left isolated in the opposition area any more than Rush was for Liverpool when they were at their most effective, or than he is himself with Blackburn. Obviously it is a great advantage for attackers to come into the box from deeper positions because they arrive facing the goal, which creates more options for them and for the man who is already there.'

He is fully aware of the immense value to his playing method of having a spearhead with Shearer's extraordinary range of strengths. 'A striker has to be truly outstanding in at least one department if he is to do well at the higher levels,' he said. 'If he is exceptionally quick or tremendous in the air, for example, that will give him a chance. Often a player has a combination of nearlies. He is nearly quick, nearly good in the air, he has so many nearlies that he gives you the illusion of being outstanding. There is nothing illusory about Alan Shearer's abilities. He is really solid in the air. His control is good with people tight on him and he is physically solid – you are never going to kick him out of the game, just as you don't kick Mark Hughes out of it. In fact, you don't want to make fellas like them angry. Shearer's passing is more like a midfield player's than a striker's, he has an appreciation of people around him, and it goes without saying that his finishing is excellent: confident and violently decisive. His goal against Greece was first-class. Good, intelligent movement made the space and the marvellous sting in the shot did the goalkeeper.

'I try to avoid celebrating young footballers prematurely but I have to be impressed by the way he is developing, especially by the proof that he is always thinking about what he does, the maturity that is definitely unusual in a 23-year-old. He is adapting well to the difference between the demands of the international game and those you meet in our League football. English club defenders pass the marking job on from one to the other. If the attacker is in my area, I'll take him. If he goes into your area, he is yours. The change-over sometimes leaves spaces that can be exploited. At the international level, there is tight man-for-man marking, with all sorts of quality men doing it. Because he is smart, he is quickly becoming adept at losing his man. It will be fascinating to see what the next 10 years hold for him. All he has to do now is keep delivering.'

Venables could, of course, say the same of himself as England manager, and he knows that for both of them the obligation is anything but simple. In his own case, he must seek to deliver an England team that can compete with the finest standards in contemporary football. Just how high those standards can be was demonstrated by the spellbinding performance of Milan in Athens on Wednesday night, when their classic blend of flawless organisation and surging creative brilliance produced the most uplifting European Cup final since the 1960s.

It would be foolish to draw from that 90-minute festival of the game's arts too many hopeful omens for the imminent World Cup. After all, neither of its two most thrilling influences is identified with a country that will participate in America: the tireless, subtle and endlessly penetrative Savicevic is a Montenegrin; Desailly, whose rich technique in midfield was reinforced by incredible strength and gravity-defying balance, is African–French. But the mere fact that the Italian league can provide a team as talented as Milan suggests that Italy may be a salutary catalyst in the US, helping to raise the tournament above the pervasive drabness that prevailed in their own country four years ago. Like Milan, they will start with the advantage of having perhaps the most impressive defender in the world, Maldini, who at 25 already has half a hundred caps.

As he watched Milan in mid-week, Terry Venables could afford to be more relaxed than Alex Ferguson. Venables need only attempt to emulate the European Cup holders. Next season, Ferguson's Manchester United must try to beat them.

Giggs breaks silence with sound sense

(*The Sunday Times*, 12 December 1993)

RYAN GIGGS under questioning proved no less impressive than he has been through several years of letting his talent do the talking.

When action is as vivid and graceful a language as it is for him on the football field, words must be a secondary means of expression. But he uses them with intelligent care, and the natural directness of what he says combines with the quiet strength of his presence to suggest that behind the athletic precocity is a 20-year-old of exceptional substance.

A week after the birthday that took him out of his teens, and was marked by the signing of a new, five-year contract with Manchester United that puts him among the top earners in the British game, our meeting over lunch represented another watershed, if a rather less momentous one. It was the first time Alex Ferguson, the United manager, had lifted the protective barrier he placed around Giggs during his rise to the status of most exciting footballer in Britain and allowed him to talk at length to a reporter.

The main impression left by more than two hours spent with him was that, for all the engaging residue of boyishness in his personality, this is a young sportsman with a clear awareness of who he is and what he intends to be. Such a firm sense of indentity is all the more remarkable in somebody who was Ryan Wilson until 1989 and who was a notably successful captain of England Under-15 Schoolboys (seven victories from nine matches, including the scalps of West Germany, Holland, France and Belgium) but changed national allegiance as well as his name and recently did as much as any player to take Wales to within a photo-finish of qualification for next summer's World Cup finals.

To add to the potential for confusion, there was the early aptitude he showed for rugby league, a game in which his abilities at stand-off shone through so brilliantly in a Salford boys' team regularly slaughtered by the likes of Wigan and Widnes that he was due to play a trial for Great Britain when the start of his Old Trafford apprenticeship ruled him out.

Rugby league was always certain to lose him. Its appeal was bound to be swamped by the sheer scale of his gifts as an attacker of dazzling fluency and pace in the more popular form of football, not to mention the vast disparity in the rewards provided by the two games and the fact that his physique – he is 5ft 11in and weighs 10st 6lb – is apparently better suited to one than the other. But, obviously, there was nothing inevitable about the decisions that made him Giggs and not Wilson, Welsh and not English. The purpose of the first was to disconnect him publicly and permanently from his father. The second expressed a sense of Welshness he insists was always there while reinforcing his identification with his mother, Lynne, her father (a retired policeman in Cardiff) and all the other relatives on the maternal side who have been indispensably supportive throughout his upbringing.

Giggs told me last week that he had last seen his father, Danny Wilson, who was once a rugby union and rugby league player of the highest calibre but has led a life disordered enough to put him more than once at odds with the law, 'eight months ago or maybe closer to a year ago'. There was no hint of regret about the vagueness of the memory. Everything he said conveyed an unequivocal desire to keep a distance between them: 'When I changed my name I was telling the world that I wanted to be known as my mother's son, that I belonged to her family. I am prepared to leave my father out of my life.

'I don't want to see him because it hurts too many of the people who mean the most to me. It hurts my mum and my grandparents, so I just don't see him. That last time we met it was only very briefly when he came to the hotel I was staying in for a Wales match. He knows it's his own fault things are the way they are.'

When Giggs moves, probably in January, into the house he is having built for himself in Worsley, a pleasant northern suburb of Manchester, he will still be only a mile from the family home in Swinton – well within reach of his mother's cooking or perhaps that of his stepfather, Richard Johnson, who is a chef. He is happy he has waited until now before opting to live on his own, glad of normalising influences to counter the mounting adulation and swirl of professional and commercial pressures inseparable from a career so meteoric that Ferguson has already contemptuously rejected two transfer offers of £10 million from Italy.

'I've had plenty of help in keeping my feet on the ground,' he said. 'If I come in a bit late, my mother gets on to me. She'll still give me a hard time about keeping my bedroom tidy. My two aunties, my uncles and my grandparents all enjoy taking the mickey out of me. My family and friends keep any superstar nonsense out of my head.

'I've had the same friends for 10 years, mostly lads I knew at school or played Sunday football with. Just yesterday I was telling Paul Ince, who is my best mate at Old Trafford – I room with him, go on holiday with him – that when I was a kid I used to play football for Salford Boys on Saturday, rugby league on Sunday morning and then football again in a Sunday league in the afternoon. All that laid the basis of the fitness that serves me well now and gave me a lot of good friendships.

'When I go for a drink it's usually to a local pub in Worsley among people who have known me since the family came north from Cardiff because my father was playing rugby league for Swinton. They treat me as just another customer, don't give me a second glance when I walk in.

'Sometimes after a match I'll go into a club in Manchester, make more of a night of it. It can be tough watching mates who are not in the game really enjoying themselves when you have to stay disciplined. I definitely envy them that freedom at times. So I think it does me good to get out and relax now and again.' In such thoughts any echo of the destructive restlessness of the young George Best is almost negligible, certainly much too faint to stir any anxiety at Manchester United. The club may be entitled to more long-term concern over a totally different kind of parallel with the experiences of the greatest of their greats.

Northern Ireland were never capable of putting Best on the ultimate stage of the World Cup finals and Giggs freely admits that if he suffers similar frustration with Wales, the urge to prove himself week-by-week against club football's most glittering concentration of talents might make a move to Italy extremely tempting.

'I feel this Welsh team we've got right now is probably the best we are going to have for a long time and some of the most important players are at a late stage of their careers,' he said. 'Maybe I won't be fortunate enough to go to the World Cup with Wales and signs of that happening would bring Italy more into my thinking. Nobody can question my commitment to Manchester United. I know how special the club is and how lucky I am to be part of it.

'But I wouldn't want to finish my career without convincing myself that I had realised every ounce of my potential. I do have a dream of proving my worth among the very best footballers in the world and most of them play in the Italian League. When the present deal is completed, I'll only be 25. I should be just approaching my prime and it could be that it will be right for me then to go to Italy.'

Ferguson knows that the best way to avoid that problem is for United to keep a long-term grip on the English championship and wreak havoc in the European Cup, with Giggs surrounded by internationally acclaimed team-mates. The manager will draw reassurance from the instant link the Welshman makes between his favourite player, Roberto Baggio of Juventus, and one of his current allies in Manchester. 'Baggio creates so much out of nothing and his finishing is so deadly. There is a lot about him that reminds me of Eric Cantona. Often when Eric gets on the ball you don't think the pass is on but you know you must get beyond a defender because he will thread the ball through, or flick it through. You always have to take a gamble with Eric because he is always able to pull something off against the odds.'

The perceptiveness of the compliment is no more than Ferguson would expect of Giggs. 'Ryan is a thinker about life,' the manager said amid the productive clutter of his office at the United training ground on Wednesday. 'He'll watch people's behaviour and listen to what they are saying and analyse it all. It's a capacity that sets him apart from most players. He has a shit-disposal unit in his head and much of what he hears goes into that. But if something is valid and useful, he'll store it away for the future.'

If the diposal unit is primed for use, it shows in the hardening of eyes that are never really soft, even when he is friendly. His passport says they are hazel but they seem darker, in their deep setting above well-defined cheek bones. Hard men, including Giggs's boss, have acknowledged the feeling that he was looking straight through them. There is no cheap aggression in the gaze, but it is steady and uncompromising, offering frankness and demanding nothing less in return.

At our lunch his black hair, newly washed after training, was bunched thickly around his forehead and the long, fine jaw was shadowed with stubble. In everyday terms, the transition from boy to man is palpable now but, of course, on the field he has been obliged to grow up ahead of schedule: 'When I was at school, even before I was an apprentice at Old Trafford, I was already playing with, and against, boys older than myself, never with my own generation. I suppose that experience is one reason why intimidation doesn't get to me. When players start talking to you, threatening, you know they are scared of what you might do to them with the ball.'

What Giggs can do with the ball has been making seasoned professional watchers react as uninhibitedly as fans ever since he was discreetly lured away from Manchester City's School of Excellence to play a trial for United during the Christmas period that fell barely a month after his 13th birthday.

'I was with Salford Boys then and I played for them in the match against a team of United trialists,' he recalled. 'Salford won 4–3 and I scored three. As you can imagine, some of the trialists gave me a bit of gyp afterwards. I didn't exactly help their chances.' He did his own no harm. Bobby Charlton, having seen Giggs score six in a boys' match not long after he arrived at United, threw Ferguson a slightly tortured look and said: 'Thank God we got *him*.'

The qualities that captivated Charlton then, now make Giggs at full throttle the most thrilling sight in British football. Whether breaking past an opponent from wide on the wing or erupting with dramatic suddenness through the middle of a defence, his runs are an exhilarating blend of grace and devastation. He has the attacking footballer's classic trinity of gifts: pace, control and balance. And the greatest of these is balance, since it so crucially underpins the effectiveness of the other two.

Once again Ferguson, the often demanding but always dedicated guardian of Giggs's uniqueness, is the most persuasive witness: 'If there is one factor that separates him from other very good players, and gives him a real chance of being truly great, it is his balance. He can wrong-foot anybody just by movement, and when you think a tackler is going to get a foot to the ball, he seems to float or ride or roll over the challenge. The defender always seems to go down while the lad stays on his feet.'

Because he is so perfectly balanced, Giggs creates the illusion of floating effortlessly over the ground when he is in fact generating a fierce pace that burns off pursuers. It is a priceless asset that seems to be a direct inheritance from his father. (A younger brother, Rhodri, is an apprentice right-winger with Torquay.) Danny Wilson is still remembered at Swinton rugby league club as somebody who could run like a god, though he swiftly jettisoned any traces of divinity when he left the field.

One of the bonuses of such fluidity of movement is the extent to which it reduces the risk of being badly hurt. That Giggs cannot recall having a serious injury obviously has a lot to do with luck but also relates to the way he, in common with the incomparable Best, rarely presents a stationary target for predatory opponents.

Since balance is as natural to him as breathing, it is not surprising that when the player himself is asked to identify his most telling weapon he nominates his pace. 'In football today you've got to be quick and I always have been,' he said. 'I love that feeling of knocking a ball past a defender and going. Just as he thinks he will get his tackle in, you touch it a little bit more and you are away.'

The appealing simplicity of that description leaves out the intricacy of control, the arsenal of deceptions, defenders have come to dread. By the standards of extremely skilled footballers, his feet are almost abnormally long and slim (he takes a size nine in boots) but their touch is extraordinarily delicate, especially when he is dribbling, and they can produce enough violence to make him a better finisher than his total of 24 goals from 108 appearances (plus 16 as a substitute) for United would indicate.

Recently the need to extend his repertoire of skills – in particular to improve his passing and his ability to cope with tight marking, to develop the precise awareness of when to hold the ball and when to steer it to a team-mate – have brought a pressure he had never previously known. He has started to absorb the implications of Ferguson's observation to the effect that knowing a lot of wonderful card tricks is not the same as being able to play cards properly.

'For a while after I got into the first team there was no pressure whatsoever,' Giggs said. 'I was playing as if I was in the A team or the reserves, where for me it was pretty much a case of being stuck out on the left and taking people on. But it's a different game where I am now. I am gradually learning to handle the other responsibilities, the need to pass effectively, to tackle back, to remember that our wingers are expected to tuck in and make a four across the midfield when required. It seemed I wasn't learning fast enough when I was left out for three or four games a couple of months back and I really did begin to lose confidence, which was something I had never experienced before. But now I realise the manager was resting me for my own good and I feel my play is developing a little bit with every game.

'I can still disappoint myself desperately and I did against Sheffield United last night. I don't know how many times I gave the ball away by hitting silly crossfield passes when I should have fed somebody next to me. It was the basic mistake of trying to hit the killer ball when there was something simple on. Fortunately, one of those crossfield balls did set up Eric Cantona to score a great third goal for us but that didn't make me forget the bad ones.'

Giggs's willingness to dwell on his bad times is the best possible guarantee that he will go on providing great times for those of us who watch him in wonder.

Farewell to the ultimate football man

(*The Sunday Times*, 23 January 1994)

IN THE LANGUAGE of the sports pages, greatness is plentiful. The reality of sport, like that of every other area of life, shows that it is desperately rare. Greatness does not gad about, reaching for people in handfuls. It settles deliberately on a blessed few, and Matt Busby was one of them.

If Busby had stood dressed for the pit, and somebody alongside him in the room had worn ermine, there would have been no difficulty about deciding who was special. Granting him a knighthood did not elevate him. It raised, however briefly, the whole dubious phenomenon of the honours system.

Busby emanated presence, substance, the quality of strength without arrogance. No man in my experience ever exemplified better the ability to treat you as an equal while leaving you with the sure knowledge that you were less than he was. Such men do not have to be appointed leaders. Some democracy of the instincts and the blood elects them to be in charge.

That innate distinction was the source of his effect on footballers. He never had to bully. One glance from under the eloquent eyebrows was worth 10 bellows from more limited natures. Players did not fear his wrath. They dreaded his disapproval. His judgment of the priorities of football was so sound, his authority so effortless, that a shake of his head inflicted an embarrassment from which the only rescue was recovery of his respect.

When Sir Matt died peacefully on Thursday at the age of 84, allowed to exit with the quiet dignity that was a central theme of his life, few beyond his immediate family of son Sandy and daughter Sheena would mourn more genuinely than Pat Crerand. And the Gorbals man's emotions represent a particularly relevant testimony to the influence of the manager he will never stop calling The Boss. Crerand in his playing days was street-hard to a degree that most of the notorious figures in the modern game can only imagine. He was a passer, a shaper of matches, a player of many attributes, but speed was not among them. Combativeness was. 'Where I was brought up, you had to be able to run or fight and you know about my running,' he once told me. Yet if Busby so much as looked at him the wrong way, Crerand felt like running.

There was an occasion in Europe long ago when Crerand came scrambling on to the team bus after all the other travellers were seated. 'You must be a very important person,' the manager said. 'You have kept the directors of Manchester United waiting, you have kept your team-mates waiting, you've kept the press waiting and you've kept me waiting. It must be wonderful to be as important as you are.'

'The man didn't miss you and hit the wall,' a friend said to the Glaswegian as he sank disconsolately into the nearest vacant seat. 'Don't worry about it,' Crerand said with undisguised concern. 'There's more where that came from.' But he knew Busby would forgive him the minor misdemeanour, just as he would find tolerance to cope with more serious offences born of the Gorbals temper. The reason was his appreciation of his wing-half's honesty. 'Do you notice that when Pat is having a rank bad day, when his touch is hopelessly off, he won't hide, he'll keep trying to pass the ball beyond people?' he would say with a smile of approval that precluded an answer.

The story of one footballer's relationship with his manager is worth dwelling upon because it reflects the integrity of the romantic dream that underpinned the practicality inseparable from Busby's monumental success at Old Trafford. He could be as hard as bell metal, in his dealings with other clubs or the legislators of the game as well as his own staff. If a little bit of worldliness, being a smart move ahead of the opposition in the transfer market or anywhere else, would help United, he was seldom slow. But for all his players – from the greatest, like Duncan Edwards or Bobby Charlton, Denis Law or George Best, to the most obscure – the essence of his inspiring impact was his humanity, the small miracle of a personality that embraced soaring ideals with a modesty and warmth bred in the bone.

His was a life lived with brilliance and style and more than a touch of nobility, a forceful reminder that sport, no matter how miserably it may be disfigured by the intrusion of cheap and distorted values, is still capable of providing a context in which a really big spirit can express itself. He did not have to be told that when compared with the suffering associated with the loss in the 1958 Munich air crash of Edwards and seven other members of a gloriously promising squad already immortalised as the Busby Babes, or the death of his cherished wife, Jean, anything that happens on a football field is fairly trivial.

But he knew, too, that the action out there can be magnificent, at once a wonderful respite from real life and an acceptable metaphor for it. As a player far more distinguished than the statistics indicate (his maturity coincided with the Second World War) and a manager of incomparable stature in the most truly global of games, he could be passionate about football without losing his perspective about its place in relation to the deeper concerns of the heart. His origins equipped him with such a perspective. Like his strong Catholic faith, it was merely reinforced by a narrow escape from death at Munich.

On the matter of origins, it is one of the most remarkable facts in football that the small coalfield which once spread across part of Lanarkshire and southern Ayrshire produced three of the greatest managers and most formidable individuals the game has ever known: Busby himself; Bill Shankly, the warrior-poet who created the modern Liverpool; and Jock Stein, the Big Man who made Celtic so vibrantly aggressive that they obliterated all competition in Scotland for a decade or so and became the first British club to win the European Cup, a year before United realised Busby's dream of lifting that trophy. Plainly, there were more than coal seams running through that bleak landscape in the West of Scotland. There were seams of rich humanity, of working-class pride and wit and energy and character.

The influence on Busby of his upbringing amid a loving family in the miners' rows of Old Orbiston near Bellshill was indelible. Commitment to a warm sense of family, both in his private life and at the club he made as renowned as any institution in sport, was one of the legacies. Another was the natural respect for other people's feelings that the harshness and dangers of life in a mining community encouraged. He had a gift, bordering on the magical, of making all who came in touch with him feel that they mattered.

Many have been recalling his almost eerie capacity to summon up, long after the most fleeting encounter, not only a name but a clear awareness of the person that went with it. Having the privilege of his friendship for more than three decades never diminished the awe that was stirred by the ease and depth of his courtesy. Asked to speak at a dinner in his honour a couple of years ago, I found myself expressing much of what is written here and telling of how, in the days when I regularly covered matches at Old Trafford, Matt would often take time to inquire around various groups in the tearoom afterwards until he had found me a lift to Piccadilly Station.

In the company of a Manchester audience, it had to be admitted that, yes, maybe he just wanted to make sure at least one pest got out of town. But, in fact, it was simply another manifestation of his spontaneous kindness.

Would-be sceptics used to smile and say he was a master of PR. They had it wrong. HR, human relations, were his speciality. It could be said that he conquered millions of hearts one at a time, moving out from his family through his club, and the adopted city he loved, into the world of football and the wider world beyond that. The way the huge power of his personality worked was the benign equivalent of house-to-house fighting.

All of his outstanding teams made statements about his values. United

qualified as a war casualty when he took over in 1945 but the rebuilding
began almost immediately and by 1952 he had taken them to the League
championship for the first time since 1911. Four more titles and two FA
Cup triumphs were to be added before that European Cup victory of 1968
climaxed nearly a quarter of a century of management (the knighthood
came in June of that year) but the record book can never convey the
significance of his achievement. Whether we think of the first Manchester
United he built in those austere post-war years, or the wonderful blending
of youthful verve and talent whose horizons seemed limitless until the sky
fell in at Munich, or the subsequent dazzling era of Law, Best and
Charlton, always there is in the mind a vision of football with the
unmistakable stamp of Busby upon it. He maintained an unshakable
allegiance to perhaps the most powerful basic truth about the game: that
football greatness cannot be measured or recorded in statistics alone, not
in the number of goals scored or matches won or trophies carried home.
All these are vital, of course, but the game's extraordinary grip on the
imagination of countless millions is exerted not through scorelines but
through the images of grace and skill, of courage and inventiveness it
leaves to shimmer in the memory.

The late Danny Blanchflower was not foolishly romantic when he said
the game is not about winning, it is about glory. Danny was too much of a
pro to deny that there must be sweat and grit and pragmatism in the midst
of all the romance. But he knew equally that football offers an
opportunity to produce something beautiful and that gifted players who
do not answer the challenge are betraying themselves and the game. And
if players of authentic talent apply themselves with sufficient heart and
honesty and resolution to playing beautifully, they will win plenty along
the way. They will not be short of prizes to go with the glory. If they ever
doubt that, they need only look at Busby's career for reassurance.

Nothing could have done more to warm the late twilight of this
ultimate football man's life than the resurgence of Manchester United
under Alex Ferguson. The winning of the European Cup Winners' Cup in
1991 gave him immense satisfaction but there was immeasurably more in
recapturing the League title last season for the first time since a team
under his own guidance had taken it in 1967. And the real joy of these
accomplishments lay in the knowledge that they were gained with the
kind of creative and adventurous football he had always seen as the one
true currency. For a long time his attempts to find a successor seemed
doomed to bring pain and disappointment to himself and others. But at
the end the view from the presidential chair was made cheerful by the
happy conviction that in Ferguson, another working-class man from the
West of Scotland, he had a genuine disciple and a worthy heir.

Using Shakespeare's words to praise somebody we know is bound to
be a rather wild risk, but at that dinner in Manchester I took the chance,

invoking Mark Antony's lines about Brutus: 'His life was gentle, and the elements so mixed in him that nature might stand up and say to all the world "This was a man".'

It did not seem over the top at the time. It still doesn't.

ISSUES

Having gone to Hillsborough in Sheffield on 15 April 1989 to cover an FA Cup semi-final between Liverpool and Nottingham Forest, I found instead that I was reporting on the worst crowd disaster in the history of British sport. Almost before the game was under way, a brutal crush at the Leppings Lane end of the ground had made the football irrelevant. The death toll was 95 (all Liverpool supporters) and at least 200 were injured. The piece on the aftermath of Hillsborough reprinted here was written for the leader-page of The Observer.

The other articles included in this section establish their own context.

The lost tribes

(*The Observer*, 23 April 1989)

MANY WOULD cringe last week at the pathetic resonance of the Football Association's efforts to justify their decision to go ahead with this year's Cup Final in spite of the awful happenings in Sheffield eight days ago.

The Chief Executive of the FA, Mr Graham Kelly, declared that a final at Wembley Stadium on 20 May would be a 'fitting memorial to those who gave their lives in the cause of football on Saturday'.

In the cause of football? Even normally sensible individuals can give way to jarringly inappropriate utterances in the aftermath of major calamities and – since words, good or bad, don't count for much in the overall context of suffering and grief – it is natural that spectacularly gross statements should draw no more than a passing wince. Certainly there is no virtue in being hard on Mr Kelly, who finds himself involved in a nightmare after only a couple of months in a new job.

But there is very real significance in the fact that he felt no uneasiness about saying what he did. Such language came readily to his lips because it is a direct echo of the desperately exaggerated importance which so many in Britain tend to attach to football.

Everybody knows that after the astonishingly rapid popularisation of the professional game in the latter part of the nineteenth century it grew to occupy an absolutely (indeed alarmingly) central place in the cultural experience of millions of working-class people. Inevitably less well understood is the complex way in which football, while continuing to have an extraordinarily pervasive and totemic relevance for a substantial percentage of the population, has found its total following appreciably reduced and attitudes to it considerably altered by processes of social change that have been dramatically accelerated under the Thatcher Government.

Hooliganism is only one extreme manifestation of a haphazard but profound adjustment in the nation's relationship with its favourite sport. And maybe it isn't the most telling one, since there must be a fair measure of truth in the argument that football's main contribution to the hooligan plague comes through the provision of clan banners and obvious battlegrounds for elements whose violence is too serious to be dissipated by the mere removal of such conveniences.

Thuggery had nothing to do with the terrible events at Hillsborough, but the behaviour of football supporters towards one another assuredly did. Grief over all the innocent victims and sympathy with the families left heartbroken cannot be allowed to obscure that reality. Of course, others in the end may be held far more culpable. Large, excited crowds can never be depended upon to behave rationally, even with self-preservation as an incentive. They have to be protected from themselves and at Hillsborough that job would seem to have been badly mishandled.

There was a fatal distortion of priorities that had its origins in the thinking responsible for the iniquitous and ill-designed containment fences which denied escape from the brutal crush at the Leppings Lane end of the ground. Something of the same negative cast of mind could be discerned in the slowness with which the police realised that they were dealing not with disorder but disaster. Perhaps it is understandable that policemen go to football matches these days with their thoughts concentrated on keeping hostile mobs at bay rather than on supervising the safety of a mass audience. But that predisposition carries the seeds of deadly consequences.

It is especially dangerous because of how it interacts with an unmistakable change in the mentality of football crowds. The memory of craning on tip-toe as a schoolboy in a crowd of 143,000 at Hampden Park, feeling scared for a while as others of my age and younger were passed from hand to hand down the great slope of the terracing to the perimeter track, but soon being able to relax sufficiently to enjoy a tight struggle between Rangers and Hibernian, makes me shudder now at the awareness of how much potential for catastrophe there was in allowing such numbers to cram together in vast standing, violently swaying congregations.

That more dreadful accidents did not occur in those far-off days (when 135,000 was the regularly reached capacity at Hampden, whereas 73,000 is the old ground's current limit) may have been due to the greater prevalence of a passive herd instinct among spectators. Probably there was more inclination to yield to authority, whether it was the boss or a policeman on a horse, and maybe being treated like cattle for generations had made fans almost as docile. The treatment has not improved more than marginally, though the responses can be very different.

There is an anachronistic shortage of seating at all but two or three British stadia, and some of the biggest clubs betray no embarrassment about letting the tenants of their executive boxes look out – with large drinks in their hands – on hard-core supporters who are pressed together in outrageous discomfort, lumbered with a poor view of the action and a fair chance of having their shoes splashed with urine.

To their credit, Liverpool FC have so far declined to follow the trend towards those fancy boxes for corporate clients, but there should be relief that the Kop, for all its romantic connotations, will shortly be replaced with seating. The ambiguous feelings likely to be stirred by that overdue modernisation of Anfield, and similar updating of other grounds, points to the peculiar mix of values today's football crowds are liable to take to the stadium. In many senses they are pretty much, probably too much, as they always were, but in others they are not at all the same. They are patently more fragmented and volatile than in the past and the conviction that they are definitely less easily controlled is not undermined by the knowledge that fans who broke through closed gates precipitated the crush that caused 33 deaths at Bolton in 1946.

Perhaps the frightening scene enacted outside a gate at the west end of Hillsborough immediately before the Liverpool-Nottingham Forest kick-off could just as easily have developed 40 years ago, but it is hard to believe that the presence of a few mounted policemen would not have had far more disciplining impact than was achieved last weekend. The police of the earlier era would have expected that to be the case and so would those they were marshalling.

Clearly the public inquiry under Lord Justice Taylor will have to ask if the policing in that Leppings Lane area can have been adequate and well led when three or four thousand latecomers (the South Yorkshire force's own on-the-site estimate) were able to create so much of a threat that a senior officer took the remarkable decision to open the gate. There will have to be a good explanation of why the start of the semi-final was not delayed to give time to control the seething throng outside the gate, a number of whom had been lingering in pubs, some of them still in search of tickets. Was it really only with hindsight that delay could be recognised as an option preferable to permitting the late arrivals to charge through a low and narrow tunnel, which apparently became a tomb for some and spurted others in a killing turmoil on to the already packed central section of the west end enclosure?

When it comes to deciding whether blame must be laid at the doors of the football authorities, the police, the Minister for Sport, or all identified with what passed for an emergency plan at Hillsborough, the testimony of Dr John Ashton, Professor of Medicine at Liverpool University, will surely be vital. Dr Ashton, who was attending the match as an enthusiast, had pitched in to set up a clearing station behind the Leppings Lane stand. He appeared frequently on television the day after the disaster and some of us who had been there but never in the front-line were made to shiver by the harrowing vividness of what he had to tell and the barely suppressed rage with which he told it. He makes an immensely powerful witness and his contention that the spectators at Hillsborough 'by and large were very well behaved' must be respected. Yet that assessment may be more valid when applied to the fans' reaction to the horror than to the wild clamour that preceded it.

Those hectic, doom-laden minutes and the slaughter that ensued should encourage a searching examination not only of the specifics of Sheffield 1989 but of the strange, disproportionate and often damaging role that a simple ball game has come to play in the lives of so many of our citizens.

It is 21 years since Arthur Hopcraft produced one of the best books ever written about the game, *The Football Man*, but several of the assertions he made in his introduction are as pertinent today as they were in 1968:

'The point about football in Britain is that it is not just a sport people take to, like cricket or tennis or running long distances. It is inherent in the people. It is built into the urban psyche, as much a common experience to our children as are uncles and school. It is not a phenomenon; it is an everyday matter. There is more eccentricity in deliberately disregarding it than in devoting a life to it. It has more significance in the national character than theatre has.'

Hopcraft would be the first to acknowledge that football is not basic to the fabric of nearly as many lives now as it was then. He would admit, too, that another claim in *The Football Man* – that the game's 'sudden withdrawal from the people would bring deeper disconsolation than to deprive them of television' – is now utterly untenable. Given the increasing unevenness of the contest between TV and all other leisure activities in this country – and considering the extent to which the standards of skill and entertainment offered by football have plummeted since the days when Hopcraft regularly watched such as Best, Law, Charlton and Crerand perform in the same Manchester United team – what is amazing is how much of its hold on the urban psyche this sport has retained.

There has, of course, always been a suspicion that an excessive commitment to football has had a limiting effect on the lives of too many working-class men, that absorption in its beauties and dramas has narrowed their cultural range and misapplied spirit and energy which might have been better expended, say, in political activism. However much justification there may have been for such worries over the years, they don't seem too terrifying if compared with the destruction wrought on the sensibilities of millions by the combined bombardment of pap from television and the sleaziest of the tabloid papers.

Yet it must be said that there remains something undeniably disturbing about the way the most ill-used sections of our society relate so uncomplainingly, almost enthusiastically, to the hardships of watching football. It can be argued that they have tolerated the perpetuation of insultingly squalid, often dangerous conditions at grounds because they lacked the power (short of boycott) to instigate improvements.

But not everyone craves the virtually all-seater stadia successfully created in Scotland by Rangers and Aberdeen. The plaintive protests about how much tradition will disappear along with the steep terraces of standing accommodation may represent more than just a nostalgic attachment to the game's cloth-cap origins.

At a deeper level it appears that the battering suffered in Thatcher's Britain by our industrial strongholds of the past, like Liverpool, to name the week's most relevant example, has left tens of thousands needing football as much as their forebears ever did. They need it as an escape from the drabness imposed by unemployment and poverty, and they need it for the defiant sense of unity they can find in the crowd, a rough camaraderie that was more of an everyday experience when factories were big and busy.

From the terracing they can, for an hour or two at least, look down on Yuppiedom with unanimous contempt. But at football grounds, as elsewhere, they run the risk of being too ready to accept deprivation and callous treatment as their natural inheritance. They should convince themselves first, and then those who take their money, that the old pleasure of watching football is not contaminated by a few modern comforts.

A great deal requires to be done if a repetition of the Hillsborough carnage is to become unimaginable. But it would be a crucial first step if Britain's vast football public started to press their case on the basis that even addicts have rights.

The scar on football's face

(*The Observer*, 13 May 1990)

THE VIOLENT disorders associated with English football have been with us so long that there is a real danger of coming to regard them not as a soluble problem but as a natural, if persistently offensive, punctuation of our national life.

Such pessimism may be excessive but it is understandable, given the profound advantages the dedicated hooligan will always have over all who try to eradicate his activities. In a society rightly committed to protecting civil liberties, the kind of liberty-takers who sacked Bournemouth and its environs a week ago can never be totally denied the opportunity to vent their malevolence. Even the harshest of hard-liners – those who sneer at claims that a complex interaction of social and psychological, historical and political factors has produced the plague – are forced to recognise that there is not the faintest hope of a swift or simple cure, however drastic. If football shut up shop tomorrow, it is inconceivable that the appetite for rampage so conspicuously prevalent among tens of thousands of young males here (and, increasingly, in several other European countries) would be instantly dissipated.

But there is naught for football's comfort in that reality, and certainly nothing to encourage any of the inadequates who proliferate in positions of influence within the game to indulge their habit of attempting to sidestep unavoidable responsibility. Their sport may not have created the hooligans but it is lumbered with them, and continuing efforts to distance itself from the implications are not merely ridiculous but shameful. Perhaps neither the bungling at the Football League that contributed so much to the Bournemouth mayhem nor the less spectacular instances of rowdyism elsewhere last weekend should be seen as particularly relevant to the threat of major violence at the World Cup finals which are due to begin in Italy on 8 June. Yet the general alarm about where football is heading can only be deepened by the evidence that, in England and several other significant places, the game still has a blinkered reluctance to accept the full seriousness of the mess it is in.

Of course, here there is an immediate obligation to emphasise that nothing – not even the accumulating achievements of Dutch hooligans – can obscure the uniqueness of English football's reputation in terms of the spread of ugliness at home or the virulence of the contagion so frequently exported to the Continent. Anyone seeking representative villainy need look no further than last weekend's principal wreckers, the supporters of Leeds United. Their record, stretching back to the storming of Paris at the European Cup final of 1975, reads like the CV of Conan the Barbarian.

For such a crew, Bournemouth on a Bank Holiday weekend was like an old lady waiting to be mugged. The admission that warnings from Dorset police about what was likely to happen never even reached the League's management committee, that the decision to reject police requests for the fixture to be rescheduled was taken at a lower level by 'a number of full-time officers', is staggering but perhaps not altogether untypical of an organisation which has its headquarters in Lytham St Annes, an office in London and a chief executive who operates from his home in Nottingham.

The League's bumbling insularity, the way it has so often combined a pathetic lack of worldliness with incorrigible complacency, must call into question its right to go on playing such a central role in the running of English football. Its main figures seem incapable of realising the utter pointlessness of repeating the obvious truth that the sort of damage done in Bournemouth is not a purely football phenomenon, that something similar might have been perpetrated three decades back by the Mods and Rockers and by other mobs at other stages of our history.

'Across the centuries,' wrote Geoffrey Pearson in *Hooligan: A History of Respectable Fears*, published in 1983, 'we have seen the same ritual of territorial dominance, trials of strength, gang fights, mockery against elders and authorities, and antagonism towards "outsiders" as typical focuses for youthful energy and aggressive mischief. Even under vastly different social conditions there are striking continuities between the violent interruptions to pre-industrial fairs and festivals, and the customary eruptions during modern Bank Holidays or the weekly carnival of misrule at contemporary football games – where the football rowdy, with his territorial edginess, mascots, emblems and choral arrangements in the "rough music" tradition, must seem like the incarnation of the unruly apprentice, or the late-Victorian Hooligan.'

All of that is true but the argument for historical continuity simply underlines how crass the League was in refusing to recognise that football is the main focus of youthful aggression these days and that letting the notorious marauders from Leeds descend on the South Coast during a holiday meant that there would indeed be a carnival of misrule. The dismissive reaction to recommendations from the police (who have, sensibly, since been given the power to veto fixtures they deem dangerous) will impress many people as just outrageously stupid, but at the core of the attitudes that produced it there is a depressing element of smugness.

Another manifestation of that unattractive characteristic came from Mr Ron Noades, the chairman of one of yesterday's Cup final contenders, Crystal Palace, when he declared that English clubs should not go cap in hand to the rulers of the sport in Europe with a plea for readmission to Continental competitions. 'They need us,' said Mr Noades, neglecting to acknowledge that such a claim was the truth but by no means the whole truth.

UEFA, the European governing body, are indeed anxious to end the ban applied to England's clubs after Liverpool supporters were adjudged culpable in the deaths of 39 fans at the European Cup final in Brussels five years ago. They see their competitions as severely diminished by the absence of such as Liverpool. But UEFA's eagerness for reconciliation is inevitably haunted by the memory of Heysel and the awareness that if the return of the English brought even the remotest echo of that calamity the administrators responsible would never be forgiven. They don't need anybody that badly.

Equally, if English fans visit havoc upon Sardinia or the Italian mainland during the World Cup finals, future participation in the game's greatest tournament would surely be in jeopardy. If the world governing body, FIFA, did not feel obliged to exclude England, the British Government might be embarrassed into doing so. Maybe all the toing and froing by the Sports Minister, Colin Moynihan, and his retinue of advisers, the security arrangements of the Italian authorities and the helpful efforts of the legitimate England followers who are members of the Football Supporters' Association will surprise us all by making this a peaceful World Cup. But few would rush to bet on it.

There is disagreement about whether trouble is most likely to come in Sardinia during a first phase that throws together the two most warlike groups of supporters in Europe, those of England and Holland, or to develop at the key ferry port of Genoa, or flare around other mainland cities as the tournament progresses. But scarcely anyone believes it won't come at all. And, as Lode Walgrave, professor of criminology at the Catholic University of Leuven in Belgium, has pointed out, it would be naive to assume that young Italians won't be ready to offer a little turmoil of their own. 'Watch out for the Italians,' says Walgrave, who wrote a report on football hooliganism for the Belgian Government after Heysel. 'They have heard so much about the war plans of the Dutch and the English. They will want to come and have a look. And if nothing happens, they will make sure something will happen.'

If Walgrave's words are worrying, there is even more long-term gloom in the testimony the Dutch have been hearing from one of their leading sociologists, Professor Andre Van den Burg. He says that Calvinism is still as strong in the Netherlands as it was 200 years ago and suggests that its suppression of emotion and of the outward show of feeling has much to do with the fact that 'the po-faced Dutch are renowned for sudden outbursts of violence, often quite out of proportion to their apparent cause'.

But it is Van den Burg's prognosis, with its application to soccer rowdyism as a whole, that is especially discouraging: 'Bringing in hordes of police to stop thugs from going on the rampage is like putting more bandages on a boil to stop it from erupting. You've got to tackle the root cause of the problem and, since it has been taking root over centuries, it will not be stopped overnight by police, politicians or even sociologists.'

That last line shows that the professor can make a joke against himself but nobody in football will see anything funny in the time-scale he attaches to the hooligan issue. Unless swift success is achieved in at least containing the menace, more and more devotees are going to wonder if the most popular ball game ever devised is worth preserving in its present form.

'No activity could withstand a constant barrage of the kind football has been suffering from its worst elements,' says Ernie Walker, who was until recently an exceptionally effective chief executive of the Scottish Football Association and remains an important voice in the councils of UEFA and FIFA. 'Nobody has the right to take an event to a city if it is tantamount to putting the bloody place to the sword.' Unless football embraces Walker's realism, it will remain in danger of falling on its sword.

Lights out for a lightweight

(*The Observer*, 17 October 1993)

THERE IS something traditionally English about the funeral rites attending the death of Graham Taylor's régime. It is a noisy ritual in which many of the participants have a self-satisfied, almost chirpy, air – like morris dancing on a grave.

Though it is natural to feel for a man who has suffered a depth of public pain that no job in sport should entail, sympathy for Taylor is reduced by awareness of how much energy he devoted, at least until lately, to the management of his public relations. Co-operating with journalists sometimes appeared more of a priority than demonstrating loyalty to his players. Any pact with the pack is bound to have Faustian implications and Taylor is not entitled to be surprised by devilish headlines such as 'Ta ta turnip'.

His record cannot be defended and even a plea in mitigation is unlikely to be offered in this space, where his handling of the national team has been condemned frequently during the past three years for its lack of coherence and conviction. The manager's position is untenable now that England find themselves in need of a compound miracle involving the defeat of Holland in Poland next month and an extravagant demolition of San Marino by England on the same day. Taylor has shot himself in the foot so often that the ricochets were always likely to kill off English hopes of earning a passage to the US in 1994. There is one bullet left and he knows where it is going.

However, when all this has been said, a basic concern with honesty is enough to discourage the simplistic tendency to blame the woes that culminated in Rotterdam last Wednesday entirely on one man's inadequacy. Before too many people seek the comfort of a lynching, a little reality would not come amiss. It can start with a reminder that, over the past eight World Cup tournaments, England have won their way through only three qualifying series. After being given a place in the finals as hosts in 1966 and as holders in 1970, they were frustrated in 1974 and 1978 and are all but certain to remain at home again. That is the record not of a super-power of the game but of a country somewhere slightly above mid-table in football's league of nations.

The enduring delusion that England's true ranking is among the mighty has been nourished in general terms by the continuing vigour of our domestic competitions and, specifically, by isolated flourishes in the international arena. Paramount among the latter was, of course, the winning of the World Cup in 1966. That success (like the excellent showing in Mexico four years later) clearly owed much to the simultaneous flowering of half-a-dozen exceptional talents and their confident deployment by a shrewd and single-minded manager. But, just as obviously, it was inseparable from the fact that England played every one of their matches at Wembley. (All the winners of the World Cup other than the English – the Uruguayans, the Brazilians, the Argentines, the Italians and the Germans – have taken it at least twice and all have won it outside their own borders.)

Even home advantage in the European Championship of 1996 may not be sufficient to compensate for the depressing scarcity of gifted, technically sophisticated players that is proclaimed week by week in the Premier League and was, as much as Taylor's misguided policies or a shameful failure of nerve by a referee, the cause of that shattering scoreline in midweek. Those who attacked the manager's team selection in Rotterdam plainly have a case. The only apparent justification for picking someone as deficient in technique and creative imagination as Palmer seemed to be a desire to mark Holland's most threatening forward, Bergkamp. When Bergkamp was left unmonitored (a freedom he squandered carelessly for a while but, almost inevitably, exploited in the end) and Palmer appeared as a forlorn, largely irrelevant figure on the right side of midfield, the choice was less comprehensible than the replacing of Palmer with Sinton at half-time.

Yet it is a fact that England matched Holland more effectively before the interval than they did afterwards. In both halves they were blatantly outplayed by opponents who saw and executed runs and passes with far more vision and precision. But in the first they did make a healthy number of rough-and-ready chances and, even allowing for the cancellation of a thrilling and perfectly legal goal from the majestic Rijkaard, equality after three-quarters of an hour did not flatter England unduly. They fared noticeably worse in the second half, as the Dutch grew in assurance, and losing cannot be explained away by dwelling on the cowardly refusal of Karl-Josef Assenmacher to dismiss Ronald Koeman when the contest was scoreless.

The point being made here has nothing to do with any attempt to endorse the selection of Palmer to fill the massive hole left by the enforced absence of Gascoigne. What is being emphasised is the falsity of the impression created by quite a few critics that Taylor could easily have changed everything on Wednesday had he not overlooked some notional richness of resources at his disposal. Let us remember that the favoured alternative to Palmer was not a Bobby Charlton or a Bryan Robson in his prime. It was Sinton, and anyone who believes his involvement from the start would have caused the England team to seethe with penetrative ideas has seen something this watcher has missed.

Admittedly, he could have been expected to bring more positive virtues to the party than Palmer did. It was, after all, a prompt, long and angled ball from the Sheffield Wednesday man into the path of Platt that led to the controversial Koeman incident. But, for the vast bulk of the time he was on the field, Sinton was as marginal as the rest of the English midfield (though never quite as hapless as Sharpe, who had a depressingly ineffectual night).

The truth about what was happening in the Feyenoord Stadium could be read in the contrasting experiences of Ince and Rijkaard. Ince, who has been hailed of late as an outstanding influence in the England side, spent most of his evening making hectic interventions, often with sliding tackles. Rijkaard, who has so much skill at close quarters, such balance and alertness and sense of time and space that he constantly invites the ball when he is tightly marked, was all deadly composure throughout.

Advocates of the inclusion of a calming creator from an earlier generation, such as Glenn Hoddle or Ray Wilkins, may feel the argument was strengthened by this match. They should, however, consider the possibility that the Dutch had too many good passers of the ball to permit one distinguished English veteran the luxury of purveying refinement at his leisure. A fit Gascoigne (if we are ever to see such a phenomenon again) would have represented something totally different, with his gift for suddenness and originality, either in his delivery of the ball or his explosive, dribbling spurts. But then, the boy-man always does.

Whether present or absent, trim or fat, in the mood or out of it, Gascoigne stands as an increasingly painful symbol of how much has been lost by English football. That one brilliant player of incurably erratic temperament should have come to mean so much to the immediate destiny of the national game is a succinct and devastating condemnation of the standards that have been allowed to pervade it. Gunter Netzer and Bernd Schuster were, in their time, equally glittering ornaments of German football but, without any appreciable contribution from either, the Germans kept getting to World Cup finals. And they won a couple along the way.

There are obvious grounds for insisting that the current impoverished state of the English game makes it more essential than ever before that the shrinking pool of talent available is used perceptively, and that Taylor has persistently and comprehensively failed to do so. His approach to developing a squad has been polluted with naivety, inconsistency and highly questionable judgments. The impression of a lightweight presence has been confirmed by a willingness to engage in public debates with reporters about the composition of his teams. When that tendency degenerated into absurdity at a press conference last Tuesday in

Rotterdam, it was impossible to escape images of how other, stronger managers would have responded to the badgering questions about why he had picked certain men and his intended deployment of them. Sir Alf Ramsey would have been contemptuously dismissive. A glare and a growl from Jock Stein would have dried the throat of the most aggressive interrogator. Jack Charlton might have gone off for a pint.

Such reactions would have been justified. Reporters deserve courtesy and co-operation from a man in Taylor's position. But it is madness to imagine that, before a crucial match, they have the right to be treated as equals in discussions of team selection and tactics. A national team manager is not put in the job to represent the views of the masses. He should be chosen as an expert and granted autocratic powers.

The next manager of England had better know more than Graham Taylor. And he had better make it clear to those who chronicle his activities that he knows more than they do.

Football feels the heat in the US melting pot

(*The Sunday Times*, 19 December 1993)

ANYBODY SUFFICIENTLY innocent or patronising to see this World Cup as the decisive breakthrough in converting Americans to the greatest of games, as a triumphant spreading of the true word across a heathen land, should be reminded that missionaries have been known to get themselves eaten.

In this case the threat applies not to the evangelists but to the message they hope to leave behind when next summer's finals are over. There are signs that it is in danger of being chewed up, swallowed and regurgitated in a form barely recognisable as football.

On the eve of the draw for World Cup USA '94, there is the inevitable fever of speculation. This time it ranges beyond the obvious basic issues of which countries will be thrown into opposition in the six groups of four that will contest the opening phase of the finals, of how far the organisers will go in seeking to protect the US team against expulsion at that first stage of the competition or to what extent the allocation of groups to cities will be governed by the kind of ethnic considerations that would place the Irish among their kin in Boston, the Italians near New York and the Mexicans in, say, Dallas.

Here in the Nevada desert the guessing game has embraced less familiar questions, such as whether the supreme figure in the history of football, Pele, will be banned from participating in the ceremonies surrounding the draw that begins shortly after noon today. That has become a real possibility because Pele is involved in acrimonious litigation (related to contracts for TV coverage of the tournament) with Ricardo Teixeira, who is the president of the Brazilian Football Confederation and, more significantly, the son-in-law of João Have-lange, the tireless septuagenarian wheeler-dealer who has for two decades exerted a steely, controlling influence as president of FIFA.

Yet it is conceivable that nothing said or done in Las Vegas during the past few days will have more long-term impact on football than a series of statements made at a Friday afternoon press conference which was not directly concerned with the dramatic events scheduled for next June and July. They did come from Alan Rothenberg, the Los Angeles lawyer who is both president of the United States Soccer Federation and the man in charge of arrangements for the World Cup, but he was speaking in yet another capacity when he made them. He was, in fact, issuing a declaration of intent on behalf of Major League Professional Soccer Inc., a group who propose to ignore all the daunting lessons of the past and attempt to establish football without pads or helmets on a sound commercial basis in the US. The plan, already approved in principle by FIFA, is to launch a league of 12 clubs – with American playing staffs that would be reinforced by small, tightly-restricted quotas of foreigners – by 1995. Rothenberg spoke optimistically about the prospects of raising the initial capital of $100m, about coping with the dearth of suitable stadia (minimum requirements include seating for 25–30,000 and full-sized grass pitches), the chances of securing the indispensable television deal and several other practical problems confronting the scheme.

But it was when I asked him if Major League Soccer (the new organisation's operating title) intended to alter the laws of football to help overcome the US public's traditional resistance to the game that what he had to say became particularly interesting and, for some of his listeners, more than a little alarming. Yes, he said, they would 'consider any and all changes' in the laws and regulations and in the presentation of the game that they felt would improve its appeal to spectators. They would, however, do nothing that was not sanctioned by FIFA.

'We shall not be a renegade league,' he insisted. 'But we'll be going back to them with our suggestions. We have told them that in certain areas we would like to be their experimental league, to test ideas that people have been floating but which so far nobody has been prepared to try. There are a lot of things that could be tried that would not adulterate the game but might well improve it.'

When pressed for specifics, he mentioned the option of having the ball kicked rather than thrown in after it goes out of play and confirmed that MLS would 'look carefully' at the advantages of increasing the size of the goals to make scoring less difficult. The case for the latter proposal is that goalkeepers, in common with most people in developed societies, have grown larger since the space they have to defend was fixed long ago at eight yards by eight feet. Advocates of the change pay scant attention to the fact that the modern ball makes firing in unstoppable shots from a distance appreciably easier than it once was. And they react sourly to suggestions that the spirit of Barnum and Bailey that hovers over their thinking might be better served by the recruitment of dwarf goalkeepers.

It is a tribute to Rothenberg, a highly personable 54-year-old, that he could deal with such controversial matters without conveying the slightest whiff of revolution. But some of us in the audience could not escape the impression that he was revealing the tip of an American reformist iceberg and that football might be heading for a collision after which it would never be the same again.

There is no shock in discovering that Brazilians, the most steadfast guardians of the beautiful essence of the game, are among those most affected by such fears. A journalist friend from Rio, a sophisticated witness who has been resident in the US throughout the build-up towards the World Cup, recently warned his readers that no cultural phenomenon could be expected to emerge from a thorough exposure to American ways without being drastically altered. 'Even Carmen Miranda came back to Brazil Americanised,' he observed wryly. So what chance did football have of remaining the game we know and love?

A number of informed onlookers are, it must be said, convinced that severe misgivings are premature. They contend that Rothenberg and his associates will be unable to get their professional league project off the ground. Trying to launch it was, they point out, a condition of being permitted to host the World Cup, and the current activity is more a matter of gesture than substance. But theirs seems a dangerously cynical interpretation. If the MLS consortium are indeed determined to succeed where hopeful predecessors have failed – most notably the North American Soccer League, which had its origins in the late '60s, was lifted to brief glory in the '70s by the skills of Pele, Franz Beckenbauer and a few other immortals and died miserably in the '80s – then it is an absolute certainty that they will strive to tailor the world's favourite sport to the demands of their domestic market.

Worries about the damage such strivings might inflict on football were not eased by Rothenberg's willingness to cite his experiences in professional basketball (he was famously influential while a member of the National Basketball Association's board of governors from 1971–79 and from 1982–90) as a source of inspiration for some of the reforms he has in mind. Basketball provides splendid expression for dozens of the most magnificent athletes and brilliantly gifted games players alike but, with its staccato bursts of excitement and avalanches of scoring, it effectively demonstrates the gulf in appetites and attitudes separating American sports fans from the majority elsewhere. Spectators here want their sporting action to come in repeated explosions of drama and they are uneasy unless it can be constantly measured and recorded in statistics. They must have floods of points, percentages, yardages, goals.

At the risk of being drowned in contempt, a few of us who have crossed the Atlantic for the World Cup draw have again been quoting the old example of Brazil's 1-0 defeat of England in Guadalajara in the tournament of 1970 as proof that low scoring and the highest aesthetic standards need never be mutually exclusive. But the concept of a fluency too subtle and seamless to lend itself to crude statistical measurement is the worst kind of heresy to most Americans.

If Major League Soccer does become a reality in 1995, the natural cravings of the US sports public will surely force the promoters to distort the nature of the game in the interests of marketability. When a questioner at a FIFA press conference on Friday tackled Havelange about the fact that a Harris poll had shown only 13 per cent of Americans were aware the World Cup was being held within their borders, the president answered blithely that 13 per cent represented 'a glorious figure'. But it is hardly a glorious proportion, especially since many among the other 87 per cent are not merely indifferent but positively hostile to something they regard as a pastime for girls – never to be confused with their own version of football, which is widely acclaimed as an arena for noble warriors.

On the very day Havelange took comfort from his conviction that 30 million Americans were on his side, Tom Weir was using his column in *USA Today* to blow a raspberry he knew would be echoed by the bulk of his countrymen: 'The rest of the world, we keep getting reminded, *loves* soccer. Surely, we must be missing out on something. Uh, isn't that what the Russians told us about communism? But don't feel guilty about it. There's a good reason why you don't care about soccer, even if it is the national passion of Cameroon, Uruguay and Madagascar. It's because you are an American, and hating soccer is more American than mom's apple pie, driving a pickup or spending Saturday afternoon channel-surfing with the remote control.' Weir, in a polemic at once wild and typical enough to be worth reprinting at length, went on to stress that the sporting dramas that thrilled US spectators were 'all arms and hands, things that happen from the waist up. From Babe Ruth to Muhammad Ali to Michael Jordan, that's where the sports action that Americans love always has been ...

'Feet never have been terribly respected in the sports world. When you mess up on defense in baseball, it's because you booted the ball. You blow a big lead or throw away a game, and you must have shot yourself in the foot. In essence, soccer is to sports what athlete's foot is to injuries. So yes, the World Cup is coming. But feel free to dodge and dismiss it, and feel good about that. As somebody who knows what real sports are, you are under no obligation to play footsie with the rest of the world.'

More to the point, the game most of mankind considers the best may live to regret playing footsie so enthusiastically with America. If a nation thoroughly accustomed to the privileges of a superpower ever graduates to a consistently significant role in the running of football (some would argue it is already in that position, given that seven of the 11 principal sponsors of this World Cup are US-based) the consequences could be immense. Football, like any other human activity, must be subject to organic change if it is to survive and flourish. But there is a clear danger that the impact of the US through the turn of the century and beyond will prove to be inordinate.

So maybe we should concentrate doubly hard on enjoying this World Cup, in case future stagings are afflicted with peculiarities. Let's hope, for a start, that today's draw leaves us with a fascinating first phase, that it avoids the more dire possibilities entertained by the pessimists. As somebody said the other day, a group formed by Belgium, Bolivia, Bulgaria and Norway might defy the ticket-scalping talents of even a Stan Flashman.

The new format adopted for the draw has persuaded the most sceptical FIFA-watchers that for once the process will be above suspicion. In the past there has been speculation about the use of magnetised rings by the drawers, of the balls representing certain countries being warmed for easy identification, and other tricks of the illusionist's trade. But here it appears that sufficient precautions have been incorporated in the system to remove the temptation to indulge in creative sleight of hand. All but one of the decisions about which of the nine playing sites each group will use are to be made after the draw, and left in the hands of the American organisers. The exception is the automatic granting of a request from the holders, Germany, to be based in Chicago.

As the hours of waiting dwindled away, the Irish grew less sanguine about their chances of having the benefit of the partisan support they would be guaranteed in Boston. Sean Connolly, General Secretary of the Football Association of Ireland and the man charged with arranging accommodation and other facilities for Jack Charlton's squad, took out insurance by adding reservations on flights to Orlando, Dallas and Chicago to the bookings he already held to Massachusetts. His disappointment if obliged to make one of the alternative trips will probably be more bearable than that of many travel agents back home who have invested heavily in the assumption that there is going to be a gigantic party in Boston.

Since the Irish are capable of bringing 15,000 supporters across the ocean with them, a following unlikely to be outnumbered by any nation, it would be no more than justice if the Cup authorities decided after all to let the planned reunion of blood brothers go ahead. Whatever the verdict, Charlton will be content to learn of it in a Dublin television studio. Characteristically, he announced that he saw no point in coming to Las Vegas 'to answer a lot of bland questions from reporters and have a bunch of microphones stuck up my nose'.

Perhaps it is just as well that the Germans already know exactly where they are going in geographical terms, for there was surprising evidence in midweek that they are less certain about their precise whereabouts tactically and technically than they usually are six months before the World Cup finals. Of course, it would be ridiculous folly to read anything momentous into their 2-1 defeat by Argentina at the Orange Bowl in Miami last Wednesday afternoon. It counted for so little in relation to the excellence of their recent form that, by the time they had beaten a palpably moderate US team 3-0 in California yesterday (Moller scored in the first half, Kuntz and Thom late in the second), they were right at the top of the FIFA computer rankings, with Italy second and Brazil third.

Yet admirers of the Germans and their extraordinary achievements in previous world championships had to be troubled after a team not far short of full strength were outplayed by Argentine opponents fielding half a dozen men who could be classified (at least when the match started) as reserves. Nothing was more distressing for the Europeans than the obtrusive hints that the dream of converting their most distinguished contemporary player, Lothar Matthaus, into a sweeper in the Beckenbauer mould could lead to a minor nightmare of disenchantment. The sight of Thomas Hassler, looking tiny and frail as a jockey in the midst of crowding reporters as he tried to rationalise a collective failure from which his own memorable efforts made him honourably exempt, would have worried those who were inclined to bet Germany to take another title.

Obviously, they still have plenty of time to regain balance and momentum and come charging through the field half a year from now. But many punters may be persuaded that the search for a betting favourite should be concentrated on South America. For some that will mean siding with the promise displayed last week by Argentina, for more it will involve declaring faith in the portents of revival lately identified with the champions' champions, Brazil.

But if the form book, or the opinion of quite a few South American experts, can be trusted, Colombia are the most exciting challengers of all. My friend from Rio readily acknowledges that today's Colombians, rallying with wonderful coherence around such outstanding individuals as the superb midfielders Carlos Valderrama and Fredy Rincon and the devastating forwards Adolfo Valencia and Faustino Asprilla, are the natural torch-bearers of the kind of exhilarating football his own country gave to the world. Their 5-0 slaughter of Argentina in Buenos Aires in the qualifying series may have been freakishly excessive but it was underpinned by utter superiority.

If they can perform as magically in the summer – and stir an appropriate response from the likes of Brazil, Germany, Argentina and Holland – they will do much to discourage the vandals who seem to be closing in on football.

Rough justice puts football in the dock

(*The Sunday Times*, 26 December 1993)

THE FA's insipid acceptance of John Fashanu's version of how his elbow happened to shatter the right cheekbone and eye-socket of Gary Mabbutt helps to establish an entirely new definition of the term accident-prone. Fashanu, it seems, has accidents, but it is nearly always other players who are left prone.

There were such basic inadequacies implicit in the criteria governing the FA's commission of inquiry into the incident at White Hart Lane on 24 November that neither truth nor justice was ever likely to be served. Given that the commission concentrated at their hearing last Thursday on the issue of intent, and gave no indication of having properly addressed the more relevant question of whether Fashanu's elbow was employed recklessly and dangerously, it is scarcely astonishing that their proceedings were dismissed as 'a complete waste of time' by Ossie Ardiles, the Spurs manager.

To my eyes, and those of many professional watchers of football to whom I have spoken, the video recording of the high challenge which produced the Spurs captain's terrible injuries shows that Fashanu was guilty of a recklessness that took his action well beyond the boundaries of legitimate competitiveness. When the Wimbledon striker says the damage done was accidental, there is no problem about believing him. Nobody will suspect for a moment that he meant to endanger Mabbutt's eyesight or leave him with a metal plate fixed for life into his cheekbone.

Equally, however, if a car that is being driven at twice the speed limit swerves out of control, mounts the pavement and mows down a pedestrian, the driver might be said to have had an accident. But that does not mean he is not culpable. A flying elbow on the field may be less deadly than a hurtling car on the road but both imply a totally unacceptable disregard for the well-being of others.

Fashanu was told as much after he rang the Professional Footballers' Association to insist that he had never had any intention of injuring Mabbutt. His claim was not doubted but it was forcefully pointed out to him that his challenge had been 'dangerous and reckless' and had not shown due concern for a fellow player. (A reminder that examples of such solicitude have been rare in Fashanu's career was provided recently when *The Sun*, under the heading 'Life and crimes of Fash the Bash', carried a lengthy, chronological list of those 'crimes', starting with a sending-off ten years ago in only his second match for Lincoln. Long before the Mabbutt affair, the 1993 contribution included a collision with Kevin Moran that gave the Blackburn defender a broken nose.)

'We are in the process of trying to cut down on the 50 or so members of our Association who have to retire each year because of permanent injury,' said Gordon Taylor, chief executive of the PFA, on Friday night. 'We are not in the business of swelling that total.' Stressing the scope and seriousness of the PFA's newly launched campaign to eradicate the destructive use of the elbow from English football, Taylor added: 'We don't want football to become a fight. It should be more an art form than it is at the moment in this country, where the widespread commitment to Route One, to throwing forward long balls and letting people scuffle for them, has a lot to do with the increasing prevalence of elbowing offences – and with the fact that we are not at the races in terms of world-class competitions. These are related parts of the same overall problem.

'There is not the slightest question of a vendetta against John Fashanu. What troubles us particularly is that Gary Mabbutt – like those other recent victims of serious facial injuries, Kevin Moran and Peter Beardsley – is a lad who is known to play the game with 100 per cent honesty and openness. If the absolute fairness with which such fellas play is making them especially vulnerable, something must be done and done quickly. Every player accepts that when he goes on the field he is volunteering to risk injury. But he also has a right – and it is now a right that has been legally established in the courts – to expect that those he is competing against will recognise their duty to show proper care and concern for the well-being of fellow professionals. You don't necessarily volunteer to have somebody jumping with you who has an elbow high, cocked and rigid and maybe 15st behind it.'

As an urgent matter of policy, Taylor's organisation are demanding that any player who uses the elbow in the way he described should be adjudged to have behaved dangerously and recklessly. There should be no more wallowing around in the bog of ambiguity surrounding the issue of precise intent. The PFA want those whose elbows represent a menace to opponents to be punished with FA suspensions covering between three and six matches. They acknowledge that the power to combat the epidemic of elbowing (25 dismissals last season, 25 per cent up on the previous season) lies with their own members and they are planning an educational bombardment of the country's dressing-rooms. Posters will offer reminders of how brutal the worst effects can be and accompanying slogans will exhort players to be responsible, while warning of the probable legal consequences if they are not. 'Every pro knows the nature and the extent of the problem,' Taylor said. 'The real horrors have two main sources. One is the aerial challenge that comes from the side where the elbow is, as I said, held high, cocked and rigid. The other is where one player jumping in front of another throws the elbow behind. We have had broken jaws and noses and it is not melodramatic to suggest there might eventually be major brain damage or even fatalities.'

Another priority of the PFA proposals is recognition of the excessive burden currently placed on referees when it comes to assessing culpability in hurtful collisions. Feeling it is wrong to make one individual's interpretation so crucial, the players' union advocate the setting up of a panel of experts to adjudicate on complex or awkward cases. It would be formed by the FA under the chairman of their disciplinary committee but would include representatives from the PFA, the League Managers' Association and the Referees' Association.

Such a group would surely have brought a wider, better informed and more worldly perspective to the judgment of the Fashanu–Mabbutt affair than Thursday's commission could. Worldliness can be an invaluable asset in deliberations of this kind. Without suggesting the commission were less than objective, it must be said that there is often some difficulty in reconciling any allegations of mayhem, or even dangerous reckless-ness, against Fashanu with the polished and highly responsible persona he presents when he is out of his football kit. A tall (6ft 1in), handsome, bright and persuasively articulate 31-year-old, he has a burgeoning TV career, is conspicuously identified with good works and is noted for an admirably active involvement with black Africa. It is sometimes hard to remember that he is also known as Fash the Bash.

A further, more general complication is the declaration made by the FA's own chief executive, Graham Kelly, when he appeared as a vital witness at Salisbury Crown Court a year ago. In that court, Gary Blissett (then a Brentford striker but now a teammate of Fashanu's at Wimbledon) was cleared of causing grievous bodily harm to John Uzzell, a Torquay defender, during a match at Plainmoor 12 months earlier. Blissett was sent off in the match after a blow from his elbow so badly damaged Uzzell's face that later he, like Mabbutt, needed surgery to rebuild an eye-socket and had to have a metal plate inserted in his cheekbone. Uzzell was forced to retire from football.

Kelly's amazing evidence at Salisbury (which, in effect, condemned the referee's decision) was that he considered Blissett's challenge 'entirely reasonable'. He further testified that if he went to four matches a week, 'I probably see 200 such challenges'.

Can the FA reasonably contemplate punishing a Fashanu, who drew no censure from the referee on hand, when Kelly so unequivocally exonerated a Blissett, who was ordered off? The answer is that they can and they must. They can no more afford to be shackled by the wrong-headedness of Kelly than by the wrong-headedness of Thursday's commission.

Bad precedents belong in the dustbin.

Thomas blows the whistle on referees

(*The Sunday Times*, 16 January 1994)

IT WAS always a given that Clive Thomas would be the least retiring of retired referees. His capacity for reticence was negligible during 18 years on the Football League list and when he passed the age limit of 47 in 1984 nobody imagined that the lack of a whistle would prevent him from making himself heard around the game.

In fact, in recent years most of his considerable energy has been devoted to his central role in building up the successful firm of which he is managing director and principal shareholder. The business has 70 employees, providing a comprehensive range of services for office blocks and other sites in many parts of the country, and generates a turnover in the millions. Thomas, who still looks youthfully fit at 57, thought little of being on the road at 5.15 one morning last week to start a working day that did not end until after nine at night. But, no matter how crowded his life becomes, he will find room to be controversial about football. He brims with opinions and with a sometimes alarming respect for the personal logic that creates them. In my experience, however, his ability to interest and entertain, and to raise genuine issues, has made coping with the indefatigability of his self-belief well worth the effort. Even when he is at his most aggressively opinionated, the humour and warmth implanted by his Rhondda Valley upbringing lighten the message for the listener.

Admittedly, some of the elevated figures in the world game who have been bombarded with his views may see him differently. Sepp Blatter, the general secretary of FIFA, was perhaps less than enthralled when, immediately after the World Cup of 1990, Thomas dispatched to him in Zurich a detailed condemnation of the 'laughing stock' standards of referees and linesmen in the finals and proposed a meeting with Blatter, the FIFA president João Havelange, or any of their representatives to discuss ways of effecting improvement. Neither Blatter nor Havelange showed any eagerness to invite Disgusted of Porthcawl over for a chat. The president especially would have no trouble in recognising this correspondent as the same Clive Thomas whose highly promising career as a World Cup referee was ended abruptly by a blast on his own whistle at the Argentine finals of 1978.

It happened in Mar del Plata, where Thomas was officiating in a match between Brazil and Sweden, and the somewhat unusual point about his intervention was that he had turned towards the centre of the field and blown for time while a Brazilian corner was in the air, only to find a roar behind him acclaiming the great Zico as he met the ball with his head and sent it into the Swedish net. Brazil were convinced Zico had claimed a dramatic 2-1 victory. But Thomas produced a more prolonged drama by disallowing the goal on the grounds that he had precisely calculated the stoppage time to be added and knew the last vestige of it had been used up a fraction of a second before the ball reached Zico. He was instantly accused of letting pedantry overwhelm common sense.

Not only does he maintain that his decision was 100 per cent correct, and one he would make again without a flicker of hesitation, but he insists that the treatment he endured as a result of the episode vividly reflects the spread of weak, misguided and morally questionable attitudes he sees as having reduced refereeing throughout football to a desperate state. There was never an inquiry at which he could have put his case, just an ostracising silence that was reinforced by his fellow referees when he got back to Buenos Aires.

'Yet to have done anything other than I did in that Sweden-Brazil match would have been dishonest,' he said in his Cardiff office on Thursday. 'People say I should have waited until the ball went out of the penalty area. No doubt a lot of the referees I watch in this country now would have done that. You will notice that in 99 per cent of matches they blow for half-time or full-time when the ball is near the halfway line. Cheating is a heavy word, and not one I use often, but what those referees are doing is a form of cheating. It is part of the chickening out that is occurring all over the place, from the ruling bodies down. Most referees are more concerned with trying to anticipate what the football establishment expect of them than with what they honestly feel they should be doing. They are behaving like programmed robots, surrendering their individuality.'

He acknowledges that referees are confused by the signals coming from above. Here he singled out the evidence offered by Graham Kelly in Salisbury Crown Court, where he stated that the blow from Gary Blissett's elbow that smashed the face of John Uzzell was entirely reasonable and of a kind he might witness 200 times a week. 'That was a prime example of the need for the Association of Football League Referees and Linesmen to take determined action,' he said. 'They should have demanded an inquiry into Kelly's statement. But they won't take on the FA or the League. Kelly should have been obliged to justify those comments, to show the basis for them. The absence of leadership is lamentable. After Kelly stood up and said all that, it is not surprising that the epidemic of elbowing has gone unchecked.'

Thomas believes that the handling of the John Fashanu-Gary Mabbutt incident at White Hart Lane was calamitously wrong. 'Without the slightest doubt I would have sent Fashanu off,' he said. 'To me it was quite simply violent conduct.' And he positively seethes over the decision that enabled Ronald Koeman to stay on the field in Rotterdam after the professional foul on David Platt that probably cost England a vital goal in the World Cup qualifying match with Holland. 'FIFA should have put that referee in mothballs for the rest of his career,' he declared. 'I believe it should be possible to bring charges against referees if they are blatantly out of order. It could be a charge of bringing the game into disrepute, ungentlemanly conduct or lack of discipline on the field of play.'

Inevitably, Thomas has an array of equally radical proposals. His hectic business schedule, and the happy family life he enjoys with his wife Beryl, two daughters and two granddaughters, do not prevent him from theorising endlessly about the sport that has been a passionate enthusiasm since long before an ankle injury killed his ambitions as a player at 16 after a short spell on the Norwich ground staff. He wholeheartedly advocates the recruitment of ex-players into refereeing, rejecting the argument that becoming available at the age of 34 or 35 is a major drawback: 'The idea that an apprenticeship of 10 or 12 years is required to produce good referees is nonsense. Some may need it, but if you give me a former player with a fair amount of common sense, and a real desire to stay in the game, I'll make him a FIFA referee in four years.'

His support for full-time, professional referees represents a change in his thinking and he emphasises that he would favour their introduction only if it came as an element of an overall restructuring of refereeing in this country. He wants the appointment of a 'supremo' who, at current rates, would warrant a salary of £60,000 a year and would be supported by eight part-time assistants in charge of geographical regions.

For the Premier League, there would be 13 top referees, who would be subjected to rigorous technical and physical training and whose wages of £30,000 a year would commit them to extra duties such as meeting supporters' clubs, visiting schools and so on. Like the regional directors, they would be trained in public relations and man-management skills to help them to deal effectively with the press and television and to communicate productively with club managers and players. 'Of course, there must always be a barrier between referees and players,' he said. 'But it should be no different from that between the police and the public. At present the barrier is much too high.'

When it comes to the laws themselves, Thomas proposes an intriguing list of changes. Offside would be a priority. He would extend the edge of the penalty box to the touchlines to form two 18-yard zones over the full width of the pitch, and no player could be offside outside those zones.

Indirect free kicks he would abolish, leaving only direct frees and penalties. He is convinced that penalties are hardly ever taken legally 'because no goalkeeper can reasonably be expected to stand perfectly still while another man is kicking the ball towards him from 12 yards away'. So he would permit goalies to move on the goal-line, while insisting that they never move an inch off it to narrow the angle.

For encroachment at free kicks or persistent dissent he would penalise the offending team 10 yards. If that punishment meant awarding a penalty for what had been a free kick outside the box, he would not hesitate.

Of course, Clive Thomas was never big on hesitancy. Ask the Brazilians.

WORLD CUPS

The first three pieces in this section were written for books that I helped to produce on the World Cup tournaments of 1966 and 1970 (in the case of 1970 I had a distinguished co-editor, Arthur Hopcraft). Those competitions, like all the others through 1990, I covered for The Observer. *By 1994, I was with* The Sunday Times *and the pieces on events in the US come from that newspaper. Among the book publishers and the sports editors involved, there were different attitudes to the use of accents, etc., in names. Where there is no danger of confusion, I have allowed such minor prejudices to survive. On the same basis, England met RUMANIA in the 1970 World Cup book but Hagi played for ROMANIA in the Sunday Times piece of 1994. I have, almost everywhere, stuck with the original versions.*

My selection of material from the mass of copy I turned out on these World Cups was bound to be arbitrary but I think it reflects something of the essence of my reactions to each tournament. Thus, there is quite a lot of sourness about 1990, much regret over the failure of Holland to get their due in 1974 and 1978 and the odd hint that I regard Mexico 1970 as the most beautiful representation of football I ever expect to see.

England v West Germany

Wembley, 30 July 1966

WEMBLEY DOES NOT always stir the spirit. As a football stadium it is overrated. The slow, sweaty crush out of the tube station and the long trudge along Stadium Way, where ticket touts and vendors of smelly hot-dogs wait in ambush, are not immediately rewarded. The closer you come to the place the shabbier it looks, twin towers notwithstanding. Under the stands there is the grey, cavernous gloom of most English grounds.

But Wembley is lucky enough to have occasions that work a metamorphosis, that can make grown men persuade themselves that the hideously inconvenient journey from London is an adventure and can transmute the undistinguished concrete bowl into what the more imaginative chroniclers of our time would call 'a seething cauldron'. FA Cup finals can do that, especially when one of the clubs comes from the North of England and brings its raucous trainloads of supporters to drink at dawn in Covent Garden and spill their beery optimism over the terraces. One wondered if the World Cup could do as much for Wembley. In the event, it did far more. It was impossible to define the atmosphere precisely but it was palpable, and it was unique. It was like walking into an ordinary, familiar room and knowing instinctively that something vital and unbearably dramatic was happening, perhaps a matter of life and death. The people hurrying and jostling and laughing nervously inside had a flushed, supercharged look, but if they were high it was with excitement. 'It's bloody electric,' said one of the doormen. He had found the word.

Down on the field the combined bands of the Portsmouth Command and the Portsmouth Group, Royal Marines, had found the music, a tune for each of the sixteen competing nations. The North Koreans, whose own community singing is probably a little hard to follow, had to settle for a thing called Oriental Patrol. It did not matter much, for the roaring and chanting from the terraces, where the red, black and yellow flags of Germany were in no danger of being submerged among the Union Jacks and English banners, was loud enough to make everything sound alike. It might have been Liverpool's Anfield (England did wear red), and there can be no finer tribute. The weather was to fluctuate unpredictably between bright sunshine and squalls of driving rain, the fortunes of both teams to swing wildly between elation and frustration, but the crowd would remain constantly exhilarated, buoyed up by an incredible flood of incident. When the bands played the National Anthem the English supporters came together in a great chauvinistic choir. *Deutschland über Alles* boomed out in its wake and the battle was on.

The Germans began rather nervously, standing off from the tackle and letting the England forwards move without conspicuous hindrance up to the edge of the penalty area. Bobby Charlton and Peters were able to work the ball along the left at their leisure and there was anxiety in the German defence before the cross was cleared. But that was a tranquil interlude compared with what happened after eight minutes. An intelligent crossfield pass from Hurst set Stiles free on the right and his high centre beat Tilkowski before Höttges headed it away. The ball was returned smartly by Bobby Charlton and Tilkowski had so much trouble punching if off Hurst's head that he knocked himself out. The goalkeeper was prostrate, the whistle had gone and the defenders had stopped challenging before Moore put the ball in the net. The crowd cheered anyway, in the hope that next time it would be the real thing. They had reason to be optimistic, for England were dominating these early moments, running and passing with fine confidence on the wet surface. Without Schulz, patrolling tirelessly behind the main line of four backs, calmly averting crises, Germany would have come under severe strain. Many of their problems came from Bobby Charlton, wandering purposefully all over the field, bringing composure and smoothness wherever he appeared, again making comparisons with Di Stefano seem relevant. Beckenbauer, asked to rein in his own aggressive impulses to concentrate on subduing the Manchester United player, was in for a thankless first half.

Yet it was Jack Charlton, carrying the ball forward on his forehead with a skill that would have done credit to his brother, who initiated England's next important attack. He strode swiftly out of defence and his perfectly judged diagonal pass let Peters hit a quick, powerful shot from well outside the area. Tilkowski, already revealing an uncertainty that sharpened the appetite of the England forwards, dived desperately to his left and punched the ball round the post. Hurst met Ball's corner but sent the volley too high. At that point Weber chose to give the sort of agonised performance that had been one of the less admirable characteristics of the German players in the competition. But Gottfried Dienst quickly made it plain that nobody was being fooled and suggested it was time to get on with the game. Peters certainly did, surging in from the right wing to shoot only two feet wide from twenty-five yards.

Then, stunningly, in the thirteenth minute England found themselves a goal behind. And it was a goal that anyone who had seen their magnificent defensive play earlier in the tournament could hardly believe.

Held glided a high cross from the left wing and Wilson, jumping for the ball in comfortable isolation, amazingly headed it straight to the feet of Haller, standing in an orthodox inside-right position a dozen yards out from Banks. The blond forward had time to steady, pivot and aim his right-foot shot along the ground into the far corner.

There were fears that the Germans would try to make that goal win the Cup, that an open, invigorating match would be reduced to an exasperating siege. It took England only six minutes to reassure us. Overath had been warned for a bad foul on Ball and now he committed another one on Moore, tripping the England captain as he turned away with the ball. Moore himself took the free kick and from forty yards out near the left touchline he flighted it beautifully towards the far post. Hurst, timing his run superbly to slip through the defence much as he had done against Argentina, struck a flawless header low inside Tilkowski's right-hand post. Moore held one arm aloft in a gladiator's salute while Hurst was smothered in congratulations. It was another reminder of the huge contribution West Ham were making to England's success in the World Cup.

There were many free kicks but a high percentage of them could be traced to the officiousness of the referee. When Dienst took Peters's name for shirt-pulling, Schnellinger placed the kick carefully for Seeler to outjump the English defence and force in a header. But the ball curved tamely into Banks's hands. Seeler was generally more damaging, both in the air and on the ground, and one through pass in front of Haller demanded an alert intervention from Banks.

At that stage, however, the more sustained aggression was still coming from England. Moore was showing wonderful control and assurance, driving up among his forwards, joining readily in the moves begun by Bobby Charlton. It was unfortunate that Charlton could not be in two places at once. Several of the attacks he conceived in deep positions cried out to be climaxed with his striking power. Peters, who was his partner in much of the midfield work, was also the one who went nearest to his cleanness of shot, but so far most of the West Ham man's attempts had been from a range that favoured the goalkeeper, even a goalkeeper like Tilkowski. Thus it was Hurst, with his instinct for being in the right place at the right time and his marvellous ability in the air, who was the most direct threat to the Germans. He proved it again when Cohen crossed the ball long from the right and he rose to deflect in another header which Tilkowski could only scramble outside his right-hand post. Ball turned the ball back into the goalmouth and the desperation was unmistakable as Overath came hurtling in to scythe it away for a corner.

With about ten minutes left of the first half the Germans, quite suddenly, put strenuous pressure on the English defence. They were using the gifted, resourceful Overath to create in midfield, with Haller between him and the three striking forwards, Seeler, Held and Emmerich. Beckenbauer joined the link-men when he could afford to leave Bobby Charlton, but that was a luxury he rarely enjoyed until the Englishman's selfless running began to slow him down in the second half. Held was the most persistently dangerous of his team's forwards throughout the two hours of the match and it was his determination that began this period of German ascendancy before the interval. Ball and Cohen made the mistake of toying with him near the byeline and Jack Charlton, who was maintaining the remarkable standard of his World Cup performances, had to come in with a prodigious sweeping tackle to rescue them. It cost Charlton a corner and the corner almost cost England a goal. The ball went to Overath and from twenty yards he drove it in fiercely at chest height. Banks beat it out and when Emmerich hammered it back from an acute angle the goalkeeper caught it surely.

After forty-two minutes Hunt had the kind of miss that was bound to revive comparisons with Greaves. Wilson headed into goal and Hurst again soared above everybody to steer the ball down to Hunt. But the Liverpool man came round behind it rather ponderously and by the time he forced in his left foot volley Tilkowski was in the way.

One of the features of the play was that defensive errors were occurring far more frequently than they had done in most previous games in the series. After Wilson's disaster, the Germans had been slightly the shakier but they could be excused their bewilderment as Bobby Charlton stroked a subtle pass into their midst. Peters could not quite reach it. Then, to stress the hectic, fluctuating pattern of the first half that was just ending, Overath had a bludgeoning twenty-yard shot turned brilliantly over the crossbar by Banks.

The rain came again at the beginning of the second half, falling like sequins in the sunshine. Charlton fell, too, rather more heavily, after being tackled by Schulz, but the claims for a penalty were understandably half-hearted. The first to assert himself was Ball, and it was no brief flourish. From then until the Cup was won he was the most impressive player on the field. In the first half he had worked with his usual inexhaustible energy but had never quite shaken off Schnellinger, who set out to track him everywhere. A redhead and a blond, they were invariably close enough to be advertising the same shampoo. But after the interval Schnellinger, who has held some of the most menacing forwards in the game, found Ball too much. The little man simply went on and on, becoming more impertinently skilful, more astonishingly mobile by the minute. However, in the long period of deadlock following the interval, when both sides were steadying their heartbeats after the tumult of that first three-quarters of an hour, even Ball's dynamism was not enough. Charlton was suffering for the way he had punished himself to mould England's pattern in the first half and, if Hurst was still outleaping the

German defenders, Hunt lacked the pace or inventiveness to outwit them on the ground. Both defences were in command, England's closing on the opposition with consuming vigour, Germany's blocking the path to goal like a white wall in which the cement was hardening.

Fortunately for England, the wall was not as formidable as it looked. With thirteen minutes to go Ball won a corner, took it himself and saw the ball diverted to Hurst. His shot from the left was deflected across goal by a defender and Peters, strangely neglected by the Germans, came in to take the ball on the half-volley and sweep it in from four or five yards. It was another West Ham goal, and there were more to come.

With only four minutes remaining, England had a chance to crush their opponents. An inspired pass from Ball sent Hunt clear on the left. Bobby Charlton and Hurst were on his right and only Schulz stood between them and the goal. It was a three to one situation, something that should bring a goal at any level of football. But Hunt's pass was ill-timed, slackly delivered and too square. Bobby Charlton was committed to a hasty swipe and the result was a mess.

In the very last minute England were made to pay a cruel price for that carelessness. Jack Charlton was doubtfully penalised after jumping to a header and from the free kick Emmerich drove the ball through the line of English defenders. As it cannoned across the face of the goal Schnellinger appeared to play it with a hand, but the referee saw nothing illegal and Weber at the far post was able to score powerfully. The fact that these German defenders were crowding in on Banks indicates what a despairing effort this attack was. Such an injustice, coming just fifteen seconds from the end of the ninety minutes, would have broken most teams. But England, after a momentary show of disgust, galloped into extra time as if the previous hour-and-a-half had never happened. Appropriately, it was Ball who showed the way with a wonderful run and a twenty-yard shot which Tilkowski edged over the bar. Bobby Charlton followed with a low one that the goalkeeper pushed against his left-hand post.

The Germans looked weary but their swift breaks out of defence were still dangerous. A pass from Emmerich gave Held an opening and only unaccustomed slowness in controlling the ball enabled Stiles to clear. Held compensated for this by sprinting away from all challengers and turning the ball back invitingly across goal. But there was no one following up.

Having lost their lead through one controversial goal, England now regained it with another in the tenth minute of extra time. Ball made space for himself on the right and when the ball went across, Hurst resolutely worked for a clear view of goal. His rising right-foot shot on the turn from ten yards was pushed against the underside of the crossbar by Tilkowski and when it bounced the England players appealed as one man for a goal. The referee spoke to the Russian linesman on the side away from the main stand and, after an agony of waiting, awarded a goal. The delayed action cheers shook the stadium.

But this match had not yet taken its full toll of our nerves. The hammer blow England had received at the end of the hour and a half was almost repeated in the final minute of extra time when Seeler lunged in and narrowly failed to make decisive contact with a headed pass by Held. And that was only the prelude to the climax. Nonchalantly breasting the ball down in front of Banks, Bobby Moore relieved a perilous situation and then moved easily away, beating challengers and exchanging passes with Ball. Glancing up, he saw Hurst ten yards inside the German half and lifted the pass accurately to him. The referee was already looking at his watch and three England supporters had prematurely invaded the pitch as Hurst collected the ball on his chest. At first he seemed inclined to dawdle-out time. Then abruptly he went pounding through in the inside-left position, unimpeded by the totally spent German defenders, his only obstacle his own impending exhaustion. As Tilkowski prepared to move out, Hurst summoned the remnants of his strength, swung his left foot and smashed the ball breathtakingly into the top of the net.

The scene that followed was unforgettable. Stiles and Cohen collapsed in a tearful embrace on the ground, young Ball turned wild cartwheels and Bobby Charlton dropped to his knees, felled by emotion. Within seconds the game was over and the players, ignoring the crippling weariness of a few minutes before, were hugging and laughing and crying with their manager, Alf Ramsey, and the reserves who must go through the rest of their lives with bitter-sweet memories of how it looked from the touchline. 'Ramsey, Ramsey,' the crowd roared and in his moment of vindication it was a tribute that no one could begrudge him.

Eventually Moore led his men up to the Royal Box to receive the Jules Rimet trophy from the Queen and the slow, ecstatic lap of honour began. 'Ee-aye-addio, we've won the Cup,' sang the crowd, as Moore threw it in a golden arc above his head and caught it again. England had, indeed, won the Cup, won it on their merits, producing more determined aggression and flair than they had shown at any earlier stage of the competition. As hosts, they had closed their World Cup with a glorious bang that obliterated memories of its grey, negative beginnings. In such a triumph there could be no failures (the very essence of Ramsey's England was their team play), but if one had to name outstanding heroes they were Ball, Moore, Hurst and the brothers Charlton, the one exhibiting the greatness we always knew he had, the other attaining heights we never thought he could reach.

The Germans had been magnificent opponents and they deserved their own lap of honour at Wembley and the acclaim that awaited them at home. If they were in the West End of London that Saturday night they must have seen some interesting sights. The area was taken over for one great informal party. Some people said it was another VE night, but perhaps that was not the most tactful analogy. At the Royal Garden Hotel, where the English team were spending the night to unwind, there were visits from Harold Wilson and George Brown, who joined in the singing with the crowds outside. Hundreds of people were still dancing a conga around Charing Cross Station at midnight and nearby, in Trafalgar Square, there was the ritual of leaping into the fountains. For most of the nation, however, it was enough to be bathed in euphoria.

England 4   West Germany 2

Brazil v England

Guadalajara, 7 June 1970

THE DAYS LEADING up to the meeting of England and Brazil had that intensity of nervous excitement that settles on a crowd in the minutes before two heavyweight boxers enter the ring to fight for the champion-ship of the world. It is an almost painful sense of anticipation, as much to do with dread as exhilaration. The time of preparation, filled with comforting repetition and the luxury of analysis and prognostication, is over. Someone's ambitions and dreams, perhaps even someone's dignity, may soon be broken. A man you have talked with and admired and grown to know in the quiet of the training camp may be battered helpless in front of you. Even those who can keep their stomach muscles loose and their throats from drying up, do not feel like talking much. Such moments are not morbid but they have a solemnity that no amount of cynicism can undermine.

Football is very different from boxing. Its beauty is not burdened with the same physical and indivisibly personal penalties. Defeats for the most part bring only psychological suffering (the financial loss is rarely important to the players) and even that can be shared among eleven men. Yet at its highest levels the game can acquire something akin to the concentrated drama of the prize ring. Players go into some matches with the certain knowledge that the result will stay with them, however submerged, for the rest of their lives. Defeat will deposit a small, ineradicable sediment, just as victory will leave a few tiny bubbles of pleasure that can never quite disappear.

Brazil *v* England was that kind of match. There was never any possibility that it could be mundane. Apart from the status of the two countries as champions and former champions, and their fierce pride in their separate philosophies of the game, there was the realisation that the football world was watching for a sign. This scrutiny imposed the greater strain on England. Four years of Latin American scepticism would spill over into outright derision if England failed to answer the challenge of Brazil's rediscovered exuberance. Mathematical interpretations might appear to diminish the importance of the match (either side could lose and still qualify for the quarter-finals) but there was no sense in denying that it had a retrospective as well as a current relevance. England's validity as world champions had been persistently and sneeringly questioned since 1966 and those who argued that the dice had been blatantly loaded at Wembley would not forget to gloat if they fell. While the battle was still comparatively remote the hotel lobbies of Guadalajara were loud with English – and, disconcertingly, Scottish – voices insisting that this could not happen. Tommy Docherty and Charlie Cooke wagered on England with an enthusiasm calculated to cause mass resignations among Scottish Nationalist election agents. The city buzzed with hyperbole and esoteric tactical theory, like a saloon bar on a Saturday night. But as Sunday drew near, banter gave way to tension and in places to bitterness.

On the Friday and Saturday nights crowds of Brazilian and Mexican youths congregated outside the Hilton Hotel for a raucous assault on the peace of the England team. The footballers were kept awake into the early morning and some were forced to change rooms. When the malicious cacophony was at its worst on the Friday night the England team bus – whose importation from Britain had been seen by the Mexicans as yet another provocation ('Do you think we have not yet discovered the wheel or the internal combustion engine?') – was driven off as a decoy, but without much success. The policemen assigned to protect the England squad stood passively inside the glass doors of the hotel, apparently satisfied that they were doing enough if they prevented the mob from barging their way in. 'If I'd been there I would have directed the bus to the Brazilian camp and given them a taste of that mob,' said one British journalist. 'But I suppose the bastards would have whispered three cheers and gone home.'

As it happened, the Brazilians had a problem sufficiently serious to keep them off their sleep. The pulled muscle in his right thigh which had caused Gérson to leave the field before the end of the match with Czechoslovakia was still restricting him painfully and he was arguing against pessimistic medical opinion. 'This is the match that stands between us and our third World Cup,' Gérson declared publicly. 'The pulled muscle is not severe at the moment. If I am to damage the leg badly it is better that I should do it against England. There is a chance that I could help to defeat them before I come off.'

In his desperation to play Gérson underwent the most intensive treatment he had ever received. He agreed, for the first time, to have cortisone injections and he submitted readily to the constant attentions of Mário Americo, the vast, waddling black man who has been repairing the violated muscles of Brazil's great footballers since 1950. Americo, whose bulk and hairless head give him the appearance of a darker and more benevolent Odd Job, ministered to Gérson, a tough, independent man, with the gentleness of a mother. Even while Gérson slept Americo slipped into his bedroom, turned him over delicately and applied a short-wave machine to the injured thigh.

It was easy to understand the depth of Brazilian concern over Gérson. Apart from his brilliance as an individual – the alertness with which he read situations, the subtlety of his running, the deadly variety of his left-footed passes and shots – he contributed a sophisticated tactical intelligence and a fierce, infectious will. He, even more than Pele, was the team's formative thinker on the field, compulsively driving, instructing and cajoling throughout the ninety minutes. Many Brazilians felt that, in the context of a match so tense that even those who would only watch were inclined to catch their breaths at the mention of it, Gérson could be more influential than Pele.

That tribute was the measure of the disappointment when the doctors made their pronouncement, for they decided that Gérson could not be risked and Paulo Cézar was named in his place. Rather, Paulo Cézar, a gifted player with a refined and powerful right foot, took over from Rivelino as a midfield man with a licence to run free on the left whenever possible. Rivelino inherited for the time being Gérson's more general responsibilities in the middle of the team, leaving Brazil confident in their strength. They were becoming impatient about being told that if Kvasnak had not missed an easy chance for Czechoslovakia shortly before Jairzinho scored an apparently offside goal to give Brazil a 3–1 lead, the previous Wednesday's match would not have turned into a joyful rout. 'We were always going to have too many goals for Czechoslovakia,' Mário Zagalo said tersely. 'Maybe we will have too many for England also.'

The English players did not think so. According to Alan Ball they had been 'frightened to death' of having a bad result against Rumania and their win had rid them of their nerves. 'We got the hardest over and now we think we can beat these,' Ball said. 'I only hope England can go ahead as early as the Czechs did because England would beat Brazil by three or four. I think the Latin Americans have to be a success to play in a game.' Jackie Charlton thought the Brazilians did enough ball-watching in defence to give England a good chance of taking a lead, especially if the combination of Hurst and Peters operated at full efficiency. And he was sure Zagalo had been deprived of his best player by the injury to Gérson.

At Suites Caribe, squinting into the sharp sunlight by the swimming pool and moving his head occasionally to prevent a microphone from going down his throat, Gérson acknowledged that England would be more difficult than Czechoslovakia. 'Their defence will not be so naïve. They will not play a straight line across the field like old-fashioned soldiers. But if England gain an advantage by having so many men in front of their goal, such depth in defence, are they not handicapped by having only two men in attack? How long did they take to have a real shot against Rumania – half an hour?' Gérson agreed that it was not too much of an over-simplification to say that when England lined up against Brazil the finest defensive team in the world would be confronting the finest attacking team. He considered that Brazil's infinitely superior ability to make the killing break would settle the match. Even without him there would be Pele, Tostão, Jairzinho, Rivelino, Paulo Cézar – all regular scorers of goals – and Clodoaldo, Carlos Alberto and even Everaldo capable of coming threateningly from behind. There would, Gérson and many others suspected, be one menace too many for England to watch.

The new menace that had emerged since England lost narrowly to Brazil in Rio a year previously was Rivelino. He had the handsome, moustachioed and sideburned face of a playboy but his body was thickly athletic and the legs bulged with power. On the field his left looked dainty enough to put a match football in an eggcup but the shots when they came were intimidatingly violent.

'Is Rivelino going to be a world star?' Pele was asked at the Suites Caribe. 'Rivelino *is* a world star,' Pele said quietly. The greatest star of all had made a late descent from his room into the babel of a press session. There was first a hush and then an engulfing clamour. He took it all as natural, even when reporters unashamedly asked him to autograph their identification cards. He repeated that he was in the best condition he had known for six or seven years. Yes, it was true that the improvement in Brazilian organisation compared with 1966 had restored his appetite for the World Cup. Yes, he believed Brazil could win it and he could do much to help.

When we recalled seeing him score superbly unexpected goals over the heads of goalkeepers who had drifted off their line, and asked if his unforgettable looped shot from his own half against the Czechs had been an attempt to realise a lifelong ambition, he looked even happier than before. It was an eloquent affirmative, but for those with English sympathies there was something disturbing in that expression. This was a different Pele from the dejected figure of 1966. The smile was back on the face of the tiger.

That smile could only be widened by the conditions at the Jalisco Stadium on June 7. Some time before noon the ground was filled with close on 75,000 people and a hard, inescapable heat from the high sun. The Guadalajara climate, like the population, was giving its vote to Brazil. It is a mistake to think that Brazilians, white or black, actually enjoy playing football in high temperatures. Most matches in Rio are timed for the cool of the evening and some in the far south of the country can be played on snow. All players prefer the mild, still weather that allows them maximum exertion. But extreme heat is a fact of life for most Brazilians to an extent that it can never be for people from northern Europe. Psychologically as well as physically, they are familiar with it and they do not find it alarming, whether they are walking in the street or playing football. That was Brazil's advantage. Since the sun was an enemy to England, it was an ally for them. The alliance was strengthened as the thermometer climbed to an enervating 98 degrees Fahrenheit.

England had other problems but nothing to produce despondency. Mocanu, the Rumanian left-back who, as Pele remarked, appeared to confuse tackling with street fighting, had succeeded in making Newton an invalid. But Wright, despite his rather stodgy physique, was seen as a competent deputy, especially against the Brazilians, who might have punished the openness of Newton's game.

The hostility of the crowd would have dented the spirit of most teams. Partisan aggression was to be expected of the Brazilians, with their flags and chants and the tireless rhythm of their drums, but through all this there ran the harsher, more gratuitous enmity of the Mexicans. They dearly wanted to see a Latin American side humiliate England, but in the absence of Latin Americans Martians would have done. There were, of course, two or three thousand friendly voices, led by that of Ken Bailey, the quasi-official mascot. Dressed in a tail coat of hunting pink, with a black top hat, and showing an expanse of Union Jack across his chest, Bailey carried a cloth bulldog and flaunted the ensemble as publicly as possible wherever he went. But he and his flag were all too easily submerged in the mass opposition of the locals. At the Jalisco Stadium the cheers of the British sounded small and plaintive as the voice of a genie locked in a bottle.

In this setting the demeanour of the England team, their unforced indifference to the strident resentment evoked by their presence on the field, was an extraordinary achievement. As they kicked around before the start, several of them gave the crowd a slow, appraising look, then turned back to the ball as if they had seen nothing worth their attention. And when the game began they went to work with a relaxed matter-of-factness that controlled and concealed the extreme tensions they must have felt. For ten minutes the ball was rarely out of their possession. Passing it unhurriedly from one to the other, they sought skilfully to eliminate the risk of those early errors that so often settle such a match. They probed cautiously but without nervousness, like a good climber securing holds on a treacherous rock face. Soon they were steady enough for Ball and Bobby Charlton to emphasise the edginess of Félix. Then, in the tenth minute, the mountain almost fell on them. Carlos Alberto gave the ball along the right to Jairzinho and the winger accelerated dramatically beyond Cooper to the byeline. From there his centre was pitched towards the far post, some seven or eight yards out. Pele, reading the situation flawlessly and moving as perhaps only he could, had come in on the far side of Mullery and now he rose in an elastic leap, arching his back and neck to get behind and above the ball. The header was smashed downward with vicious certainty, aimed just inside the upright Banks had been obliged to neglect as he went to the near post in an effort to cover

Jairzinho's cross. Pele, Mullery reported later, shouted 'Goal' as the ball flew off his head. So did nearly everyone else in the stadium. But Banks, hurling himself back across his goal at a speed that will never cease to awe those who were there or the millions who watched on television, was already twisting into range as the ball met the ground two or three feet from his line. When it rose again venomously, he managed to flick his right hand at it and divert it miraculously over his crossbar. Much later Banks was to bring an incredulous expression to Cooper's face by saying the ball had been about shoulder height when he reached it, then amending his assessment to thigh height. In fact, the ball had been a foot or at most two feet off the ground when he saved it. He had reacted so quickly, so instinctively, that even his own mind did not have time to record the exact details of what he had done. There was no confusion, however, about the uniqueness of it. 'That is without question the greatest save I have ever seen,' said Bobby Charlton, who has seen a few.

Charlton was one of the players most immediately encouraged by Banks's virtuosity. With the surviving strands of blond hair glistening behind him, the face strained by effort, he was to be found wherever there was action. He had made a vigorous start and now, incredibly, he was stepping up his pace, running like a man who had recently passed twenty rather than thirty. It was a sign of his effectiveness when Rivelino, who was regulating the pulse of the Brazilian midfield in the manner of Gérson, came so far out of character as to attempt a foul on Charlton. Even that did not work, for Rivelino merely succeeded in hurting himself. When his verve carried him through on goal Charlton forced Félix to save at his feet, then hurdled two rough tackles before shooting too high. The Brazilians were at their most dangerous when Jairzinho and Paulo Cézar were dribbling or sprinting wide of Cooper and Wright to turn the ball back into the penalty area. But the covering in England's central defence was quick and sure. Moore, as always in this World Cup, was magnificent, interpreting the designs of the opposition with clairvoyant understanding and subduing their most spirited assaults with brusque authority. Mullery was marking Pele with the good sense and energetic persistence he had shown in Rio a year before and, though the Brazilian attack was ripplingly alive with one-twos and sharp progressive triangles, England were doing more than holding their own.

It was already a marvellous football match, tensely balanced and overflowing with high skills and intelligence. It was, as Mário Zagalo would say later, a match for adults. Far from being negatively defensive, England were retaliating with swift breaks that promised a goal. When Wright's cross was edged on by Lee, Peters headed over the bar from a position he would normally consider a scoring one. After thirty-one minutes a fine pass along the right wing by Mullery saw Wright spin on the byeline to screw back a wonderful centre that left Félix's goal open to

Lee. Unfortunately, the ball came to Lee's head, which is by no means his most powerful weapon, and the header was well taken by Félix. Lee, running in, kicked the goalkeeper and was warned by Abraham Klein, the Israeli referee. The forward's impetuosity, which had earlier produced an undamaging kick at Everaldo, brought retribution from Carlos Alberto, who went violently across the ball to foul him. (Carlos Alberto apologised at the interval and the match was never again to fall below its impressive level of integrity.)

Ball, who was pumping ceaselessly alongside Charlton in the middle, exposed a great gap in the left side of Brazil's defence with a superb pass forward to Hurst and we waited for the famous athletic rush on goal. But the big man loitered almost diffidently before pushing the ball on to Lee and a definite chance was lost. There were Brazilian demands for a penalty when Mullery, finding his job more taxing by the minute, crashed into Pele and both sprawled face down in the box. The referee might have been more sympathetic if Pele's fall had looked less like a crude impersonation of the cliff divers of Acapulco. No one, however, could question the award of a free kick when Cooper fouled Jairzinho just outside the area. Employing the ruse that had been so successful against Czechoslovakia, the Brazilians put Jairzinho in the English wall but Moore, who could play tag with a fox and never get caught, simply stood behind him. As Rivelino's shot raged through, Moore killed it as coolly as he would have taken a lobbed tennis ball and strode upfield. The word 'majestic' might have been invented for him.

At the interval the ferocity of the conditions was graphically indicated when the shadow of the public address loudspeakers, which were suspended on wires high above the middle of the pitch, was seen to be resting dead in the centre circle. Brazil delayed their appearance for the second half, leaving England to swelter in the vertical glare but Ramsey's players sat around in unconcerned groups, casual as sunbathers. They are too mature in the ways of international football to be affected by a little gamesmanship.

There was nothing gradual, however, about the entry into the second half. Almost at once Hurst went close to making decisive contact with a Peters cross and then Paulo Cézar struck a long right-footed shot that dipped and swerved before Banks lunged to push it round the post. A through pass by Pele, quick as a mongoose to punish any hint of vulnerability, sent Jairzinho raking through to the edge of the penalty area but Banks careered out to kick the ball away. Soon Pele, jinking and jostling through a pack of white shirts, was only stopped by Mullery's final tackle. Then Banks had to punch out a worrying shot from Rivelino.

Yet, for all this momentum, Brazil's goal when it came after an hour had a quality of surprise. Its immediate origins were deceptively innocent. In fact, it began with a lucky break of the ball. Tostão, spurting at Moore out on the Brazilian left, played the ball through the England captain's legs and had the satisfaction of seeing it ricochet between them and bounce out conveniently on the other side. Even then, Tostão seemed to have nowhere to go but, twisting and pivoting away from the closing defenders, he turned back brilliantly on his right foot and centred. He admitted later that he had aimed the ball for the danger area rather than for any specific player. Disastrously for England, it went straight to Pele. With Labone looming in front of him and Cooper straining to come across from his right, Pele decided against a shot. Instead, letting himself fall away to the left, he stroked the ball delicately at a slight angle in front of Jairzinho on his outside. Cooper's last hope of an interception went when he lost his footing and Jairzinho was clear for a shot. As Banks came plunging off his line and Peters struggled vainly to reach the ball Jairzinho hammered his cross shot in high with the right foot.

Sir Alf Ramsey had detected signs of tiredness in his team as the pressure on the defence mounted and he had one substitute warming up on the touchline before the goal was scored. Now, with twenty minutes left (and soon after Jairzinho had brought further alarm by shooting over, following passes by Paulo Cézar and Pele) he put Astle on for Lee and Bell for the overworked Charlton. Astle's principal virtue (some would say his only virtue) as an international forward, is his ability in the air. Hoisting himself above defences as smoothly as a performing seal rises from the water, he heads the ball with tremendous power and flexibility. That skill showed with heartening promptness for England when he knocked the ball back towards Ball. Unluckily, it was on Ball's left foot and the attempt at a volley was abortive. The other side of Astle was then sadly revealed. Everaldo, in a moment of terrible aberration, rolled the ball to the Englishman near the penalty spot, leaving him with generous time and an unobscured target. An equaliser seemed assured but Astle hit the ball slackly with his left foot and it slid past Félix's left-hand post. That, for England, was the most disappointing miss of the World Cup.

But they were not beaten yet. With twelve minutes left and Roberto on the field in place of Tostão, Moore went driving down the left, steadied and crossed for Astle to head on to Ball. A little way inside the eighteen-yard line and at an angle on the left, Ball made a calculating pause and carefully passed rather than shot the ball high beyond Félix's left shoulder. It was a beautifully deliberate effort and Ball was entitled to his agonised gesture of frustration when the ball, having beaten Félix completely, bounced on the top of the bar. Soon afterwards, as the goalkeeper punched the ball away, the small red-haired forward volleyed it back but again it did not stay low enough. He was playing splendidly, demonstrating every asset a great, foraging player needs, except luck.

To help wash the taste of injustice out of English mouths, Brazil finished with a flourish. Roberto, fed by Clodoaldo, made Banks dive to save at a post, then Pele sent one of those sinister chips close to Banks's crossbar. But it would have been blatantly wrong if Brazil had taken a two-goal victory from a match which, ideally, should have ended in a draw. England, who lost because they did not take the chances they made, had the substantial consolation of knowing they had conducted themselves like world champions, sharing equally in the honour of a genuinely great match. After watching the film of it, Bobby Charlton said: 'Even *we* were impressed. You could take that film and use it for coaching. That is what the game at the top is all about. There was everything in that, all the skills and techniques, all the tactical control, the lot. There was some special stuff played out there.'

There was indeed, and despite this setback, England were still very much alive and ready to provide more special stuff.

Brazil 1   England 0

Brazil v Italy

Aztec Stadium, 21 June 1970

THERE IS A BEAUTIFUL self-contained quality about a World Cup final. All the other matches, whatever their own vivid excitements, can only nourish the expectations of that last collision. Earlier days offer sudden death but this is the only one that offers instant immortality. Now the thousand background noises of the competition, the politicking, the training camp gossip, the accusations and insinuations, the boasts and hard luck stories, are stilled by the imminence of a pure climax. The thousand complex pressures that shape a World Cup have squeezed out all irrelevance and left the single thrilling reality of a game of football. That process of simplification is not always fair but its drama is to do with irrevocability rather than justice. No matter how many start out, in the final only two can play, and only one can win.

To those of us whose childhood and adolescence left us permanently impregnated with the mythology of football, it is inevitably a moving occasion. Sprinting through the rain to the bare, hard-seated buses that were to take us from the Maria Isabel Hotel to the Aztec Stadium on the morning of Sunday, June 21, we had that heightened sense of anticipation that invests every trivial preliminary with a tremor of pleasure. Every joke seemed funnier, every face friendlier. You could say that our behaviour was childish or you could say that we were reacting normally to the prospect of one of the last great communal rituals available to our society. You can say what you like. We were just glad to be going to the World Cup final.

The rain thinned and the exhaust fumes thickened as the bus hurried in a series of lunges through traffic that was even more raucously lively than usual. Brazilians, with vast flags streaming behind tall poles thrust from their car windows, weaved hazardously between lanes, seeking Italian victims for their banter. The Italians, for their part, were a minority but not a meek one. Disembarking in a gentle smirr at the Aztec, we were happy to let them get on with it. We could not lose. And yet it would be dishonest to claim total objectivity. Seeing the Brazilians come to this last obstacle was like watching Arkle gallop into the last fence of a steeplechase. A bad fall, even an ungraceful stumble, would be a painful blow to anyone who loved the sport. No one would begrudge Italy victory so long as they beat Brazil at their best. Indeed, if Italy rose above the highest standards of Pele and Gérson and Tostão and the rest, the world would be obliged to acclaim them great champions, a team fully deserving to keep the Jules Rimet trophy as their own property. What no neutral wanted, however, was to see Brazil undersell themselves. It can happen to the finest teams: the brutal anti-climax of an unworthy performance in the final. We suspected that it would not happen to Brazil, that their thinking players, and above all Pele, would not let it happen. We had flown up with them from Guadalajara and been impressed by their deep calm. Most of the damaging tension had been drained out of them by the defeat of Uruguay. They would obviously be nervous now as the kick-off approached but theirs would be an alert, stimulated edginess, uncomplicated by neurotic apprehensions. At the technical level they admitted that they would have been far more concerned if set to face England, whose zonal marking presented much greater problems than the man-for-man covering of Italy. But no opposition would have frightened them. They believe Brazilian football is made for World Cup finals and could not wait to prove the point.

In the press room beneath the stands, we drank the last cups of coffee and exchanged hopes and speculations about what would happen in the next two hours. The Italians, so patiently defensive in the earlier matches that they sometimes appeared willing to wait for opponents to grow old before striking at them with Riva, Boninsegna, Domenghini and the others, were not short of supporters, a few of whom were interested in taking a shade of odds. For the other side, the most compellingly specific argument was put forward by Armando Noguerra, a Rio columnist. Noguerra is not given to extravagant statements or claims to omniscience but now he shook us by saying there was one simple, technical reason why Brazil would definitely win. 'The Italians, who use a sweeper, cannot mark everyone and the Brazil player they will not mark is Gérson. He will be deep in midfield at the start and they will leave him alone. He will have space, he will move through to shoot, probably score and certainly decide the match.' On our way upstairs to our seats, we were tempted to tap his pockets for the clink of a crystal ball.

Outside the stadium, the three preceding nights of thunderstorms had left a scene that was almost Mancunian in its dripping greyness. But here inside, the colour and spirit of the crowd had splintered the dullness of the day. Dressed defiantly for sunshine, the spectators rippled down in a dazzling mass from the high rim of the arena, like garish wallpaper hung under a dirty ceiling. The field looked as lush as an Irish meadow, greener than the Brazilian flags that easily outnumbered the Italian tricolours. On the rich grass the military band, in full battle order and with rifles slung over their shoulders as they played, looked incongruously warlike. They were equipped exactly as they had been at the opening ceremony, as if to remind us that in a country as politically tense as Mexico a festival like the

World Cup must be parenthesised with steel.

When the teams came out the Italians threw flowers to the crowd. Whether as a reward or because they were viewed with morbid fascination as condemned men, they claimed almost the entire attention of the photographers thronging the pitch. The Brazilians were left in comparative peace to limber up and even in this exercise Pele caught the eye, opening his legs with a peculiar sideways motion that carried him round in jaunty circles. At last Herr Rudi Glockner was in the centre circle with his whistle in his mouth, Gérson was impatiently waving the last straggling photographers on to the sidelines and the match these players had been dreaming about for four years was just a breath from beginning.

The first aggressive gesture had, to Italian eyes, the quality of a portent. With only two minutes played, Mazzola made a square pass from the right and Riva stepped forward unhurriedly to meet it twenty-two yards from goal. There was that familiar impression of cold anger as he swung the left foot and the next time most people saw the ball clearly it was above Félix's head. The goalkeeper touched it over his crossbar without attempting to conceal his discomfort. Such a blow might have acted as a slap on the rump to many teams, sending them galloping eagerly into attack. But the habits of generations are not easily forgotten and Italy quickly restrained themselves in readiness for retaliation. Brazil did not let them down. A foul by Bertini on Pele thirty yards out brought no worrying consequences and a simple shot by Everaldo was equally negligible but there was real concern when Jairzinho sprinted for goal after intercepting a misplaced pass. Facchetti interrupted Jairzinho's progress at the cost of a free kick. We had foreseen that the Italians would concede many such kicks dangerously close to their penalty area and had guessed that Brazil, with their mastery of set-piece manoeuvres, would punish them for it. But, while Tostão and Gérson scuffled distractingly in the defensive wall, Rivelino shot unthreateningly high. Rivelino was blatantly ill at ease in these early minutes and for some time afterwards. He was the worst affected of several Brazilian players who were finding difficulty maintaining balance on the wet surface, in spite of having overcome their traditional reluctance to wear long studs. When Carlos Alberto's dangerous centre pressed Albertosi into punching the ball behind, Rivelino was again unsure of his footing as he prepared to take the corner and the kick spun away on an aimless trajectory.

Jairzinho's wanderings were already dragging Facchetti far from the left-back position and leaving room for Carlos Alberto to move up the wing. This had been a basic element in the strategy laid down by Zagalo before the match but, as he sat on the touchline with his clipboard in his hand, the manager must have been pleasantly astonished by the naïve reaction to his ruses. Above all, he must have been even more gratified than Armando Noguerra to find that Gérson was indeed left unmarked in midfield, that the Italian man-for-man covering stopped short of perhaps the most influential builder in the Brazilian side. For the moment, however, it was Carlos Alberto, tall and powerfully upright, who made most impressive use of the freedom he was given. After careful possession play had trapped the Italians into giving space yet again on their left, the full-back drove a low centre across goal and saw it stay just out of reach of Tostão's lunge.

Albertosi's anxiety was balanced at the other end when Riva took the ball through on the left with Domenghini waiting, free and poised to shoot, on the other side of the goal. Untypically, Riva shot wastefully at Félix and Brazil relaxed. But not for long. Having seen his goalkeeper make an uneasy save that left the defence in confusion, Pele tried to dribble forcefully upfield but was penalised a dozen yards outside the penalty area. Mazzola's free kick from the left took the ball to Riva but, though the header was struck solidly, it carried slightly too high. Almost as soon as the goal-kick had swept the ball away from Félix, the Italians brought it back. Facchetti sent it out of defence to Domenghini, who beat Clodoaldo and passed to Boninsegna. With his long, thick hair slapping the nape of his neck, Boninsegna began one of the thrusting, tenacious runs that would soon make him, and not Riva, Italy's most dangerous attacker. This time he was smothered in yellow shirts on the edge of the area. His disappointment was instantly doubled by a goal for Brazil. It was a fine example of their gift for transmuting the apparently innocent into something deadly.

Facchetti, hurriedly clearing a cross from the Brazilian left, gave away a throw on that side. Tostão threw to Rivelino and he quickly found room for a crisp, well-judged centre high over the six-yard line. Pele, just short of the far post and facing squarely on to the goal, planted both feet firmly for the jump and rose far above Bertini, his hapless marker. Jerking his head back and then forward like the firing hammer of a pistol, Pele smashed the ball down past Albertosi's left side. We remembered something else the perceptive Noguerra had said. 'For the first time Pele and Brazil share the same destiny,' he told us. 'In the past there were always two entities, Pele and Brazil. Their objectives may have been similar but they moved towards them separately. In the past he was never a leader, not even at Santos. Now Brazil and Pele are integrated. He is leading this team to their destiny.' That goal, its timing and its uncompromising character, represented the best kind of leadership.

It was a commodity Italy were apparently lacking. Their response to the goal was to acknowledge the obvious: that it had been an error to allot to Bertini, an attacking wing-half, the job of subduing Pele. Feruccio Valcareggi could perhaps advance the unusual excuse that he had long since lost control of team selection. Whoever had control on the field did not improve dramatically on the original miscasting of Bertini. He was moved to right-back, allowing Burgnich to switch on to Pele. So instead of being an inept central marker, Bertini became an inept right-back. At least he could console himself with the certainty that Burgnich had the worse of the deal, although it did not look that way when Bertini was bustled into fouling Rivelino, justifying a free kick that nearly brought a goal. Rivelino readily misled the defenders by shaping to take the kick, then darted forward on to Pele's chip. But his feet were still behaving like a comedy skater's and he had to let the ball run past. A moment before, the alarm had been elsewhere as Carlos Alberto, attempting a fancy pass, gave the ball to Riva. Félix raced out to kick away from the Italian's feet but the goalkeeper could only pray when a high, diagonal centre from Mazzola eluded everyone. The crowd sighed, too, as the ball fell wide.

There was further encouragement for Italy in the sight of Tostão (who was normally to be found far upfield, stroking off his cogent passes under heavy pressure from Rosato) chasing far back to clear off his own penalty line. And if Burgnich was sufficiently troubled to earn a caution for hitting Pele from the back, Piazza was far from composed when he pushed Riva while both may well have been inside the Brazilian area and not outside, as the referee decided. Bertini's free kick was eased wide to Riva but his shot died in the cushioning barricade of defenders.

Boninsegna, harrying with keen intelligence, tirelessly putting himself in those positions that offered his own players a target and denied the opposition peace of mind, was now clearly the searching point of Italy's attack. This was demonstrated once more when he took a pass from Riva, beat Brito and drove the ball a few feet wide. The one other Italian who equalled and perhaps outshone Boninsegna was Mazzola. Mazzola was, unmistakably, the heart of the team, pumping out spirit and purpose from midfield. He is a strong, resilient, abundantly skilled player but his performance was probably even more a definition of courage than of talent. His family has a proud tradition in the game and he seemed determined that his contribution to the World Cup final would be worthy of it, that his team would never surrender quietly. None of the 112,000 people who filled the Aztec Stadium is likely to forget how he played.

De Sisti, whose imaginative persistence had been a pleasing motif in earlier matches, was largely submerged and it was almost a surprise when he contrived a graceful series of passes with Mazzola on the left. Mazzola was given the shot but Gérson and Carlos Alberto combined to smother it. Gérson, despite the absence of any shadowing opponent, was still content to operate from deep positions. He, and indeed the whole Brazilian team, gave an impression of great patience. That quality had been discernible in Italy, too, since the start of the competition and the loss of a goal had not ruffled them excessively. Yet the attitudes of the two sides, and the emanations that came from them, were fundamentally

different. Italy had Cera sweeping behind a back line of four, and
Mazzola, De Sisti and Domenghini as a middle line that only occasionally
released a man to support Riva and Boninsegna at the front. Theirs tends
to be the patience of a garrison that has laid in supplies to withstand a
siege and hopes to step from the fort eventually and find the attackers
dead of starvation. Patience with them was a weapon in itself. With the
Brazilians it was a launching pad for more spectacular weapons. We
assumed confidently that the period of calculation, of weighing up,
would be limited, that Gérson would soon come forward, that Pele would
begin to turn the screw as he had done in previous games, that Carlos
Alberto would make more runs along the right wing and that Tostão,
who was unsuppressed by the adhesive thoroughness of Rosato, would
increase the rate of those passes that run out from him like live fuses. All
this was different from assuming a Brazilian victory, though some of us
did that too. The point was that we were sure the Italians would have to
cope with these problems, that in their attempt to find answers would be
the resolution of the match, the climax of the World Cup. We sensed in
Brazil's restraint during that first half a promise as palpable as the ticking
of a time-bomb.

The ticking was temporarily drowned, however, when the Italians,
armed by an outrageous error, produced a blast of their own. Jairzinho
had just made a splendid run that led to passes between Tostão and Pele
and a shot from Tostão which had to be right-footed, and therefore
comparatively weak, when Italy found a surge that pressured Brazil into
rough defence. A foul by Pele on De Sisti was swiftly followed by Brito's
on Riva. Before the strain had eased Brito, in a tightening situation in
front of goal but perhaps thirty-five yards out, played the ball square
towards Clodoaldo on the Brazilian left. It was, blatantly, a time for a
simple, forceful clearance but Clodoaldo chose to be clever and
attempted a back-heel flick to Everaldo. If Clodoaldo had been unaware
that Boninsegna was descending on him, he soon saw the implications of
the forward's presence. Boninsegna snatched the ball away and sprinted
for the penalty area. He might still have been delayed crucially, for Carlos
Alberto and Brito were striving to converge on him. But Félix, fatally
miscalculating the percentages, ran from his line. In the muddled
collision over the ball on the edge of the area, the bones that crunched
most loudly were those of Brito and his goalkeeper. Boninsegna regained
his balance long before they did and pursued the ball as it broke out
towards the left. When he reached it, Riva was also in attendance and
might have scored. But, fittingly, the man who had made the chance was
permitted to take it. He did so briskly, turning the ball back into goal
ahead of the scrambling Brazilian defenders.

The eight minutes that were left of the first half were tense with the
knowledge that another loss on either side could be permanently

wounding. Bertini hurriedly surrendered a corner when Gérson threatened to dribble through. Then Carlos Alberto and Boninsegna crashed
painfully together as Italy broke to take a retaliatory corner. The trainers
returned to their benches in time to see a long shot by Domenghini
fumblingly saved by Félix. Rivelino, having been aggravatingly fouled,
replied by stamping his heel over the ball on to Bertini and was rightly
cautioned. The free kick awarded for the original foul was taken by
Gérson and brought a much more controversial decision from the referee.
Gérson lifted his kick over the entire Italian defence and Pele, killing the
ball with relaxed deliberation, slid it easily past Albertosi. But Herr
Glockner's whistle had ended the first half before that last blow was
struck. The electronic clock showed a few seconds remaining but, of
course, the referee is his own timekeeper. Brazil made a muted, confused
protest as they left the field.

A Mexican journalist who seemed inclined to use the interval to put
the complaint more aggressively through the wire fence separating the
press seats from the Italian supporters found himself heading away a few
small flagpoles. By the time he had been dragged out of range and we had
noted that the sun – having won *its* fight – was now shining with a slightly
glazed confidence, the teams were out for the second half. Brazil, who had
climbed nearly two-and-a-half thousand feet from Guadalajara to face
men who were actually reducing their altitude problem by playing in
Mexico City, had been urged by Zagalo to be wary with their energies in
the first forty-five minutes. Now whatever had been saved must be let
loose on Italy. Like a racehorse that has been hard-held into the straight,
Carlos Alberto's team must try to quicken and leave the opposition
standing. The captain himself took only three minutes to give a firm
declaration of intent. Released by Jairzinho's pass, he moved along the
right for another of those low centres across goal. Pele, sliding in with the
alarming suddenness of a skidding motor bike, rammed the ball just
outside the far post. Burgnich, discomfited by the evidence that Pele was
about to become even more threatening, responded with fouls that could
easily have been self-destructive. The first, thirty yards out, gave Rivelino
the opening for a swerving shot that Albertosi beat down as he dived to
his left. The second, a bicycle kick on Pele's head as the forward sought to
capitalise on a one-two between Gérson and Tostão, resulted in an
indirect free kick two yards inside the penalty box. Pele passed to Gérson
but his shot was unexpectedly harmless. Gérson's next intervention,
another effort at a break into the area with Tostáo, also misfired but there
was no mistaking the significance of the contribution he was now
making. His reticence in the first half had persuaded the Italians that they
were justified in leaving him without specific cover. Free to build
composure in his side and to scan the enemy at leisure for the principal
points of weakness, his play until the interval had been in the nature of a

preparation. He was like an arsonist who had been allowed to stoke up
with matches and petrol. Now he was ready to set the game alight. Bill
Shankly, the manager of Liverpool, has said that nothing in the World
Cup impressed him more than the patience with which Gérson stayed his
hand. 'He discovered before half-time that he could move up and put
Italy in trouble,' said Shankly. 'But he knew if he did too much of it they
would see what was happening and try to find a solution at the interval.
So he waited until the second half. Then the Italians had no chance to
discuss the problem. They were sunk.'

Even judged as a reaction in the heat of battle, however, the Italian
dithering over Gérson was lamentable. They should surely have known
that to neglect him in the first place was a huge risk, that they might be in
need of a quickly arranged compromise. They managed none. The
consequences of that failure were briefly concealed by two stirring
assaults on Félix's goal. After Facchetti had slipped away on the left and
Boninsegna swung the ball out wide for Domenghini to deliver a shot that
was deflected for a corner, De Sisti set the splendid Mazzola on a thrilling
run. His shot was powerful but he did not keep it low enough. Before they
could draw encouragement from these endeavours Italy were swept back
as if by a landslide. Amid the debris of their crumbling assurance, Bertini
pulled down Rivelino. When the same happened to Jairzinho as he went
for Tostão's return pass on the eighteen-yard line the referee charitably
placed the ball five yards farther out for the free kick. But it was still
nearly disastrous for the Italians, though they crowded every man back
into the box. Gérson merely pushed the ball square and Rivelino,
swinging the right foot that is supposed to be no more than a crutch for
the left, lashed it brutally against the crossbar wide of Albertosi's left
shoulder. Rivelino had fully recovered from his early nervousness and
soon he was bearing down on Albertosi to shoot again. The ball rose
wildly high but Riva, almost as big and bony as Henry Cooper, kept his
team in difficulties by backhanding Rivelino on the mouth as the
Brazilian followed through. That free kick brought a scramble of shots
but none that counted.

Italy, stretched to the limit, retained the elasticity to snap back
dangerously. Facchetti passed down the left to the untiring Boninsegna
and when the cross beat a puzzled, scurrying Félix, Riva struck an
excellent header from beyond the far post. The goalkeeper was lucky to
see the ball bounce off Everaldo, lucky again when a foolish attempt at a
punching save produced nothing worse than a moment of hectic
confusion. At this point Gérson, presumably worried by the possibility
that Félix was about to make some fatuous interpolations in the script,
took the sensible precaution of scoring a magnificent goal.

Spinning clockwise in a deep inside-left position, Gérson sent a blind
but unerring pass to Everaldo on the wing. Everaldo pushed the ball

straight ahead to Jairzinho and the forward, after starting to dribble inside, saw the advantage of rolling it back to Gérson. With that carefully schooled left foot, Gérson first dragged the ball outside a tackle and then cracked it with the clean force of a perfect one-iron aimed under the wind. It flew more than twenty yards in a killing diagonal and was still only waist height when it hit the far side-netting. That goal, scored in the sixty-fifth minute, gave formal recognition to the fact that Gérson was the central influence of the match, the hub of the wheel that was grinding Italy down. Within five minutes he was helping to squeeze the last of their resistance into the damp turf. A foul on Pele was punished with the twelfth free kick given to Brazil in the second half and Everaldo used it to make a short pass to Gérson. The balding head flicked up to take in the sight of Pele sidling behind Burgnich beyond the far post. No one in the world passes the ball more accurately in the air than Gérson does. Now it was lifted in a precise, elongated arc over the head of Burgnich on to that of Pele. An immediate strike at goal would have been in order but Pele, whose mind is quicker than most men's eyes, coolly headed down to Jairzinho. The manoeuvre was so deadly in its simplicity that Jairzinho could afford to miskick and still have time to run the ball into the net.

Italy faced a further twenty minutes on the rack. Bertini, at least, was spared the torture. He collapsed in the centre circle, with a pulled muscle in his right thigh, and was replaced by Juliano. One of Juliano's first contributions was to give the ball to Gérson, which is about as profitable as throwing live grenades against a rubber wall. This time Gérson made a chance for Rivelino but he did not connect adequately. Brazil, who might have become drugged with their own brilliance, instead emphasised the tactical discipline inculcated by Zagalo. The idea that their football in 1970 was all some kind of beautiful, primitive dance is charmingly absurd. Of course, there is an elemental rhythm about their play, a natural gymnastic grace and flexibility, but their game is as rational as it is instinctive. Can anyone seriously argue that the stunning subtleties of Gérson, Tostão and Pele do not represent the highest form of the games-player's intelligence? It is questionable if any team in the World Cup other than England equalled the tactical sophistication shown, individually and collectively, by Brazil. The recurring weaknesses in their defence were flaws of temperament and technique, not errors of innocence. In this last quarter of the match the strong personalities in the side organised the total manpower to make sure that any kamikaze inclinations among the Italians would not bring late embarrassment. At one moment every Brazilian was working in his own half. Thus when a mistake by Piazza let Boninsegna through there was an extra man, Brito, to fill the gap with a superb tackle.

That moment marked the exhaustion of Italy's spirit and Brazil were free to finish with the sort of rich flourish that suits their natures and the

dramatic range of their talents. Those last minutes contained a
distillation of their football, its beauty and *élan* and undiluted joy. Other
teams thrill us and make us respect them. The Brazilians at their finest
give us pleasure so natural and deep as to be a vívid physical experience.
This was what we had hoped for, the ritual we had come to share. The
qualities that make football the most graceful and electric and moving of
team sports were being laid before us. Brazil are proud of their own
unique abilities but it was not hard to believe that they were anxious to
say something about the game as well as about themselves. You cannot be
the best in the world at a game without loving it and all of us who sat,
flushed with excitement, in the stands of the Aztec sensed that what we
were seeing was a kind of tribute.

No player's statement was more eloquent than Gérson's. One
marvellous run on the left produced a cross that was just too high for
Tostão, then a great pass to Everaldo sent the full-back careering in on
goal to be denied by Albertosi's brave save at his feet. The sympathy that
was due Italy was tempered by continuing disappointment at their folly.
It was almost unbelievable that a country with a neurotic obsession about
tactical theory should reveal such an elementary lack of foresight and
imagination. With less than seven minutes left they again betrayed their
masochistic eccentricity. Despite being two goals behind and glaringly
short of firepower, they withdrew their one consistently effective
forward, Boninsegna, and substituted the delicate midfield player,
Rivera. To have any relevance Rivera would have needed much longer on
the field. Bringing him on at this point simply meant that an angry man
(and Boninsegna had a right to his show of disgust) was replaced by a
sulky one. The only benefit Rivera earned from his promotion to active
service was that he had a closer view of one of the best goals scored in the
World Cup. Naturally enough, it was scored by Brazil. Barely four
minutes remained when Clodoaldo, whose donation of a goal to Italy had
been isolated in an otherwise excellent performance, began the attack
with a dribble that was as brilliant as it was untypical. Normally he is
happy to apply his skills with firm economy but here, wriggling and
feinting in the manner of Rivelino, he mesmerised five challengers and
from the left-half position passed the ball forward to Jairzinho. Moving
inside from the left wing, Jairzinho sent it on to Pele, who was twenty
yards out in front of goal. Yet again Jairzinho had drawn Facchetti far
out of position and Carlos Alberto was coming through on an angled run
with the intimidating directness of a torpedo. Pele, seeing him come,
turned unhurriedly and rolled the ball into his path with the relaxed
precision of a lawn bowler. Without having to check, deviate or adjust his
stride, Carlos Alberto smashed the ball with his right foot low into the
side-net behind Albertosi's right-hand post. It was an unforgettable goal
and its seeming inevitability increased rather than diminished its
excitement.

Dozens of photographers and supporters were sufficiently overcome to invade the pitch while the match was still going on. They were made to retreat but stayed near enough to lead the massed charge that came when the referee did signal the end. Pele and Tostão ran to hug one another but were soon in the more hazardous embrace of their admirers. Tostão was stripped boot by boot, sock by sock and had a struggle to keep his shorts. Vast flags, acres of green and yellow, swam above the delirious mob. Men with banners danced until they collapsed exhausted on the grass. There were now thousands on the field and in the middle of this South American celebration was the marching, bowing figure of Ken Bailey, the English cheerleader. As usual, he was dressed in a tail coat of hunting pink and black top hat. He was carrying his toy bulldog and waving a tiny Union Jack. But for those unreal happenings in León, some less outlandish Englishmen would have been entertaining the crowd at the Aztec.

There was no discrimination about the laps of honour. Anyone could join in and it was not easy to pick out the players in the swarms of supporters. One local patriot made himself prominent with a placard reading 'Mexico – World Champions of Friendship'. Sir Alf Ramsey would have savoured that one.

Zagalo was still carrying his clipboard as he rode round the arena on an uncomfortable platform of shoulders. The presentation by the Mexican president, Gustavo Díaz Ordaz, which was loud with the music of naval and civilian bands and bright with the flags of all the FIFA members, was a moment of profound satisfaction for Zagalo. He had been accused of a defensive approach to the challenge in Mexico but in the event his team scored nineteen goals, more than Brazil had taken in 1958 or 1962, and an average of better than three a match. In the process they beat three former champions, Uruguay, Italy and England, and proved they could match the tactical discipline and physical condition of the Europeans. Stamina and composure helped them to score important goals in the last twenty minutes of their games.

The manager could claim another more personal achievement. He overcame at last the resentment that had persisted among the men, notably Pele, who had played with him in 1958 and 1962. No one questioned the value of his contribution in those years ('Zagalo was the one who showed the world 4–3–3,' says one Brazilian, 'who made it clear to all of us that a footballer must have two shirts – a defender's and an attacker's'). But his team-mates felt that his luck, which is legendary, had kept better players out. In 1958 and 1962 Pepe, the great goal-scoring winger of Santos, was removed by injury and Germano was similarly unfortunate in 1962. Pele was one of those who believed the Zagalo luck had put a jinx on his rivals. It was an intriguing scene, therefore, when Pele and Zagalo came face to face in a momentarily quiet corner of the dressing-rooms after the final. Pele put down the glass of water he was drinking and, without a word, they ran to each other for a long, tearful embrace. Later Pele gave the manager his shirt. (Tostão gave his, along with his winner's medal, to the doctor who operated on his eye in Houston, Texas.)

At roughly the same time as Pele and Zagalo were burying past differences the President of Brazil, General Garrastazú Médici, was draping a national flag round his shoulders and going out of his palace to play informal football with the crowds in Praça dos Tres Poderes, the main square of Brasilia. The one player President Médici strenuously advocated, Dario, a centre-forward, did not help directly in the winning of the World Cup but he was of some assistance in keeping it. Carlos Alberto, while being buffeted around on his lap of honour, failed to notice that the gold top of the Cup had slipped to the ground at his feet. Dario, following on behind, saw a small boy pick it up and after a brief chase was able to retrieve it.

Paulo Cézar had to survive a chase to hold on to another prize, the match ball, which he snatched on behalf of a friend who is a fanatical follower of Brazil. When he was pursued by an Italian player, Paulo Cézar had an unanswerable advantage. He had been resting on the substitutes' bench throughout the match.

Long after the final was over some of the Brazilians still found difficulty in absorbing what had happened. Pele says that when he woke next morning he seriously wondered if he had been dreaming. The sight of his medal at the bedside only partially reassured him and he telephoned his wife Rose at home in Brazil to ask: 'Are we really the champions?' Rose, who was seven months pregnant with their second child, told him she had felt a severe pain when he scored the first goal. She must have been one of the few people in Brazil who did. Even the Italians in the Aztec Stadium could not have found the experience of this final too hurtful. Football, and all of us who regard it as something worthwhile, can only gain from such occasions. As tons of coloured confetti were spilled from the roof of the stands to drift down upon us in a dry, bright rain we realised that the mood of schoolboy expectancy with which we had come to the match had been sustained. The afternoon had become cool and mild once more but we had enough Brazilian friends to make us suspect that a long, hot night of revelry lay ahead.

Outside the ground we were met by vendors offering pennants commemorating Brazil's World Cup victories in 1958, 1962 – and 1970. They had mass-produced the mementoes well in advance. It was not much of a risk.

Brazil 4   Italy 1

How it dawned on Ormond that his crew were rocking the boat

(*The Observer*, 19 May 1974)

WHEN OUTRAGEOUS fortune came at Willie Ormond in mid-week it was with nothing as dramatic as slings and arrows. The blows had, rather, the impact of a wet flounder across the whiskers.

A few worrying injuries apart, his troubles in the home international championship before yesterday's triumph over England had been of a kind to produce embarrassment rather than a sense of crisis. They began with an Irish raspberry at Hampden eight days ago and, although that red-faced occasion was followed by a competent win over a ramshackle Welsh team, any brief swelling of the martial music was quickly drowned by the mocking shanties that were readily improvised when Jimmy Johnstone (the smallest sea-dog ever to ask to be clapped in irons) gave an unconvincing impersonation of Hornblower in the rowing-boat that went drifting helplessly away from the beach at Largs shortly after dawn on Wednesday.

That bleary episode, coming at the end of a night in which quite a number of the Scotland players avoided the beds of the team's hotel as if they were English defenders, might easily have led to one of those messy little tragedies that occur so often when people forget that salt water and the old illusion juice don't mix. Johnstone, who was cheery enough to spend the first few minutes of his ordeal standing up in the boat, waving the single oar in his possession and chanting 'Scot-land, Scot-land', was soon reduced to a less celebratory waving as he bobbed towards the horizon, pursued by the noisy advice of his team-mates on the shore. 'I thought about gaun ower the side and swimming for it,' he said later, when his teeth had stopped chattering, rescuing fishermen had been paid off and the local constabulary had been placated. Had he taken such a decision the wee man would have had less chance of finishing on the beach than in the submarine boom a few miles down the Firth of Clyde. And he could easily have had company, for two other players had rashly elected to go to his aid in an inflatable dinghy that subsequently proved to be holed. By the time they, too, were assisted ashore, the water in the dinghy was rising above their bare feet.

The darker possibilities were swiftly forgotten when a safe landing restored the entire incident to the level of farce, but at midnight Willie

Ormond, with the thought of the headlines and the Knoxian homilies that were bound to be carried in Thursday's papers, was still tense enough to wash down a sleeping pill with a gin and bitter lemon. 'I don't know whether to seek political asylum or settle for an ordinary, old-fashioned asylum,' he said, managing the smile that is the most natural expression on his round and friendly face.

As a Navy man he survived the wartime convoys to Murmansk but nothing he saw on those Arctic seas was ever as unnerving as the sight of his right-winger floating off in the morning sunlight towards Dunoon. 'Come in No. 7, your time is up,' was the line the cartoonists couldn't resist. If the impromptu cruise had been a solo enterprise Ormond could have felt that he was merely the latest victim of Johnstone's seemingly impenetrable and incurable waywardness. But the noisy crowd who stood at the water's edge, rousing a fair part of the population at Largs with their shouts, included the most senior and experienced footballers in the squad. Having allowed the nonsense to develop, because of a trust that he now recognises as naive, the manager could not opt for fierce disciplinary action. Any applause he received for dismissing more than half his first-choice players from the party would have come mainly from future opponents.

So Ormond, having to some extent invited the blow, had to take it with no more than a threatening lecture as retaliation, perhaps consoling himself with the thought that it could have been worse – he could have had a Stan Bowles. 'I've told them that they've misused the trust I put in them and that from now on there would just have to be a kind of curfew system. And the next one to step out of line knows its bingo, pack the bags and home. That's the only good you can get out of a mess like this, to learn a lesson from it. It's better that it should happen here and now instead of a month later in Germany.

'Maybe I'll finish up being grateful for this week of the home championship because of things like that, because it put a lot of people under the microscope for me and showed me something basic about them. You could argue that the players would have been better having rest instead of football at this stage of the preparation for the World Cup, that shoving them into three matches now after an exhaustng League season would simply drain some of them and encourage others to be non-triers because they didn't want to risk their legs, especially after seeing the injuries Tommy Hutchison and Willie Donachie have got already. All that makes sense, and yet I am glad we've had this hard week. It's told me a few things I couldn't have known without it.

'You can learn as much about men watching them day in and day out around the hotel – at training, at meals, in front of the TV – as you can seeing them play at Hampden Park. In the end you are not just sending out footballers in the World Cup, you're sending out men and I've seen into the character of a few of these in the last week or so. Some, like Danny McGrain, have risen even higher in my estimation. He's not only just about the best full-back in the game, he's a great character, a fellow you could trust with your life. But there are a couple who act like layabouts. They don't do it for you on the park and they don't look as if they even want to try to do it here at training. They're either too idle or too big-headed to commit themselves.

'Don't think I'm stuck with the pool of 22 we've got for these games. There will be a change or two next week when I announce the party for Belgium and Norway at the beginning of June. That will be the World Cup party, so there will be no room for the doubtful cases.'

It is not too hard to identify the two men he is inclined to jettison. One is a skilful mid-field player, whose talent so outstrips his industry that it was being suggested at Hampden last Tuesday that anyone who spotted him in action should be awarded a free trip to the World Cup finals. The other is a home-based defender who appears to be burdened with the fantasy that his abilities are so remarkable that breaking sweat will somehow soil them. By losing favour they have opened the way for the recruitment of equivalent players from the overall pool of 40 and, although half a dozen names might be considered relevant, the outstanding candidates are Cormack of Liverpool, as a man who could help to build in the middle of the field and strike usefully at the front, and Munro, of Wolves, as someone whose experience and controlled distribution of the ball might diminish the huge sense of loss caused by the injury to Connelly. With Jardine finding such marvellous form against Wales, the position that would have been filled by Connelly is the major worry in the defence.

The Celtic man himself is sweating through regular training sessions at Parkhead, driven on by the minimal hope that his recovery from a fractured ankle may be so accelerated that he will be able to play in Germany. Thinking of his value to Scotland – of the way his coolness and the elevated quality of his football blur the jagged edges of Holton's game when he operates alongside the centre-half, of the way his long, ambitious passes widen the horizons of his team – every Scot is willing that ankle to turn supple overnight. But Connelly is not yet kicking a ball in earnest and Jock Stein says dolefully that we must consider his class a frozen asset.

Sitting in the Celtic boardroom, with the Scottish Cup on the table by his elbow, Stein smiles ruefully at the thought that the two members of his playing staff who have been giving him most worry over recent seasons should be proving so crucial to Scotland's chances of making a flourish this summer. Connelly and Johnstone are in their different ways intensely private, impulsive and frequently aggravating men. Both have left Scotland parties in the past without seeking permission or offering excuse, departing with such abruptness that they might have parachuted from the team plane.

'I think Connelly was geared up for this World Cup,' says Stein. 'The thought of earning 10 or 12 grand out of it would have helped to maintain his concentration. But who can tell about the wee man? He lives in a world of his own. In our dressing-room before a big match all the rest are stamping about, working themselves up, talking about getting a result. He is sitting in a corner with his legs crossed, looking at nobody in particular, remote from it all. "Are you all right, wee man?" I'll say, and he says: "Aye, I'm fine." And that's all you get out of him. Then he goes out on the park and he looks like no footballer you've ever seen. He's like a wee old man. You feel a top hat would suit him better than a football strip. But when the mood takes him, he can do a job for you. It's not just his skill, that low-slung action with the sudden stops and all those feints packed into the one dribble, the technique of lifting the ball over the feet instead of dragging it wide so that the tackler has to be deadly accurate to make contact.

'There's all that, but there's also the sight of him. Most foreign opponents have never seen anything like him before, and they can lose concentration for 20 minutes trying to work him out. What will the fellas from Zaire think of him? They'll take him for a leprechaun or a hobgoblin. Even the Brazilians have never seen anything like him. If Willie Ormond can keep a grip on him, Jinky may show some of the old stuff.'

At least the Scots will be inland in West Germany, and their accommodation may be better calculated to keep them securely indoors than the little hotel they have been using in Largs. There are only 14 rooms (just two with baths) and the ladies sipping afternoon tea were liable to be alarmed by the spectacle of a Scottish defender stepping past their table in nothing but a towel. Even the exceptional kindness and enthusiasm of the staff could not make up for the claustrophobia that gathered day by day.

The Inverclyde National Recreation Centre on a hill behind the town might profitably have been used for living quarters as well as training facilities. It would bear some comparison with the Brazilian 'concentration' in Rio. A tiny hotel with rooms devoid of phones and television, is perfectly designed to massage the traditional self-destructive urges of Scottish footballers.

Ask Willie Ormond. Or ask Jimmy Johnstone if you can reach him.

The week that Scotland were out of this World

(*The Observer*, Frankfurt, 22 June 1974)

SCOTTISH FOOTBALL suffered perhaps the cruellest and least deserved blow in its history tonight when one of the most impressive teams the country has sent on to an international field frightened and outplayed Yugoslavia but had to settle for a draw, and then found that they had been removed from the World Cup by a goal scored in a stadium 150 miles away.

The electronic scoreboard here in the Waldstadion told the Scots that Brazil had beaten Zaire 3–0, and they knew that their own record of remaining undefeated in their three group matches was not enough to keep them alive in the competition. The failure to take more than two goals against the Africans left them equal on points with Brazil and Yugoslavia, but behind both when goal difference became the eliminating factor. Salt was shovelled into the wound by the knowledge that the Scots had demonstrated themselves superior in the drawn matches with their two major challengers, and that Brazil's third goal against Zaire had come from a shot that most goalkeepers in the park on a Sunday would be expected to save.

'At least we did not lose our pride,' said Billy Bremner, seeking to cheer himself and the grey, drained faces around him in the dressing-room corridor, after today's disembowelling experience. Neither did the supporters lose their faith. At least 200 of them, having presumably escaped the mayhem that broke out around the ground when rival groups collided during the evening, waited with their flags and their undaunted chants to see their players off towards a wake in the hills outside Frankfurt.

It might have been a vastly enlarged, vastly different scene had Jordan, that splendid fighter for the cause all through the last ten days, succeeded in dragging the ball away from Maric when a wonderful chance fell to him in the first half; had the referee acted more strongly in response to the harsh misdemeanours of the Yugoslavs (it was outrageous in the end that with Jordan and Hay joining Oblak, Katalinski and Bajevic in the referee's book, the cautions were only 3–2 against the Slavs); had Hutchison been brought on much earlier than he was for the fading, sadly unconvincing Dalglish . . . the possibilities, slipping like bright images through the mind, make an agonising list.

But what happened was that the opposition, having been scared virtually from the start into abandoning their greatly admired attacking skills, and relying on more negative, less honourable expedients, did score first through their substitute Karasi only eight minutes from the end. Scotland, spurred to still higher levels by the fresh energies of Hutchison, contrived a thrilling equaliser. But if the Scots deserved more than equality on that field, they were given less than overall equality on the electric scoreboard. 'The best team in the group are going home,' said Jim Holton, speaking sadly over the heads of the sympathisers who crowded round his tall figure. 'What a sickener to be all over Brazil and Yugoslavia and have to get on the plane for home on Monday.'

Holton's words had double significance, because they came from one of the men judged to be vulnerable and probably beneath World Cup class in the Scotland squad. When it came to the test, Holton was a giant in every sense, a man who pitted his simple, effective abilities against some of the best forwards in the world and subdued them. All around him other players made a heroic success of their contributions. Jardine, McGrain, Buchan, Hutchison and, of course, the thrustingly dangerous forwards, Jordan and Lorimer, will remember this World Cup with a welling of personal satisfaction to balance the collective frustration. But the greatest eulogies should be reserved for Bremner, a captain with a heart as big as a church and the talents to go with it, and Hay, his ally in midfield and the biggest of men in a crisis.

The nervous strain on the Scots today was hardly reduced by the intensive security measures taken by the German police after a letter claiming to come from the IRA had threatened the assassination of two Protestant players. Yet even the presence of scores of police wherever they went, and the noisy company of low-flying helicopters, could not unsettle them. This team did far more for Scotland than any of their predecessors in the World Cup and, with a little luck, they might have been too much for any other side in the competition.

The Scots withstood the remorseless sun, the early violence of the Slavs and their subsequent passage of smooth and probing aggression to finish the first half looking the stronger and less worried side. Bremner, who was on the ball as much as any other two players combined, maintained a sense of composure in front of the Scottish back line and broke forward into damaging spaces whenever they showed. He did lose his calm abruptly late in the half when Acimovic stamped viciously over the ball on to his left leg. As the disturbingly lenient Mexican referee, Señor Archindia, gestured restrained annoyance with Acimovic, Bremner struggled to his feet and hobbled towards the Yugoslav in a red fury. Luckily, he was intercepted long enough for his anger to subside below the explosive level.

The earlier fouls by the Yugoslavs were not as malevolent as that one, which appeared to have come from some grim list of secondary means of stopping Bremner, but they were sufficiently harsh and certainly sufficiently frequent to warrant a much greater reaction from the referee than they evoked. Time after time – on no fewer than seven occasions in the first six minutes – one Scot or another went tumbling under the impact of illegal treatment from an opponent, and the aggravation was not lessened by the irony that the victims were wearing an all-white strip that might have been England's, while their abusers were in a blue only a shade lighter than Scotland's own traditional colours.

The pattern of those first disreputable minutes was set when Hadziabdic hurt Lorimer and Oblak blatantly fouled Bremner. Scotland's captain, who was already spreading the inspiring authority that so healthily infected his team against Brazil on Tuesday, was cut down again almost immediately, and those who celebrate the Slavs as one of the last romantic influences in European football must have questioned their values at least for a moment or two. Without their ugly methods, Mr Miljanic's widely acclaimed players would have been severely strained to hold out against the spirited advances of the Scots, who were ambitiously making full use of the fluid running of Jardine and McGrain along the flanks. Having climaxed that particular series of crimes with a double assault on Morgan, the Slavs at last sought to play attractively and with legitimate purpose. Surjak worked skilfully with Djazic on the left, and when the winger crossed long beyond the far post Petkovic met the ball with a hammering volley and Harvey, for all his coolness and subsequent assurance, must have been happy to see it soar wide. Djazic, vividly representing the leisurely, self-indulgent attitude that seems to ooze into his countrymen's play from the southern streak in their natures, was not yet the constant threat his publicity had suggested he would be. But he did emerge again briefly now from Jardine's smothering attentions to take Petkovic's cross, steady, and chip over the crossbar. There was a foot or two to spare, but the Scottish supporters in the colourful crowd that roasted on the terracings sighed in unison.

They did not have the breath to sigh shortly afterwards when Buljan came loping through from right back to make a marvellous reverse pass to Petkovic on his outside. A centre, hard and low, reached a lunging Bajevic at the near post, but the forward was effectively shut out by Holton. Scotland recovered from their period of inferiority and Jardine's shot from 25 yards eluded Katalinski and caused Maric to fumble. Jordan rushed in from the goalkeeper's rear with a clear chance to steal a goal, but for once he seemed excessively gentle, and the groping hands survived the challenge of his feet.

Then Oblak's name was being taken for refusing to stand back from a free kick, but that offence compared feebly with the foul Acimovic was allowed to perpetrate on Bremner without similar punishment. Jardine was still moving forward with an ease that alarmed the Yugoslavs, and one cross from the byeline would have won reward if the ball had not fallen awkwardly to Dalglish. His improvised shot was beaten away almost as soon as he struck it.

It took a memorable tackle by Buljan on Lorimer to rebuff another Scottish attack before the interval, and Katalinski was once more obliged to employ his technique of deliberately barging Jordan in the air. If one country deserved to be in the lead as they went to the dressing-room, it was not Yugoslavia.

Djazic was apparently determined to alter that first-half emphasis swiftly, and when he beat both Jardine and Morgan down the left as soon as play had restarted, Buchan had to demonstrate his remarkable defensive alertness to close Oblak's way to goal. Even now Yugoslavia were not above some rough-housing, and Katalinski received a caution for hacking down Jordan. The roles were reversed when Jordan was booked after kicking Katalinski as the centre-back dived low to make a headed clearance to the Jardine shot that ended a six-man Scottish attack.

Yugoslavia were wearying, and their defensive marking was not as thorough as it had been, so that Jordan had more space in front of Katalinski and Bremner and Hay were able to come upfield more regularly. But some of the Scots, too, were tiring, and no one was surprised when Dalglish was replaced by Hutchison with 25 minutes to go. The young Celtic player had performed to much greater effect than in either of the previous World Cup matches, but his contribution was diminishing, and Hutchison promised an extra dimension in attack as he at once began a search-and-destroy operation against the right flank of Yugoslavia's defence. The match almost took a decisive swing when Jordan crossed to the far post and Lorimer promptly lobbed the ball over Maric. Hadziabdic managed an anxious clearance near a post. Holton appeared to have hurt a hand at that point and needed treatment, but nothing short of a broken limb could have kept that huge spirit off the field for more than a moment or two, and soon he was back dominating Scotland's central defensive area with a seemingly inviolable aplomb.

As the minutes dripped away, as sickeningly as blood for the Scots, there were dangerous breaks and nervous moments around both goals, but when something decisive came it was at the wrong end for everyone British in the stadium. There were only eight of those minutes to go when the ball was played out to Djazic on Yugoslavia's right wing, and his extreme coolness in the face of opportunity compensated for all his earlier lack of energy. His cross was unhurried and calculated, and it carried beyond Harvey to the head of Karasi. This forward had only just substituted for Bajevic, and now he gave himself the memory of a lifetime as he threw himself against the flight of the ball and steered it back past Harvey's left shoulder into the side-netting.

With so little time left, Ormond decided to put Johnstone on as a substitute, but could not find a gap in the action long enough to let him catch the referee's eye, and the idea had to be dropped. It is doubtful if even the extraordinary dribbling of the wee man could have improved upon the final magnificent surge that Scotland offered. The official time of 90 minutes was already up when they gained the goal they had deserved for so long. Hutchison darted clear again on the left, and his cross was edged on by Lorimer to Jordan, who spun on the ball and, with his left foot, swept it efficiently inside Maric's left-hand post.

Even tragedy seemed almost a justifiable word when the sound of the final whistle was followed in an instant by the electronic scoreboard's declaration that Brazil had beaten Zaire 3–0 and would qualify by the minimum margin.

The shadow of history across Holland

(*The Observer*, Munich, 6 July 1974)

A CHILL BREEZE, laden with echoes, blows across the years, and as we wait for a World Cup final that should be a coronation, we shudder at the thought that the inspired footballers of Holland, like those of Hungary in 1954, may be ambushed in the last strides by anticlimax.

The fear is more superstitious than rational, bred on a welling desire that the best team Europe has produced in two decades should be left where they deserve to be tomorrow evening, alone on the victors' podium. No such dread infects the Dutch players. In them, as they take the field at the Olympic Stadium, the normal flutter of nerves is likely to be tranquillised by a deep conviction that they have the talent, the courage and the collective maturity to lay emphatic hold on the championship. All who have seen them play, who have thrilled to an attacking style at once so spirited and so cuttingly precise that the effect is of a cavalry charge of surgeons, must share that belief. Yet, for some of us, those echoes of events that took place so many seasons ago tend to form ice cubes in the blood.

In 1954 the Hungarians stood where the Dutch stand today, probably even higher in their unrivalled mastery of all that is creative and exhilarating in the game. But they were denied the ultimate reward, and comparing their path then with Holland's path now, it is hard to dismiss the possibility that history is bent on callous repetition. To reach that fifth World Cup final, Boszik and his apparently irresistible little army had to survive a war with a Brazilian team driven to violence by their frustrating inability to succeed with the defensive methods wrong-headedly imposed on them. To make this tenth final, Johan Cruyff and his men had to come through a similar, though appreciably less severe, ordeal against Brazilian opponents reduced to desperation by their failure to harness their instincts to the disciplined negativism of Mario Zagalo.

West Germany were waiting for Hungary and, in an epic final, genius fell to the condition and the will of a team whose crescendo was a miracle of timing. The Germans wait again, and the shadow they cast is broadened and darkened by the fact that they are on their own soil and have the fierce commitment of their people pressing at their backs like a forest fire. Whether we like it or not, such confrontations are inclined to reveal atavistic prejudices that go as deep as the marrow, and many who travelled here as neutrals become tense as they talk of their hunger to see Holland win.

Even without such natural but dubious attitudes, however, it would be hard for those of us who have enjoyed personal contact with the Dutchmen, who have known the private grace and warmth behind the public brilliance, to avoid identifying with their cause. They have an appeal that goes far beyond the capacity of Cruyff, the team coach, Rinus Michels, and one or two others to be engagingly articulate in several languages. Agreeable hours spent in their lakeside hotel at Hiltrup, north of Dortmund, on the day before and the day after their jarring collision with Brazil, confirmed the earlier impression that the leading personalities in the team have an intelligent alertness to the world outside the game they play so superlatively well.

'In culture, they are 100 years ahead of our players,' said a journalist from Rio, as he moved from the knot of rapt listeners around Cruyff to that around Michels, to that around Suurbier. 'Most of ours are barely literate. Of course, a man does not need education to be a great player. Garrincha and many others have proved that. But surely in modern football it is an advantage to be able to communicate, to be able to discuss and understand tactics, and to react intelligently to all the commercial and other pressures. Michels can treat players like adults and demand responsible behaviour. Ours are treated like children and locked up in their camp for four months before the World Cup. Perhaps one of the things Holland are showing is that this is now a competition for adults.'

Disappointed by his own team's performance, captivated by the Dutch, that Brazilian was being self-consciously hard on his countrymen. Mention of Garrincha, who could never have passed exams, but found passing defenders no problem, indicates an awareness of his own oversimplification. But his argument about the value of mental sophistication seems to have much validity when applied specifically to Holland and what they have achieved with a squad that assembled raggedly and in an atmosphere of squabbling dissatisfaction only a few weeks ago. 'It helps us that we have players with education,' says Cruyff. 'They understand better their responsibilities. They are more mature. It is possible that this helps us to win the championship.'

Credit for the miraculously swift realisation of that dream – for the phenomenon of having seven Ajax or former Ajax players and three from Feyenoord in one team and seeing them truly represent the sum of their genius – he attributes in large measure to Michels, his coach at Barcelona as well as here. 'Everyone in Holland wanted to say how the team should play, but he refused to have anything from outside interfering with the team. Suddenly there was one boss. He made the discipline and the tactics. There had been so many problems with everyone, but under him the team came together mentally. The players knew they had to give something, and they gave it. We knew we had the gifts to be a great team, and this maybe was the only chance to show how great we could be. For after the World Cup things will change: there will be a new manager, and perhaps all the players will not be available. So we came together.'

Cruyff's own influence as a central magnet for that process has been considerable. It could scarcely have been otherwise. He has more than his status as the finest of contemporary footballers to make him an immensely attractive figure. His physique, like his play, is made up of sharp edges rather than curves. The face is small, thin and fresher than his 27 years should have left it, with only the lightest stubble fighting through on an unaggressive chin. Even scuffing in loose slippers through the public rooms of the Wald Hotel at Hiltrup, exchanging pleasantries with the Dutch reporters who have chronicled his rise since his days as a schoolboy prodigy in Amsterdam, he moves on those extraordinary long legs with a contained, unaffected grace.

On the field he is as straight and incisive as a knife. His physical skills (electrifying pace and control, flawlessly crisp striking of the ball) and his absolute awareness of where the areas of danger and opportunity lie at any moment, enable him to organise and build superbly in deep positions and to materialise in front of goal with interventions that are as final as death.

That he is equally happy to arm team-mates or to do the killing himself was perfectly demonstrated by his side's two goals on Wednesday. All Brazil's venom could not save them against the skills implicit in those blows. There were one or two occasions in the first half when Holland were lucky to find offside decisions in their favour, when their opponents' tactic of chipping the wet ball briskly over the snowstorm of white shirts that came exploding out of the Dutch area deserved to yield reward for the breaking forwards. But from the interval onwards there was only one conceivable result, and by the end few Brazilian reputations had been salvaged from the wreckage of their World Cup challenge. Of those that were, the most solidly established is Luis Pereira's, and it was de-pressingly ironic that this splendidly equipped defender, perhaps the best in the competition apart from Beckenbauer, should blemish his contribution by being ordered off. His foul on Neeskens was undoub-tedly wild, but the punishment might have been less drastic had there not been such a general accumulation of violence.

If this championship has made Pereira internationally, it may well have shattered the career of the black Paulo Cezar, who came to Germany as a star and goes home branded a failure and a coward by his own people. His is a sadness much greater than that of Zagalo, who sought to fight from a trench and cannot complain now that its walls have collapsed on him.

While Brazil headed gloomily for the third-place final, the Dutch were politely shrugging their way through requests for a definition of their playing method. Arie Haan, whose own flexibility has enabled him to switch from midfield so that he can do a sweeper's job, mainly in front of the back line, was more explicit than most. 'People talk of "total football" as if it is a system, something to replace 4-2-4 or 4-3-3. It is *not* a system. As it is at any moment, so you play. That is how we understand. Not one or two players make a situation, but five or six. The best is that with every situation all 11 players are involved, but this is difficult. In many teams maybe only two or three play, and the rest are looking. In the Holland team when you are 60 metres from the ball you are playing.'

The swirl of movement this involvement produces often makes it difficult to discern a pattern, largely because their patterns are usually organic and spontaneous, rather than preconceived. They can be extremely hard and when they lose the ball they harry and pressurise to get it back. Perfumo, the vastly experienced Argentine defender, whose already miserable World Cup was made worse by the Dutch, recalls an example. 'I received the ball from a short free kick, and I looked up and there were seven Holland players running at me. It was unnerving.'

Rinus Michels smiles at the image. 'There are some of our players who never lose their view of the field. They always know where they should be and they guide the others. I did not believe six weeks ago that we could play so well with so little preparation. Normally it is impossible in such a short time that you form a team that express themselves as a great unit. The most important reason is the responsibility that has taken the players. Now we are calculating everything to make certain they can express themselves again in the final.'

Their determination to do so is hugely intensified by the identity of their opponents. Any softening of their attitude towards the Germans was abruptly arrested by stories in *Bild Zeitung* alleging that the players, despite a longish visit from their wives last week to remove the strains of celibacy, had held a wild party with local girls on Sunday night, and suggesting, too, that an assistant coach had been sent home after drunkenly hurling bottles at a bar wall (the official version is that club obligations made it necessary for him to leave Hiltrup and rejoin the party in Munich).

Michels, an embittered expression on his sea-captain's face, steadfastly refused to speak German at his press conferences and players such as Cruyff and Suurbier mutter about a campaign to undermine morale by worrying their families. Tonight the talk in Munich is of whether Bonhof or Vogts will be asked to subdue Cruyff, of whether Michels will compensate for the possible absence through injury of Rensenbrink by fielding the ageing Keizer or the inexperienced René van der Kerkhof, of whether Beckenbauer or Overath or Muller, Neeskens or van Hanagem or Rep will emerge as a decisive figure tomorrow.

But in the end such technical and tactical considerations may be secondary. Holland's flood of talent and feeling may sweep them through the hostile gauntlet of the Olympic Stadium to the crown that is theirs of right.

The Dutch were beaten 2–1 by the Germans in the final. West Germany, with Beckenbauer at the back and Muller at the front, were outstanding. But the Holland led by Cruyff were undoubtedly the most inspired and inspiring footballers of the 1970s. When their defeat in Munich was followed four years later by disappointment against another host nation in Buenos Aires, they had the right to feel that a serious injustice had been done.

The pride of our Ally

(*The Observer*, 28 May 1978)

IF, AS EVERY Englishman suspects, the Scots ingest a weakness for hyperbole with their mother's milk, Ally MacLeod would seem to have been breast-fed until he was 15. The race's traditional love of vaunting ('See you, know whit Ah'm gonnae dae wi'ye . . .') finds a rough-hewn apotheosis in the former left-winger who has managed the Scotland team through the qualifying series of the 1978 World Cup and is now come to Cordoba to lead them into the final.

During the past six months, MacLeod's pronouncements on his assignment have shown all the objective restraint of the Highland Light Infantry going over the top. He is the rich man's version (very much the rich man's version if we add up his World Cup pickings) of the bedraggled patriot who, having reeled off a team of all-time Scottish greats that had Alexander Fleming as stopper centre-back, Robert Burns as midfield creator and David Livingstone as probing centre-forward, declared to a crowded Wembley tube train: 'We are the greatest wee nation ever Goad put braith in.'

It is a widely held view, but not all of us from north of the Solway are so convinced of our superiority, in football or anything else, that we would insist on being under-strength when we take on the rest of the world. Presumably, Ally MacLeod's confidence does not stretch to that approach either, but it's hard to be sure after looking at his squad of 22 for South America. In the minds of many of us the omission of Andy Gray from that group is a calamitous error and marks the point at which the manager's admirable independence of mind spills over into self-destructive stubbornness. And the same pattern may be discerned in his determination to adhere to the midfield that served him well in his earlier matches, in spite of the evidence that Rioch and Masson (though they played well enough against England at Hampden) should be making way for a middle line drawn from Hartford, Souness, Gemmill and Macari.

MacLeod gives the impression of relishing the controversy his selection has generated. Perhaps his childhood experiences have persuaded him that he has a happy capacity for weathering hostility. He was born on the south side of Glasgow, a part of the world that tends to stimulate the survival juices, and when the family moved to the Clydebank area because of his father's work with the Singer sewing machine company they were welcomed by a German bomb that destroyed their home. The MacLeods then went to Moffat in rural Dumfriesshire but when another bomb landed on a neighbouring farm the mother decided that Glasgow might be safer after all and returned the clan to the Mount Florida district of the town. Their home there was between Hampden Park and the Cathkin ground of Third Lanark, a club that contributed a good deal to the mythology of Scottish football before it went out of business. It was natural enough that his talent for the game should take him to Thirds. The great Bobby Mitchell was the resident outside-left at the time but he was transferred to Newcastle six weeks after MacLeod arrived and the precocious new boy found himself in the first team at the age of 16. The difference between then and now in professional football is suggested by the fact that in those days he played for Queens Park School on Saturday mornings and for Third Lanark in the afternoons. Having had seven years at Cathkin, he went briefly to St Mirren and then on to Blackburn, where he played in an excellent side that included such as Vernon, Douglas and Dougan.

MacLeod's playing career ended with three years as captain of Hibernian and he went on into management with Ayr United. His 10 years there were characterised by valiant efforts to lift the club above the reality of its resources. Then there were the 18 months at Aberdeen that proved he could operate at a higher level. He did much more than put together a good team, he stirred the whole town and created an atmosphere of pride and confidence around Pittodrie.

It was inevitable that he would bring the same declaratory aggression to the job of managing Scotland. Some of his fellow countrymen are inclined to cringe when Ally, his face glowing with conviction under the straight fair hair, appears on the television screens of the nation to tell us that we are in danger of becoming the new superpower of world football. Even he has the odd moment when he begins to suspect that he may have been overstating the case.

'When I took the job I started talking about how it would be *when* we won the World Cup. Now I say "if we win the Cup". But the punters won't have that. "What do you mean if," they shout at me. "To hell with that if nonsense." They are really carried away but what's wrong with a bit of euphoria. Whatever happens, the country has had a terrific six months. I'll bet there are thousands of wee businesses that are flourishing because we are going to Argentina. And there is a serious advantage in putting myself out front to shout the odds a bit. It takes the pressure off the players. If things go wrong everybody's going to blame me. I have been the big mouth and I will take the rap. That's the way I want it to be. I think that's what I am paid for.'

Of course, he is also paid to pick the best men to wear the colours and even those of us who might be attracted by MacLeod's openness and appetite for life find difficulty in endorsing all his views about the squad. We are those who believe that the first essential in approaching a World Cup is to reach for whatever really special players you have available, the men that no other country in the finals is likely to duplicate. Scotland lost the most striking embodiment of that quality when McGrain, the best full-back in the world, was removed from the lists by injury. Now McQueen – another who qualifies as an outstanding asset, if some way behind McGrain – is hurt and may have to suppurate with frustration in Argentina.

The loss of McGrain and the possible loss of McQueen make it even more vital that any other special men who are to hand should be sent into the line. Dalglish is such a footballer, one of the shrewdest and most insistent predators in the opposition's penalty area, and he will be a key figure in South America. His chances of being a decisive influence must be lamentably diminished by the absence of Andy Gray. MacLeod watched Gray five times recently and says with some regret that the forward never once showed evidence of the killing touch that has convinced so many of us that he is one of the deadliest and most exciting front players in the game.

Gray has had an excessive strain imposed on his physique over the past year or two by Aston Villa and his fitness has often been questionable of late, but despite that handicap he has managed to score 20-odd goals this season, a total that represents on average about three years' work for Joe Jordan, the manager's first choice centre forward. Yet Gray, unbelievably, was not even second choice. Ally MacLeod says he has opted for Joe Harper because the little Aberdeen man offers specific cover for Dalglish. 'You can play short to Harper as you do to Dalglish. He comes off his marker in much the same way and works the same space on the park, complementing Joe Jordan who breaks to the left.'

What is left unsaid is that when Jordan breaks he frequently does so with cumbersome predictability that anaesthetises the electric spontaneity given to the Scottish attack by Dalglish, Hartford and Johnston, thus by breaking left he clutters the space so thrillingly exploited by Hartford and the surging Johnston when they shredded the right side of England's defence in the first half at Hampden. Supporters of Jordan extol his heading ability, but most of his headers simply direct the ball in a hopeful upward arc, requiring the creative intervention of another forward to bring profit. That both he and Harper should have been preferred to Andy Gray is masochistic eccentricity.

There will be plenty of other issues to be talked into the sawdust over the late-night bevvies between now and the big kick-off in Cordoba. But no one has a hope of persuading Ally MacLeod that he should alter his opinions. 'The squad probably pleases only one man and that's me,' he says doggedly.

There is no doubt that he will go on blowing the trumpet. Good luck to him. Maybe he is right to be unaffected by the thought that in the past Scottish Joshuas have had the knack of bringing the walls down on their own heads.

Scotland: The party is over, 3–1

(*The Observer*, 4 June 1978)

BARRING THE kind of miracle that no one here is prepared to believe in, the party is surely over and the Scots are left with little but dirty glasses and the stale smell of spent euphoria.

This embarrassing and unquestionably just defeat by Peru left them without a sliver of an excuse. They had every break that any contenders for the World Cup could desire, including the reassurance of a stylish early goal and an opportunity to retake the lead in the second half through a penalty which, though legally correct, had a substantial element of luck.

But none of this was enough against the superior fluency, ambitious directness and powerful shooting of Peru. While the South Americans could applaud superb performances from Cubillas, who has been stirring them with the brilliance of his control and his finishing authority for more than a decade, and the remarkable contributions of such as Cueto, Munante, Oblitas, Velasquez and Diaz, the Scots were mainly concerned with a list of failures.

Their full-backs were thoroughly tortured throughout the hour and a half. Buchan, at least, had the defence of having been played out of position but Kennedy's international career must suffer from a night when his greatest asset, his speed, was utterly invalidated. There were other sadnesses, like the unproductive quietness of Dalglish, the scuffling ineffectiveness of Jordan (apart from his simple goal), the late labourings of Masson and Rioch and the frequent untidiness even in the middle of the defence. Hartford took most of what little credit there was but he will consider such a tribute poor consolation on such a depressing night for his team.

The graceful blow that Scotland struck after a quarter of an hour might have stunned Peru into an acceptance of inferiority. Instead it seemed to encourage the Scots to assume a languid smugness and before they realised the dangers of that attitude the match was being thrillingly transformed. Peru, set flowing through the middle by the intricate skills of Cueto and the lively veteran Cubillas, and given surging threat along the flanks by Munante and Oblitas, soon began to regard the ball as private property and the Scottish defenders were constantly and painfully late with their cover and too often reduced to a shouting turmoil of uncertainty. The Peruvian equaliser that came one minute short of the interval was not only overdue but an ominous indication that there would be more anguish for the noisy enclaves of tartanry scattered around the Cordoba stadium.

Yet at the start the South Americans, with their tiny, apparently edgy goalkeeper, and several outfield players who would never be contenders for places in a basketball team, had looked vulnerable in the extreme. The Scots, who had their own share of nervousness, were admittedly slow to thrust at the opposition's throat but once neat work by Dalglish's right foot and Jordan's head had sent Masson free at inside-right for a shot that Quiroga held, there were accumulating signs of coherent aggression. Hartford and Dalglish combined to create an opening that was improved upon by Masson but the final shot was innocuous.

Nothing of the kind could be said about the attack Scotland produced in the fifteenth minute. Johnston, out on the left, steered a subtle little pass into Dalglish and he in turn moved the ball sweetly on to Hartford. When Hartford served Rioch the captain's shot was too firm for Quiroga to hold and his pushed save left Jordan to slide the ball comfortably into the net from the far post.

If the behaviour of Velasquez, who was shown the yellow card after two heavy fouls on Jordan, suggested anxiety among the Peruvians, the impression was rapidly dispelled by the excellence of their attacking play. It was no surprise when, after 44 minutes, Peru scored. Velasquez rode a tackle and angled the ball towards Munante who stabbed it on the Cueto. As Forsyth attempted a challenge Cueto swept past him, controlling the ball with his body, and then drove it low into the net.

The second half, like the first, had a deceptively happy beginning for the Scots. Jordan had a header that glanced off the top of a post and Dalglish had a shot on the turn that spun over the bar off a defender's foot before the Scots were awarded what might have been a decisive penalty in the 63rd minute. It was certainly a fortunate one because the ball had already sailed over the byeline before Diaz clattered Rioch down with a wild tackle. Masson's effort at scoring was just about as wild in its own way, a slack, shoulder-high shot with the right foot that Quiroga (having prophetically favoured the right side) slapped away after the minimum movement of his feet. Peru now chose to substitute Sotil for La Rosa but they were about to show us something much more dramatic than any substitution.

With 20 minutes remaining Cubillas took a square pass from the right and, as the Scottish defence sought apprehensively to rearrange themselves in front of him, swung his right foot to pulverising effect. The ball flew from just outside the area into the net wide of Rough's right shoulder. Four minutes later Ally MacLeod opted for the midfield that many had favoured from the start by withdrawing Masson and Rioch and drafting in Macari and Gemmill, but all this was much, much too late.

Just how hopeless Scotland's predicament had become was battered home to the far-travelled patriots who were already shivering from a chill that had nothing to do with the dropping autumn temperatures of Cordoba. Cubillas, the unchallengeable star of the evening, provided its conclusive declaration with another splendid goal.

Shaping to take a free kick on the fringe of the Scottish area near the point from which he had delivered his earlier murderous stroke, he allowed a team-mate to make a dummy run and then swerved the ball bewilderingly with the outside of his right foot, curving it round the left-hand side of the defensive wall and up in a blurred arc inside Rough's near post.

Before the finish Peru substituted Rojas for Cueto but in their dazed state neither the Scottish players nor their supporters were likely to notice.

Scotland followed this defeat with an inept draw against Iran and then, astonishingly, gained a handsome victory over Holland, who were on the way to their second successive World Cup final. Against the Dutch, Scotland were considerably strengthened by the overdue inclusion of Souness in midfield, an injection of substance and quality that had an uplifting effect on all the other players, notably Gemmill, who dribbled several opponents dizzy before scoring an unforgettable goal. But too much damage had been done in the earlier matches and the Scots, as always, found themselves dumped out of the World Cup finals at the end of the first stage.

The articles that follow were, obviously, written before the face-saving defeat of Holland in Mendoza but the conclusions of the 'Kamikaze' piece held up readily enough.

A *case of kamikaze in Cordoba*

(*The Observer*, 11 June 1978)

IF THERE IS EVER a World Cup for self-destructiveness, few nations will have the nerve to challenge the Scots. It seems astonishing that the race has never produced a kamikaze pilot, but perhaps the explanation is that all the volunteers insisted on attacking sewage farms.

If that line is more bitter than funny, the reader should remember that it comes from an unobjective source. What has been happening around Cordoba over the last week or so has been enough to turn Scottish blood to sludge. Reminders that football is just a game that we have encouraged to get too big for its boots bring less than total comfort. Some of us have been acknowledging through most of our lives that the game is hopelessly ill-equipped to carry the burden of emotional expression the Scots seek to load upon it. What is hurting so many now is the realisation that something they believed to be a metaphor for their pride has all along been a metaphor for their desperation.

To the Scots, a cosy, domesticated sense of identity, a national persona in carpet slippers, would never be enough. They want instantly to be making aggressive declarations about themselves to the rest of humanity. For many decades now the nearest thing to a gunboat they could send out into the world has been a football team, and to see the current model holed by Peru and Iran and possibly sunk by Holland today in Mendoza, is more than tenaciously preserved illusions can bear.

When the most glaring causes of this squalid failure have been measured and given their due emphasis – when attempts have been made to calculate the harm done by irrational selection of players and the irresponsibility of some of those chosen, by the negligible preparation and tactical organisation and the millstone of the team manager's naivety – there remains, stubborn as ever, the evidence that the seeds of the small disaster are to be found deep in the natures of the people most devastated by it.

As they approached the World Cup finals, most Scottish supporters gave every indication of being happy to be on the march with Ally's Army, of sharing the outrageous, patently unjustified optimism of Ally MacLeod. He told them they had the players to win the Cup (that third place was the worst they were entitled to expect) and they believed him, in spite of the overwhelming reality that only five countries have won the championship in its 10 stagings during nearly 50 years. They believed him because they wanted to believe him, because he talked like one of them, indeed could contrive, when utterly sober, to sound as the wildest of them might sound after a night on the liquid hyperbole. In the run-up to the tournament he behaved with no more caution, subtlety or concern for planning than a man getting ready to lead a bayonet charge. The fans echoed his war cries, never bothering to wonder if the other contenders for the world title would be willing to stand still and be stabbed.

This past week has seen Ally MacLeod impaled on his own boasts, and obviously he cannot complain too much about that. But the truth is that his principal crime has been to be himself, the same loud and hopeful extrovert he was when he was picked to do a job for which he was never really fitted. A manager at the highest levels of football, and particularly in international competition, can be effective in many different ways, but to succeed he will require some combination of remarkable qualities.

Apart from a keen intelligence that is inclined to manifest itself in cunning, and a reasonable depth of perception about how the game works, the ability to see what makes one player or one team, one formation or one style of play more successful than another, the best managers tend to have a gift for charting psychological tides, for reading entrails while they are still inside the rib cage. In all these areas MacLeod has been found wanting to some degree.

The Scottish training camp at Alta Gracia, near Cordoba, is the rumour capital of the world this month, but there is sufficient reliable testimony available to confirm that a group of footballers who should have been as tightly integrated and specifically prepared as a commando unit have had more in common with the Home Guard on a bad day. 'We look disorganised on the field because we are disorganised,' I was told by a player who is among the most senior and, as it happens, was among the least culpable in the two calamitous matches that have been played. 'For all we achieved in the week we were here before the first match we might as well have stayed at home. I don't think we worked on one free kick in that time.

'I am not one of those who will be turning on the manager. At the end of the day you've got to admit that he is not out there kicking the ball, and if we aren't good enough to beat Iran we are in a bad state. Still, it's a fact that the trip has been a bit of a shambles off the field from the start. We were told we were coming to luxurious accommodation and we find here at the Sierras Hotel that we are cramped two to a bare little room, in a place that is isolated and with hardly anything to occupy our spare time. We have an hour's travel to a training pitch so bad that the cows won't eat the grass on it. Three or four of the lads have gone over on their ankles because it's so rough.

'Then there's the question of the money. It doesn't excite me very much. I'm fairly well paid back home and anything I got here would go in tax. But it was a mess. When we arrived here, Ally told us the squad would share £15,000 if we qualified from the first series of three matches. Most guys were pretty unhappy about that figure and there was some argument. Then it turned out that Ally got it wrong and we were actually on £30,000 to qualify. If a manager can be as far out about something like that, it's a bad sign.

'Of course, it's not as important as Ally's failure to organise us or the fact that he had nothing worthwhile to say at half-time against Peru, when we were already letting them take over a match that should have been won, surrendering the midfield to them and letting them work their quick one-twos on the edge of our box. After such a performance I wasn't surprised to find some Scottish punters battering on the sides of our bus and shouting abuse. Coming 7,000 miles out here wasn't quite like taking a bus along the road to Hampden, and they have a right to tell us what they think of us.

'My own feeling about what has happened here is genuine shame. But there are plenty of players who don't appreciate how much we have let down ourselves and the people back home. They just don't realise the impact of it all in Scotland, or the kind of reception we'll go back to. In any squad of 22 footballers you're bound to get quite a few whose heads are full of mince.'

According to the harshest of their travelling critics, the Scottish players have more serious deficiencies around the heart than around the head, but these accusations of collective cowardice, or at least indifference, are extravagant interpretations of the torpid inadequacy on the field. The problem is better defined as one of impotence, an inability to translate desire into fulfilment. Perhaps, after a prolonged and heavy season of League football, the desire is less compelling than it might be.

Certainly the footballers cannot duplicate the raw, unreasoned passion of their supporters, and no one should imagine that it would be helpful if they could. Lou Macari, the midfield player from Manchester United, though he is far more of a patriot than many a man with an och-aye name, is one who is convinced that efforts to respond directly to the relentless exhortations of Scottish crowds generate in the team a hysteria which – when found to have no relevance against the skilled defending, probing and counter-punching to be faced in a World Cup – can give way all too readily to the kind of hapless languor the Scots have exhibited in Argentina.

The Mexican squad, who have shared the Sierras Hotel with Scotland, would trace that listlessness to the orgiastic activities of rivals they have reported to FIFA for roaming the corridors in the early hours, drinking whisky by the litre and fooling around with girls. One cannot resist pointing out that the Mexicans had better grounds for complaining about the German players who roamed so freely in their penalty area in the course of a 6–0 drubbing.

Although this Scottish party may be no more monkish by inclination than its notorious predecessors, and although there have been deviations from the straight and narrow dating back to the week spent at Dunblane for the home international championships, there is little to suggest that the days and nights at Alta Gracia have been lurid with dissipation. For once it would seem that dope-taking did more damage than drink-swilling in a Scottish camp, and that hurt was political rather than physical.

So Macari's theories on morale are worth consideration. 'If clever people had been in charge, they would have taken the pressure off by telling us we were coming to play against the best players in the world,' he says. 'Instead, we were bombarded with crap about beating the rest of the world into the ground. How could anyone be so optimistic about our chances? When did you last see Scotland play really good football, play with a positive rhythm and a consistent pattern? In the home internationals and the qualifying matches before them it was a fight, a case of charge, a battering-ram job. It was a fight when we beat the Czechs and a fight when we beat the Welsh at Anfield. Meanwhile, the likes of Tunisia and Iran would be slogging away in their little training camps for the last two months with the World Cup as the only target.

'Tunisia and Iran are better prepared than we are. In our last match before coming here the lads exhausted themselves trying to beat England. It couldn't be any other way with 85,000 mad Scotsmen yelling, "Gie us an English heid".' Macari is in the minority of his countrymen who are not now asking for that famous Scottish head, with its sparse fair hair and pinched, painfully drawn face. 'I like Ally a lot as a guy and what has happened here won't change that,' he says.

Sadly, we must assume that it will change everything for Ally MacLeod. This experience could bring recurring cruelty in the years ahead for him and his family: side-of-the-mouth nastiness in a restaurant, frontal hostility in the street, and – most heartless of all – taunts in the playground. Before long all the celebrity and all the money made from his promotional activities, and from his wife's commercial for the Co-op and a newspaper, may strike him as very hard-earned.

The irony is that for the Scots as a people the episode may have its benefits. Maybe at last they will see that they have been asking too much of football. If you try to go to Heaven in a handcart, you are liable to find the wheel coming off.

Call-up for Ally's chocolate soldier

(*The Observer*, 11 June 1978)

IF THE CAVALRY are to arrive in the last reel and save Scotland in Mendoza today they will have to come charging up from the midfield. Ally MacLeod, the most grimly beleaguered manager even the Scots have known, yesterday named a team that will play a basic 4-4-2 formation against the Dutch, who are themselves noted for seeking to smother the opposition with superiority of numbers as well as talent in the middle of the park.

The key to MacLeod's tenuous hopes of survival into the second phase of the World Cup is clearly Graeme Souness, of Liverpool, who will be making his first appearance of the tournament. In the bitter raking over the ashes of that inept draw with Iran on Wednesday the one unambiguous regret that the manager admitted about his team selection was his failure to make use of Souness. 'Throughout my career I have always gone for a player of his type in front of the back four,' he said. 'But I went against that principle in the belief that the three little men, Macari, Hartford and Gemmill, would be effective busybodies and enable us to camp in Iran's half of the field. It didn't work and I know now that Souness would have been a better answer.'

There will be no argument from the Liverpool man himself, for he is not afflicted with any crushing sense of inferiority. 'If he was made of chocolate he would eat himself,' said one team-mate last week.

As far as his game is concerned, Souness is entitled to self-confidence. Since going to Anfield he has sharpened the skills that were always there, and now with his bitingly competitive tackling, sure control and imaginative distribution, he is distinguished enough to command a place in sides much less discredited than Scotland's.

Souness will be joined by Hartford, Gemmill and Rioch in the effort to subdue a powerful Netherlands midfield that will have the forceful brilliance of Neeskens and the finer creativity of Willy van der Kerkhof reinforced by Poortvliet and either Jansen or Haan. If we were not familiar with MacLeod's enthusiastic loyalty to him, the choice of Rioch might occasion surprise because the Derby County player has not had a conspicuously happy time here, either as an individual performer or as captain of the party.

In contrast, Jardine can think of himself as unfortunate to have been dropped after achieving the outrageous distinction of looking competent against Iran. But presumably young Kennedy has been recalled to right-back to ensure adventurous pace along the flank and carry regular support to the front men, Dalglish and Jordan. Their form in Córdoba suggests they will need all the support available. Some of us could not be disappointed in Jordan, having recognised him long ago as the eternal blunt instrument, but the catatonic displays of Dalglish have been a misery for his admirers.

Macari, Burns and Robertson are the other casualties of the side that trundled to disgrace last Wednesday. All three will be on the bench today along with Johnstone, who would appear to be the most wronged man of the expedition. The big Rangers forward, who has scored 41 goals this season, has the ability and the form to justify inclusion in a team that have an aversion to scoring, and if MacLeod has other reasons for leaving him out some public indication might have been given. By the kick-off today Scotland will have employed 18 members of their squad of 22, so anyone who is omitted must feel as if he has the plague.

Against Holland, the Scots' prospects of maintaining security at the back, while thrusting clusters of players forward in search of the three-goal margin of victory they need to save themselves, must be improved by the presence of Buchan. He has a heavily scratched right eyelid and a wound on his forehead that needed two stitches, but is able to joke now about the swinging kick from Willie Donachie that did the damage in the Iran match. 'Willie is my best mate, so I suppose it sums up how things are going for us when he nearly kicks my head off,' says Buchan.

Holland would seem likely to inflict a more general injury. With Jongbloed in goal, Suurbier, Krol and Rijsbergen at the rear, Rep, Rene van der Kerkhof and the deadly Rensenbrink in attack, and the midfield already identified, they will field eight of the team unluckily defeated by West Germany in the World Cup final of 1974. Scotland have every right to pessimism.

Even their gloom will be merely a little cloud in the South American sky, however, if Brazil fail to qualify from Group Three. And they cannot be certain of doing so unless they manage in Mar del Plata today to beat Austria, whose two victories have already guaranteed them a place in the last eight. Shabby draws with Sweden and Spain brought the inevitable clamour for the removal of Brazil's manager, Claudio Coutinho, but the senior members of the CBD delegation in charge of the party settled for reducing him to the level of a committee member when team selection decisions are being made. There is now considerable doubt about whether his opinions will carry more weight than those of Admiral Heleno Nunes, the president of the Brazilian sports authority, and the three senior officers who accompany Nunes. It is quite certain that Coutinho will lose not only his vote but his job unless a respectable performance and the right result can be produced against Austria. 'Admiral Nunes has told Coutinho that he can play any tune so long as it is a waltz,' one Brazilian official told me. 'The admiral has offered his humble opinion of what should be done, which means he has given an order.'

The order included insistence on several team changes, the first of which drafted in Roberto, the Admiral's favourite centre-forward from his own club, Vasco da Gama, in place of Reinaldo, whose weakening series of cartilage operations seems to have left him unable to score goals at this level.

Battle of the River Plate

(*The Observer*, 25 June 1978)

AS THEY APPROACH what must surely be the most emotional World Cup final in history, the brilliant footballers of Holland are in less danger of being beaten by superior talent than of being drowned in a Niagara of adrenalin. In the River Plate Stadium today they will be opposed not only by the skills and spirit of another team but by the concentrated pride and desire of an entire people.

With every nervous touch of the ball in the first 15 or 20 minutes an inhuman volume of sound will roll down from the high rim of that beautiful arena to remind Rudi Krol and his men that they are, in a frighteningly basic sense, taking on Argentina. That noise, and the passionate identification it expresses, will stimulate the Argentine players, expanding lungs and quickening legs and clearing minds of everything but the thought of winning. The decisive question is whether it will break the Dutch.

Against it, the morale of most national sides would offer as much protection as a plastic raincoat in a typhoon. But the Dutch are not like most national sides. They are the best and they admit, without bombast, that they know it. Whatever happens today in Buenos Aires their performance here has reinforced their status as the outstanding football nation of the '70s.

Now, as in West Germany in 1974, they have travelled all the way to a World Cup final on foreign soil and find themselves faced at the end with the need to overcome a host country who were realistic favourites from the start. And this they have done after leaving behind in the Netherlands enough players of the highest quality to provide the foundations of a second championship squad.

Van Beveren, rated the finest goalkeeper they have ever had, declined to play in the competition just as he did four years ago and refusals came, too, for a wide variety of reasons, from outstanding figures like Geels, van der Kuyler and Dusbaba. Hovenkamp was removed by injury. Van Hanegem asked to be guaranteed a key role, Ernst Happel as manager would not make such a promise, and that great left foot and combative presence were lost, widening the gap created by the earlier decision of Johan Cruyff that his allies of 1974 would have to win their battles in South America without benefit of his inspirational genius. So apparently raw young men, men who were still first or second season novices in the senior professional game, Wildschut at 20, Brandts and Poortvliet at 22, were brought abruptly under the orange banner, hurriedly integrated into a party that had 10 survivors from the challenge in West Germany. All three of those recruits played with distinction on the way to the final.

In the Holland camp at Moreno, an hour and a half by road from Buenos Aires, there is a tangible satisfaction at the way they have overcome the absence of some great stars and, after a miserable stumble through the initial round on a Mendoza pitch that they hated, have rapidly gathered the convincing momentum that took them out of trouble and on to successful results against the Germans and the Italians. Mixing with them on Friday, as they spread eddies of relaxed, intelligent comment on their prospects around the dining hall of their headquarters, it was easy to feel again the warmth for their cause that we experienced before the Munich final. There was something poignant about their predicament then because a few of us sensed that history would regurgitate an injustice and the Germans would defeat a better team, as they had beaten Hungary 20 years before.

The vague resentment that we harboured when Holland did lose in the Olympic Stadium will not be repeated if they are beaten today. No one with half a heart could begrudge the Argentine people the celebration that will flood the streets with undiluted and undestructive joy if their team take the World Cup. They are by nature a generous, appealing race and if too many of them seem to have allowed the political areas of their minds to be anaesthetised, if a majority are content to let the ephemeral dramas of football obscure the deadlier games played out at the centre of this military dictatorship, who among the outsiders has a right to offer rebuke?

The Montoneros guerrillas themselves acknowledged before the start of the tournament that their countrymen, having been denied so much, should be left alone for a month at least to wallow in their consuming love of football. To witness the enthusiasm that has swept Argentina, the joyous, boozeless clamour that has engulfed every town and city after even negative results, and the spectacle of literally millions of all ages and all classes chanting and dancing through the streets of Buenos Aires when the slaughter of Peru made a place in the final certain, has been to appreciate that the Montoneros were merely bowing to reality. The masses would brook no political interfering with their enjoyment of the Cup.

To wish for a more legitimate interference from the Dutch, when a home victory means so much to so many, when one crucial save by Fillol or a couple of explosive shots by Luque and Kempes might detonate the happiest party South America has ever known, may suggest an unnatural churlishness. Yet Holland have a special claim on our feelings. There is

the impression that they and their travelling support could be accommodated in a single Jumbo. They are like a tiny commando trapped far
behind the enemy lines, but determined to fight their way out with the
booty. As always, they will seek to do so by marrying subtlety to verve,
sophistication to courage. Refinement and versatility of technique, a
profound collective understanding of how skill, perception and speed
should be used to bring flexibility and fluent effectiveness to the team –
these are their essential assets, but they have the stomach to trade in a
rougher currency if the need arises. They are the best representatives
Europe, and perhaps football, could have at this time and I find it
impossible to avoid siding with them.

Personal contact does not diminish that admiration. In a hotel bar in
Buenos Aires on Thursday night Rene van der Kerkhof – using the
English that is commonplace in the team – was engaging and interesting
enough even to draw the attention away from a barman wearing a locally
conceived kilt that reached to the middle of his shinbone. Van der
Kerkhof was with his wife and his twin brother Willy, enjoying a full day
of liberty from the training camp in keeping with the Dutch tradition of
treating their footballers like responsible adults. Other players were
scattered around the city, some with wives or girlfriends, shopping,
having leisurely meals, letting the blood cool after the previous day's
tense entry into the final at the expense of Italy.

What Rene had to say about that match emphasised the fascinating
distribution of roles between Holland's Austrian manager, Ernst Happel,
and Jan Zwartkruis, the Dutch Air Force officer who is his assistant and
will succeed him after today. 'Happel does not spend much time working
directly with the players,' said Rene. 'He picks our teams, decides on the
tactics and passes on the detailed instructions before matches to each of
us. He is a great man in football, a strong personality and wise in the
game, a man on the same level as the 1974 manager, Rinus Michels, but it
is his way to leave most of the day-to-day work with us to Zwartkruis.

'So it was Zwartkruis who was waiting for us when we went in at half-
time against Italy, one goal down and knowing it should have been
worse. We had been too conscious that a draw was enough, so we played
with too little aggression. We were terrible. Zwartkruis said: "This is not
Holland I have seen. You have not played like Dutchmen." He made us
understand that we had 45 minutes to take a place in the final. We
changed the team – Neeskens stopped marking Rossi and went to
midfield and my brother marked Rossi – and we changed our attitude and
took control.

'People say that we do not have the passion to win a World Cup, that it
does not mean enough to us. But to me it means everything, the absolute
climax of a footballer's career, the peak. Club football gives us good
rewards. I earn more than £1,500 a week with PSV Eindhoven, but this is

above money. This is the end. On Sunday I will give everything. All of us will, and I honestly believe it will be enough.

'I think we are stronger than in 1974 with Cruyff, more collective. Cruyff is a wonderful player but he dominated other players, the team revolved around him. Now he is gone such as Rep and Rensenbrink and Krol come out and show their true worth. The strength of Dutch football is team strength. From the age of eight or nine we are taught the importance of running without the ball. Always we have movement. When I have the ball there are three or four others running, open for the pass. With that, we have the capacity to counter-attack against Argentina. They come at the goal with great speed, with many players pressing forward, but they leave spaces behind and we can use them. Kempes is a marvellous forward, a player of the top class, and Luque is powerful and always dangerous but if we can neutralise those two they have not too much left.

'Of course, there will be great noise at River Plate, much nervous pressure at the start, but we are not afraid. We have faith in ourselves. We have a good 50–50 chance and who can ask more in the World Cup final?'

The following day Happel, a small, greying man with a pouchy, expressive face and the steadiest eyes of any manager here, talked quietly in German and Dutch of how he wished the match to go. Said Willy van der Kerkhof: 'He will want us to lock them up in the middle of the field. South American teams must not have the freedom to flow. If you let them move easily to the edge of your penalty area, as Scotland did with Peru, their quick interpassing can give them scoring shots. We can make them struggle in the midfield where they are less strong and then hit them hard in the counter-attack.' The locking up will be a job for Willy van der Kerkhof himself, Haan, Jansen and Neeskens, who looked formidable in the second half on Wednesday in spite of a chronic knee injury that threatens drastic consequences in later life.

As the final neared, the only threat Neeskens wanted to discuss was that of Argentina. They have ridden thus far on erratic form, their spectacular surges punctuated by periods of sweaty ineptitude, lucky escapes and rescuing saves by the excellent Fillol. Ardiles, Bertoni and Luque have also made a splendid contribution but it is the thrilling Mario Kempes, moving and striking with more grace and authority than any other forward in the competition, who has done most to feed their optimism.

He made a personal swagger of the match with Peru on the night when Argentina scored the six goals that denied the late run of a Brazilian team who had already outplayed the hosts in a goalless draw. The air was thick with talk of corruption and Peru began that match with the indignant fury of honest men whose integrity had been questioned. They might have scored twice before Kempes hit them with a fine, cool goal that had the effect of a rock on a windscreen. The Peruvians' game blurred, then fell apart. Suspicion persisted but in the end the thought of bribing them seemed as superfluous as offering a contraceptive to a eunuch.

Holland should not fall apart, however much passion pours over them. The bleakest possibility is that Argentina, faced with such brilliance and toughness, will find themselves prised away from the uncharacteristic restraint they have shown so far and permit frustration to beget violence.

But dark thoughts should not be uppermost on the morning of the World Cup final. We should be looking for a result that truly measures the qualities of the two teams. Such a result today will leave Argentina with a lump in its throat and a lead weight in its stomach.

A bandage for injustice

(*The Observer*, 2 July 1978)

EVEN HERE ON Copacabana, where the sun shines and there is so
much that bounces more interestingly than any ball, the images of the
World Cup final and the hours immediately after it refuse to go away.
The most persistent memory is of the streets of central Buenos Aires in
the middle of Monday, when the schoolchildren had taken over the
celebration of Argentina's victory, jogging past us in an endless stream of
shining faces, chanting in high, exultant voices or piping rhythmically on
whistles, creating a din to suggest that all the starlings on earth had settled
in one square mile. They would have brought a smile to the face of a man
who had bet a million guilders on the losers.

It had been less easy to smile in the first hours of that Monday, standing
around the bar of the Sheraton Hotel with the Dutch footballers who, for
the second time in four years, had swallowed a bitter reminder that being
the best does not guarantee the big prizes. Their performance in the River
Plate stadium on Sunday afternoon had confirmed something most
people in football already accepted, that for nearly a decade now their
collective talent for the game has been notably greater than that of any
other nation. Yet they had lost and as they drank in restrained,
unmournful groups we wondered along with them whether they will ever
see a glimmer of justice in the supreme competition of their sport.

'Twice we have shown the world that we can play very well and twice
when it is finished we have nothing,' said Johan Neeskens. It was hardly
the moment for pointing out that players of his quality do not need cups
or medals to anchor them in the mainstream of the game's folklore. 'In
this final we had no luck,' he said. 'Here it has been the same as in 1974 in
Germany. When Rensenbrink turned the ball in at the end of regular time
it seemed it must be a goal and that would have been the true result
because we had been on top all through the second half. But the ball came
back off a post. In the extra time again we are pressing, pressing, but in
the first counter-attack Argentina scored. The goal was by Kempes, who
is a very great player, at least 50 per cent of his team, but even he needs
luck before he can score such a goal. The bounces went with him and not
with Jongbloed or our defenders. That is how it is with us in the World
Cup.'

There was more than the simple harshness of rebounds to handicap the

Dutch at River Plate. There was, for a start, the lamentably soggy and uneven pitch, which interfered with the fine margins of Holland's passing far more than it did with the charging style of Argentina. Then there was the referee, Signor Gonella, an unforgettable experience.

We should have known how miserable Gonella's contribution would be, and how damaging to Holland, the moment he showed himself so ready to be swayed by Passarella's protest over the small plaster cast on Rene van der Kerkhof's right hand. The plaster had been there since van der Kerkhof damaged the metacarpal bones of the hand in his country's first match of the competition, against Iran, and he had worn it through five matches without objection. Yet the Argentines having operated the old boxing trick of letting the opposition enter the ring and then delaying their own arrival by almost five minutes, let the national anthems and other formalities pass and waited until the last seconds before the kick-off to complain through their captain, Passarella, that the plaster violated FIFA regulations.

'I asked Passarella what kind of regulations could allow Rene to play five matches with the covering on his hand and then send him out of the field in the minute before the World Cup final,' Neeskens remembered. His rage had long been spent but grimness returned briefly to the handsome, sharply defined face as he thought of the attempt that had been made to unnerve his team. 'Gonella was listening to the nonsense, looking as if he would be influenced by it, so I said to Passarella: "All right, if van der Kerkhof goes we all go. You can play the World Cup final alone."'

'That was it,' said Rene. 'Ruud Krol called for all of us to leave the field and Gonella knew we meant it, so he said: "No, no, wait, he can put a soft cover over the plaster and it will be OK." When I had put some padding and a bandage on my hand and we were walking back to kick off Johan Neeskens turned to me and said, "All right, let's go and get them."'

Holland are always capable of being a jarringly physical team but there is no doubt that their rugged, indeed violent entrance into this final had much to do with the provocative impact of those preliminaries. The ruse was obviously contrived to leave them disconcerted, shaking with nervousness. But they are not boys and its main effect was to kindle a deep anger that was still showing itself when they declined to attend the banquet after the match.

The attitude was much too hard to be mistaken for petulance. The ordinary knocks and disappointments of the game they take philosophically. Neeskens, as he talked, was fingering a nasty little bruise and cut beneath the right side of his mouth. It had, he explained, been done during the match by Passarella's elbow but when I winced sympathetically he shook his head. 'No, it's not important,' he said. 'At the time I was angry because we were far away from the ball. But the anger goes soon. In the World Cup final you must expect these things. It is a game for men.'

The Dutch clearly felt that the gamesmanship that was tried before the kick-off, and the operatic variations employed during the action to manipulate the weak match officials and the powerful crowd, were not conspicuously manly. But Neeskens and the rest were quick to acknowledge that Argentina had substantial legitimate strength. Above all, they had Mario Alberto Kempes, the outstanding figure of this World Cup, a forward of genius who competes intensely but remains sporting enough to be almost benign. When Argentina were at their groggiest Kempes was the horseshoe in their glove. His two goals in the final owed little to the passes that preceded them, almost everything to his own beautiful, swooping infiltrations from midfield, his untroubled control of the ball at speed on the difficult surface, the inexorable directness of his running and the sureness of his finishing.

In the end – as Holland's relentless movement throughout the second half told on them in extra time and their hopes of neutralising that half-hour and girding themselves for a replay began to crumble – Kempes again rampaged gracefully through their tiring ranks to set up a goal for Bertino and give the impression that his team had won going away. If such a modern young man has anything resembling a sideboard, the World Cup should sit on it for the next four years. There were other distinguished players who brightened a competition that was erratic but by no means lacking in excitement or entertainment (Fillol, the Argentines' invaluably excellent goalkeeper, Platini and Tresor of France, Torocsik of Hungary, the boyish, thrillingly ambitious Rossi of Italy, Oscar, Batista and Dircun of Brazil and, of course, a whole clutch of Dutchmen) but none will deny that Kempes was the star of the occasion.

If his contribution was pure joy, there was much else about this World Cup that was disturbing. Most alarming of all was the talk of enlarging an event that is already becoming overblown, both in size and in its assumed importance, to accommodate 20 or 24 finalists and all the additional nationalistic and commercial madness such a change would imply. That thought should be buried at once and so should the system of playing the second round on a league basis. This year's pattern created the lunatic situation in which Peru, bereft of all hope and all but a dribble of morale, were left in their match with Argentina to decide the destiny of Brazil. After the first round, there should be sudden death, with quarter-finals, semi-finals, a third-place match and a final.

That would not guarantee justice. Football, as a microcosm of the big bad world outside, can hardly do that. But at least sudden death would mean that countries were blasted from the Cup rather than killed by the fall-out from someone else's failure.

An unknown upstages Maradona

(*The Observer*, 28 March 1982)

THE SIGHT OF A 21-year-old footballer doing something extra-ordinary on the field has come to be expected in Argentina this season but for nearly 80,000 people in the River Plate Stadium last week there was a strangeness about the experience. They found it hard to accept that the young man whose performance demanded so much admiration was not Diego Maradona from the poor streets of a Buenos Aires suburb but Lothar Matthaus from a small town in Germany.

Maradona is deservedly recognised by just about everyone from here to the Angel, Islington, as the most exciting talent in football. Until a few days ago Matthaus was, as they say, scarcely a household name in his own house. But when their contrasting abilities collided head-on in Argentina's international with West Germany on Wednesday night the genius that has encouraged slightly fevered talk of a £4 million transfer to Arsenal was thoroughly obscured.

Since Matthaus had at the Maracana in Rio last Sunday celebrated his 21st birthday by imposing similar anonymity on Zico, whom many Brazilians discuss in superlatives that seemed to have become obsolete with the departure of Pele, he was completing a win double too outrageous to have a racing equivalent until the Guineas and the Derby are run in the same week. In both matches his concentration, the swift authority of his interceptions, his confident, skilful use of the ball once he had won it and, perhaps above all, his judgment of when he could leave some distance between himself and his famous opponents and when he had to make them feel he was as close and uncomfortable as a hair shirt, were all astonishing. It was almost unbelievable that he had earned only three caps with West Germany (and all of those by being drafted in from the substitutes' bench) before he ran out in Rio to quieten a crowd of about 170,000 at a ground that can be the most exhilarating or the most intimidating in the world.

Jupp Derwall, the German manager, takes considerable credit from his decision to employ such a young and relatively inexperienced player in a role so exacting. This two-match tour in South America has been used by Derwall to wean his squad away from the system of man-to-man marking that has been a tradition of his country's football. Only two of his men were asked to operate on the old principle and it was an inspiration to choose Matthaus as the chief jailer, an inspiration crucial to the success of an expedition whose achievements have significantly strengthened belief in West Germany's challenge for the World Cup that Argentina won amid such irresistible euphoria in this city four years ago.

There were only seven minutes left to be played last Sunday when, as they began to show the combined effects of heat, humidity and a plane journey from home that had ended only 36 hours before, they fell victim to a flighted pass from Adilio and a volleyed goal by Junior so classically brilliant as to be unmistakably Brazilian.

In Buenos Aires they led Argentina for much of the match and outplayed them for even more of it. A draw was the least they were due. Derwall's imaginative integration of the wide range of skills at his disposal will make betting against his team in Spain this summer a hazardous business.

It will be particularly so if threats like Zico and Maradona are as marvellously contained there by Lothar Matthaus as they were on this tour. Few men in the game, however seasoned, could have achieved such control without resorting to far more physical harshness than was applied by the midfielder from Borussia Mönchengladbach, who is neither very tall nor ostentatiously powerful.

He did dig into Maradona a couple of times, once at the beginning of the match and once near the end, and that early foul ('I had to introduce myself,' the young German said afterwards with exaggerated innocence) was reported to have bruised the great Argentine forward's left ankle so badly that it was still in need of an ice-pack as late as Friday afternoon. But there was no evidence on the pitch that Maradona's pace or agility had been dramatically impaired. What counted was that his opportunities to exploit those and his other assets were deliberately and drastically limited.

'It was not a good night for Diego but all great players have such matches,' said Jorge Cyterszpiler, the star's commercial manager and his friend since they were boys together on the streets of Villa Fiorito, an impoverished neighbourhood on the edge of Buenos Aires. 'He will forget it.'

He is entitled to do that and so are his admirers. Not many of them will be inclined to abandon the view expressed succinctly by Cesar Menotti, the man who steered Argentina to their World Cup victory in 1978. He is optimistic about the defence in Spain now that Maradona will be supported by the thrilling gifts of the 20-year-old centre-forward Ramon Diaz in attack, Passarella in defence will be inviting comparison with a diamond as much because of his hardness as his brilliance, and Ardiles will be back to bring fluency and variety to the midfield. 'Maradona is the best player in the world" Menotti declares unequivocally. 'He does things no other footballer would attempt. At 21 years old he is a miracle.'

Whether the miracle can be transported to North London must remain extremely doubtful. There is almost sure to be an exodus of leading Argentine players after the World Cup finals, a flight from an economic shambles in their domestic game that makes the financial difficulties of British football appear trifling. 'The clubs here have had to cope with terrible inflation and devaluation in the last year and some of the best players will have to be sold,' claimed Jorge Cyterszpiler when we talked in the office of Maradona Productions at the end of last week. 'It is not possible to say at this moment if Diego will go to Europe. All I know about Arsenal's interest is what I have read in the newspapers. There has been no official contact.'

The approaches of Barcelona have obviously been more determined and more formal and Helenio Herrera was here again in midweek representing the Spanish club and assuring anyone who would listen that Maradona will be signing for them in late summer. Maybe he was right to make light of the legal confusion that currently envelops the player's present club, Boca Juniors, and his previous employers at Argentinos Juniors.

Boca took him on a 16-month loan from Argentinos Juniors with an option to pay for his transfer when the loan expires in June, but it seems that the flow of cash from Boca has been sluggish, to say the least, and the two parties have gone to law over the question of which has proprietorial rights to his contract. To an outsider it looks like a good old-fashioned impasse but veteran observers of the local customs will tell you that the shrewd deployment behind the scenes of large bundles of pesos can resolve such problems overnight. Herrera definitely has the air of someone who reckons he knows how to work the trick.

If it is any consolation to Arsenal supporters, and to every other British fan with the sense to see that our enjoyment of the game could only be heightened by such a distinguished import, their cause has drawn potent backing from Cesar Menotti and Ardiles. Ardiles, while playing with Maradona in the so-called Little World Cup in Uruguay at the beginning of 1981, urged him to think about moving to England and the advice has been reinforced in telephone calls since then. Menotti, who is serious about his job and has principles firm enough to make him bravely outspoken about Argentina's military regime, is nevertheless much warmer and more friendly than the lugubrious face within the frame of long, lank hair would suggest. However, his expression is genuinely sombre when he talks about the treatment Maradona might encounter in Spain.

Making a severe chopping gesture of his right hand into his left palm, Menotti says: 'I do not like Spanish football. Often it is more concerned with crippling opponents than with technique. I would prefer Diego to play in England than in any other country. I have a great affection for English football.' The affection owes a lot to the co-operation he has been given by Tottenham Hotspur over the release of Ardiles to play for Argentina in important competitions and especially in the World Cup. Ardiles comes home at the beginning of April to prepare for that but the national team manager made a promise in the week that he would allow him to return to England briefly if Spurs reached the FA Cup final. 'Keith Burkinshaw and all the people at Tottenham are gentlemen and my friends. Always Tottenham have said yes, yes and yes again to Menotti. Now it is impossible for Menotti to say no if they need Ardiles for the Cup final. Ardiles will decide.'

Spurs can be happier about that than Arsenal are entitled to be about their prospects of buying Maradona. 'The last word will, of course, be with Diego himself,' insists Cyterszpiler, speaking more like a 23-year-old chum than a manager. The tone changes when he adds: 'He will perform where his talents are best rewarded. At present he is paid about 65,000 American dollars per month before bonuses for playing and his annual income from other sources is around $1,500,000. We would expect to improve on those figures if he became known to a wider public in Europe. They say that tax would be a problem in England but maybe that could be solved.'

Just paying his wages might be a big enough snag for Arsenal. The virtuoso himself was not preoccupied with money when interviewed on the day of the West Germany match out among the green acres of Argentina's heavily protected training camp at Tortuguitas, a 35-mile drive from Buenos Aires. He was standing under tall trees to shield himself and his visiting parents from the fierce sun that would still be holding the temperature in the nineties when the kick-off came.

His mother, a plump, pleasant matron in glasses, was taking the weight off her feet and his father was leaning against a handsome white car his son's success has brought them. It is from the father that the player has taken his broad, muscular shoulders ('Bumping into him is like hitting cement,' said Alfredo Di Stefano when we talked on Tuesday) but the immensely formidable legs are his own creation.

He was happy enough to address himself to the question in the British visitor's mind. 'Ardiles has told me that I would be a better professional, that I would complete my education as a footballer, if I played in England,' he said. 'He says that the way the game is played there and the way clubs respect players is different from anything here or in other parts of Europe. Ardiles thinks that time spent in England would benefit my career. But so far there has been no real contact from Arsenal. It is crazy for anyone to say we are close to making a deal.

'Of course, I'm interested. Arsenal is one of the great names of football

I have known since I was kicking a ball in the streets. But decisions about where I will be playing after the World Cup are so important that there must be a lot of talking and thinking before they are made. I remember watching Arsenal against Manchester United in the 1979 Cup final on television. Apart from that I know little about British football. Of course, when you feel as deeply about the game as I do you are aware of great players around the world. I know about Kevin Keegan and Johan Cruyff just as I know about Zico and Junior and, naturally, the greatest of all, Pele. When people tell me that I am the greatest footballer in the game today it is not for me to say that they are right. But if they believe that, it means I have a special responsibility. I must go on to the field knowing that they're looking for something extra. I am sure I could still provide that in England. I'm still young, so learning the language would not be too hard. And so·long as the ball is round I can play football anywhere.'

It would be nice to believe that he could be making his point in the First Division next season but the hope is not sufficiently realistic to justify going out to steal an Arsenal season ticket.

Beating the big drum

(*The Observer*, 20 June 1982)

IT IS NEVER easy to be philosophical about being outclassed but as Scotland's footballers nurse their bruised spirits and dehydrated bodies on the Costa del Sol this weekend they are entitled to reflect that Friday night in Seville did not have the remotest echo of all those disasters their predecessors brought upon themselves in past World Cups.

The hurt they feel over the four goals dazzlingly inflicted on them by Brazil should be no more tinged with shame than the sense of inadequacy experienced by every golfer who has been buried under a tide of birdies from Jack Nicklaus, every fighter overwhelmed by Sugar Ray Robinson or all the Grand Prix drivers who have ever had Juan Fangio's exhaust fumes blowing in their faces. When you lose to the best, self-recrimination is a graceless irrelevance. You have no option but to own up, salute the brilliance that has done you in, and go wholeheartedly for the next opportunity to prove that you, too, are pretty good at your game.

That was the essence of Jock Stein's immediate reaction to the routing of a Scottish team who had performed bravely and, for half the match, with exceptional skill and composure at the Benito Villamarin Stadium.

He had a right to suggest that his men had suffered much more damagingly than their opponents from the smothering heat that persisted far beyond the nine o'clock kick-off (the stadium authorities gave the mean temperature as more than 90 degrees Fahrenheit and that was mean enough to have many of the Scots moving as if through a vat of vaseline in that long and agonising second half). But Stein's admiration for the Brazilians is profound and even the depths of his own disappointment with the eventual annihilation of a challenge that had encouraged real hope after Narey scored a sudden, marvellously struck goal in the eighteenth minute could not blur the sincerity of his tributes to the winners. He has never lost his craving for the great, genuinely stirring occasions of his sport and no collision in the championship so far has generated a more theatrical atmosphere, a more contagious throb of excitement than this hour and a half that was so conspicuously unblemished by bad feeling on or off the field.

When the yellow and green of the Brazilian supporters swamped the yellow and red of the Scottish banners around the ground and the relentless drumming of cheerful fugitives from the samba bands of Rio drowned the songs and chants imported from Hampden, there was no rancour between two contingents, who revelled in the discovery that they share a taste for earthily extrovert behaviour.

Even when Socrates, Zico and Cerezo, through the middle, and Eder, wide on the left, had begun to punish with concerted brilliance the aching weariness in Scottish limbs – when Zico's malevolently flighted equaliser from a free-kick was followed by Oscar's near-post header, Eder's embarrassingly deft chip over Rough's head and Falcao's blasting low shot off an upright to lift Brazil's total to four goals – the Scots in the crowd justifiably refused to consider themselves humiliated, refused to abandon the carnival mood of the evening entirely. They seemed, like their manager, able to dilute their sadness with the knowledge that few if any collections of footballers in the world could have withstood the quality that had bombarded their men.

Looking drained but maintaining a courteous patience while his answers were translated into Spanish, Portuguese and German, Stein told a clamorous press conference that Scotland's chances of progressing from Group Six to the second phase of the competition still hinged on the result of their last group match with the USSR in Malaga on Tuesday. He stressed that a win over Brazil would have been no guarantee of qualification and a defeat need not be damning, unless the physical effects of the hard night's work or the psychological implications of its outcome reduced his players' capacity to do what was required on Tuesday. They were, he insisted, unlikely to be shattered by losing, even as comprehensively as they had done, to a team they and he had always recognised as utterly outstanding. 'The Brazilians are an excellent side, good enough to win the World Cup,' he declared with the simple conviction of one whose insides had so recently been churned by that excellence. 'I said they were the true favourites before the start and you wouldn't expect me to have a different opinion now.'

Tele Santana's attractive, intelligent face was as relaxed as a holidaymaker's once his Brazil team had ensured a place in one of the four three-nation sections whose eliminating process in the second phase will provide the World Cup semi-finalists. He was ready to praise both of Brazil's victims in the first week, Russia and Scotland, as good sides but, when he was pressed to forecast which of them would survive as the second qualifier from Group Six, honesty obliged him to say that 'Scotland may have missed the bus'.

Obviously, he based that view primarily on the fact that the Scots, having conceded two characteristically bizarre goals while erratically hammering New Zealand last Tuesday and having been carved up by the Brazilians, find themselves with goal figures of six for and six against going into their meeting with Russia. Making the legitimate assumption that the USSR were about to improve their goal difference comfortably against New Zealand in Malaga last night, Santana was concluding that the Russians would need to take only one point from Scotland to qualify. And his memory of how much anxiety Konstantin Beskov's side had caused him was bound to nourish the assumption that Beskov and not Stein would still be around as a rival at the second stage.

The Russian coach is another who saw Brazil as the likeliest champions before a ball had been kicked but he is bitterly convinced that only the outrageous decisions of a Spanish referee, Lamo Castillo, gave the South Americans victory over his own players on Monday. By the poolside at the Atalaya Park Hotel outside Marbella, renewal of acquaintance with Denis Law was made all the more agreeable for Beskov when Law offered the opinion that denial of two penalties claimed by Russia was disgraceful. 'I think the referee may be going to Rio for a long holiday after the World Cup,' said Law in the arch tone that is his speciality.

As he wiped the sweat away from the creases that recollection of those moments had brought to his forehead, Beskov said he had always believed footballers were the men who settled football matches but in this case it was a man with a whistle who had done so. He rather glibly attributed the blatant second-half superiority that enabled Brazil to force the Russians back on their 18-yard area (thus creating the context of pressure within which Socrates and Eder shot their stunningly decisive goals) largely to inroads made by the referee's irrationality on the morale of players never previously exposed to the World Cup.

At 62, and with more than one spell as national manager behind him, as well as many years as both player and manager of Moscow Dynamo, Beskov knows most of what there is to know about the game. Certainly, he is too calm and balanced a personality to let his own morale be seriously dented by the loss of a match in which his team – by exploiting the fast breaks of Shengelia and Blokhin on the flanks – were often thrillingly effective but still owed the lead they held for so long to a grotesque goalkeeping error. Waldir Peres reminded us that, in Brazil, the goalkeeper's jersey sometimes has scarcely more status than a leper's bell.

The Brazilians worry about Waldir Peres, as they did about Felix in 1970, but they managed to protect themselves from the full penalties of the weakness then and feel they can do so again. If an outsider were to identify another deficiency in their first-choice team it would probably be the absence of a wholly satisfactory replacement for Reinaldo, the cunning and technically gifted centre-forward lost to the squad because enforced surgery left him without a cartilage in either knee.

Serginho, the large black forward who has been leading the attack, is as yet an enigma. He has been admirably game in the face of buffetings and often tricky on the ball and against Scotland it was his sensibly contrived pass (allied with Scottish neglect) that freed Eder for his spectacular goal. But at other times he has looked clumsy and unsure when in killing positions around the six-yard box. The trouble is that he tries to do things too well – 'he must learn to score ugly goals,' said one Brazilian close to the team.

Even that observer, with fresh memories of Pele, Gerson, Tostao, Rivelino and the rest, is impressed by the refined touch, the ability to keep possession with smooth and richly varied sequences of passes, exhibited by practically every outfield player in the current side. Socrates, who plays with a balanced grace and effortless control that should be impossible for a man of his beanpole physique may be the most exciting presence but on Friday Zico was more like the galvanising influence he is for his club, Flamengo. Falcao was slightly less assertive than against Russia but unmistakably a superb player and Cerezo, of the Arthur Wint stride, was a marvel of skill, spirit and stamina.

In addition to all their individual talents, Brazil are armed with a deep understanding of the game's priorities. 'They not only have great flair – they know so much about *how* to play,' says Konstantin Beskov, and Jock Stein is inclined to agree. 'They are so good that they are willing to let you take control of the ball and then set out to kid you into passing it where they want it to go,' he said yesterday.

They were even good enough and devious enough to hold Junior, the man many good judges see as their most dramatic talent of all, in the left-back position for most of the second half on Friday in order to give Eder profitable running space. It is because he recognises such subtleties in the Brazilians that Stein is proud of how his men performed for 45 minutes. Strachan, who had done splendidly in the New Zealand match, was disappointingly quiet but collectively Scotland were magnificent and Souness and Robertson in particular played with so much composure, effectiveness and self-belief that they would not have been out of place in the colours of the opposition.

No one should be blamed for what happened subsequently. It is hard on Rough that he should be faulted in some quarters in connection with the free-kick equaliser and the headed goal. When Brazil are in such a mood a goalkeeper is liable to feel that his efforts are as futile as sticking brown paper on the windows during a nuclear attack.

Two worlds collide

(*The Observer*, 27 June 1982)

IF YOU INCLUDE all the ghosts who will join the 22 nervous footballers of England and West Germany, that acre of grass at the Bernabeu Stadium in Madrid will be a crowded place on Tuesday night. Few collisions in the game carry as many echoes of past dramas, or reach into such depths of commitment among players and supporters, as a meeting that will leave the winners with only the feeble resistance of Spain standing between them and the semi-finals of the World Cup. The admission may be embarrassing, but there is no doubt that for some people on both sides the intensity of feeling is fed by the emotional residue of the two more basic conflicts between Germans and Englishmen this century. However, for most of us who will be at Bernabeu, what they have done to each other on the football pitch is history enough to justify the special tension that will take hold of us when the teams line up.

There will be memories of the World Cup final at Wembley in 1966, when England lost a late equaliser to these opponents and then went on to crush them in extra time with the help of a goal that the Germans insist was never valid. English thoughts will be dominated by painful images from the Mexico World Cup of 1970, from a day in Leon when perhaps the strongest squad ever managed by Alf Ramsey seemed sure to ride a two-goal lead into the semi-finals until the errors of his goalkeeper and his own ill-conceived substitutions brought stunning defeat.

The overall statistics of matches between the national teams of England and Germany favour the English (the Germans did not have their first victory until 1968) but that result in Leon was followed by a 3-1 beating at Wembley in the European Championship of 1972 that was probably even more significant, if not quite as shattering in its impact on the senses. West Germany won the World Cup in 1974 and at least competed, though not very convincingly, in Argentina four years ago. England, having failed to qualify for both of these competitions and having been obliged to acknowledge that Tuesday's opponents possess a far more substantial record in the principal international events, need to win here to reassert themselves as a comparable force in football.

A few months ago the odds against such an achievement would have been long but after steering his men out of Group Four with maximum points Ron Greenwood now has a far cheerier view from the bridge. The completion of formalities against Kuwait may have bored and disappointed the television audience at home but inevitably the players' minds were already on the next stage of their challenge and in the circumstances their performance was an occasion of joy and delight when set alongside the disgraceful antics of West Germany and Austria in a corresponding match. If this non-contest had been a horse race the stewards would have held an instant inquiry and if anything similar had happened in a fight at Madison Square Garden some patrons might have made a more successful attempt at intervention than the enraged Algerians who, with a running take-off, tried to fly over the fence surrounding the pitch. There must be widespread sympathy with the official protest from Algeria but they would realise even as they delivered it that they could expect no practical response from FIFA, whose approval of the competition's structure led to the situation in which West Germany needed a win while Austria could suffer a narrow defeat and still survive.

As Franz Beckenbauer pointed out on Friday night, when teams go into a World Cup tie knowing there is one kind of result that will suit both of them, an atmosphere of co-operation is bound to develop. The atmosphere at Gijon was polluted.

Beckenbauer said he was 'ashamed' of what he had just seen from the Germans and added ominously that he was not impressed by anything he had seen from them lately. He complained particularly about the failure to achieve the sense of integration that was such a vital characteristic of the team that took the World Cup under his inspired leadership in 1974.

'There is no communication,' he said. 'It is as if each man is playing on his own.' Since Pele had been still more scathing a couple of days earlier, saying that Jupp Derwall was sending out 'Mr Rummenigge and 10 robots', there is obviously some heavy opinion to encourage Derwall's counterpart, Ron Greenwood. He is not likely to be complacent about men who were regarded only a few weeks back as being easily the best equipped to carry the banner of European football but he will recognise the evidence that the last stage of West Germany's preparation for the finals was less than ideal. Players were still engaged in League matches a week before they left for Spain and their chances of being in the right frame of mind were further diminished by the inclination of some members of the squad to spend much of their time negotiating fat commercial contracts and talking arrogantly about winning the Cup.

The voice of the agent has been distressingly loud around the England camp, too, but the work has been done effectively out on the field. 'England are the most professionally efficient team we have seen,' says Joao Saldanha, the former manager of Brazil, who is here as a journalist and broadcaster. His choice of words is carefully made, of course, to avoid too direct a comparison with the Brazilians themselves, who are outstandingly the most glamorous and exciting team anyone has seen in the past two weeks. 'England play what they know. They exploit their strengths. They are cold.' He means they are cool and he holds, reasonably, that the refusal to seize up under pressure is one of the most essential assets when you challenge for the World Cup.

Given that the semi-final place England could earn on Tuesday would offer them a great opportunity to go through to the final (the thought of facing France, Austria, or even the marvellous heroes of Northern Ireland would hardly turn their blood to water), Saldanha can visualise them as worthy opposition for his countrymen in that climactic match on 11 July.

It is not difficult to share his dismissive attitude towards Spain. But to be appalled by their miserable form and the tendency of referees to be scandalously free with favours to compensate for their inadequacies is not to belittle the extraordinary deeds of Northern Ireland, who now have justifiable hopes of battling on to the semi-finals. Their attempts to do so will, naturally, occur out on the edge of most people's vision, for the action in the second phase of these finals will be dominated by the converging powers of England and West Germany and, in Barcelona, of Brazil and Argentina. No one charges in to disagree with those South Americans who say that the meeting of the giants from their sub-continent may prove to be the real World Cup final and everyone with an ounce of objectivity admits that it was outrageous to arrange the draw so that they could not possibly meet in the last, supreme contest of the tournament.

Argentina cannot be optimistic about beating Brazil at any time. They have not beaten the masters since they overcame a hastily constructed side in a friendly match in Porto Alegre, at the southern tip of Brazil, in 1969. This reporter was present on that day but does not anticipate a similarly historic result in Barcelona.

With Leandro and Junior making imaginative plundering runs from the full-back positions while the skilled Luizinho and the impressively quick Oscar stay behind to 'keep the door shut' (Jock Stein's phrase), and Falcao adding his rich technique and huge physical drive to the more familiar brilliance of Socrates, Zico and Cerezo in midfield, Brazil have often looked unstoppable in Seville. But Argentina will hope to benefit from the problems that continue to afflict Brazil in two crucial positions: goalkeeper and centre-forward. 'Waldir Peres is the second edition of Felix, who nearly gave us a nervous breakdown as goalkeeper in 1970,' said Saldanha, 'and Serginho is not the kind of player who should be leading the Brazilian attack. It was beautiful when he went off against New Zealand. Suddenly the ball was round again.' Saldanha thinks the man who was substituted for Serginho then, Paulo Isidoro, should supplant him permanently, a small neat black man replacing a tall, gangling black man. But the current manager, Tele Santana, apparently takes a different view.

While English managers like Dave Sexton and Keith Burkinshaw volunteer breathless tributes to his team ('People tend to think of them as guys who are marvellously skilful with the ball but their tackling is tremendous, they work really hard and practically all of them look as though they could play in any position,' says Burkinshaw), Santana emphasises that an Argentine side containing most of the elements that won the World Cup in 1978 but further reinforced in attack by Maradona and Diaz could take his men to the limit.

Yet he suspects that the Argentine defence may be exposed as slightly shop-worn by the speed and fluency of his men's aggression. 'It will be a match to remember,' he said in Seville. 'These are the two great powers of South American football and the rivalry will be intense. Of course, I am worried by Argentina but I feel these Argentine players may have made their bit of history in 1978. My team is almost entirely new. I believe that my players may be about to claim their moment of greatness.'

For Scotland and Jock Stein there was to be no such moment, only a sad awareness that luck had been unkind and genuinely splendid endeavour had gone unrewarded. If they had not been burdened with the worst possible draw, if exhausting heat had not so seriously increased their difficulties, if they had fielded a goalkeeper less like Rough and more like Dasaev, who defied them on behalf of Russia in the thrillingly drawn match that so cruelly put them out last Tuesday, if . . . if . . . if. Some players, notably Souness, Robertson, Strachan, Hansen, Miller and Narey, positively enlarged their reputations but it was the collective effect of the whole Scottish presence in Spain – the warm, utterly unloutish behaviour of almost 15,000 supporters, the spirited but composed excellence of the team and the rationality and dignity of the manager – that made such a moving contrast with the dishevelled and embarrassing experience in Argentina four years before.

Jock Stein may have done much more than put a decent football team on the park. He may have persuaded one of the most stubbornly obsessive races on the planet that as far as football is concerned it is time to grow up.

Brazil beat Argentina but devastating aberrations by Junior and Cerezo did much to bring their downfall against Italy. The Italians, with Rossi inspired, went on to be popular winners of the World Cup. But the best team departed when Brazil were eliminated.

A conflict of pride and prejudice

(*The Observer*, 11 July 1982)

WITH BRITISH hopes long buried and the yellow and green of Brazil (every romantic's alternative banner) trailing in the dust, it is remarkable how much feeling will be stirred around this country's television sets by tonight's World Cup final in Madrid.

Most of it will favour Italy and not just because the people of these islands have, to say the least, something of an adversary complex about the Germans. Antipathy towards Jupp Derwall's men has been deepened by their defeat of the more graceful and imaginative footballers of France and, in particular, by the fact that their win in the semi-final probably owed much to a foul so gratuitously vicious that its perpetrator might have been taking lessons from the Spanish police.

When Schumacher, the German goalkeeper, clattered brutally into the head of Battiston, dislodging two teeth and making the basic act of breathing a problem for the victim, he remained astonishingly unpunished by the inadequate Dutch referee but audiences all round the world marked him down as a villain. Some of the dispatches from Spain I have read since making a premature return to London to cope with family responsibilities have suggested that the whole German side set out to butcher France. That is a wild accusation, fed by bitter memories of the collusion with Austria that saw West Germany comfortably out of the first phase of the competition and the negative strategy that contributed so substantially to the goalless draw with England in the second.

Derwall, who is not at all a cynical or sinister figure, insists that the first disgraceful episode was spontaneously engineered by his players on the field and justifies his refusal to take risks against the English by saying he was sure his attackers would subsequently take goals off Spain more readily than Ron Greenwood's could. Given the absence of the knockout element from the competition at that point and what everybody and his brother knows about the England forwards, was that a silly or an immoral gamble? If further argument against wholesale condemnation is needed, Derwall can point to the injuries that have beset his team and to the enteritis that made four of them doubtful about appearing in the match with France. Briegel had a touch of sunstroke, too, but when his manager questioned his inclusion the big man offered to turn out in a cap. He is a phenomenon, in morale as in everything else, and he symbolises the spirit that may overcome Italy's superior artistry.

Should West Germany win, only the simplistic and the emotionally biased will see it as the wrong outcome to a morality play, a triumph for the powers of darkness. Has everyone forgotten how long and how chillingly Italian attitudes cast a shadow over European football?

Nobody should fail to acknowledge the marvellous endeavours of the present manager, Enzo Bearzot, to wean the brilliant talents of the Italian League away from the calculation of percentages that governs mentalities there. But Bearzot, though he has survived some notable battles with the clubs and the demented sporting press of his country, has still to win the war. The tremendous performances that have taken his team to the final at the expense of such as Argentina and Brazil have been blemished by occasional manifestations of defensive paranoia and outbursts of the kind of cruelty that brought Claudio Gentile two bookings and cost him a place in the semi-final with Poland. Even more souring is the tendency of the Italians to fall so painfully as to indicate that a shoulder charge warrants a week's convalescence. When faced with the uncluttered determination of the Germans, Italy may be damned by a reassertion of ethnic neuroses.

Certainly the Germans will come back with their shields or on them. Their choice in the matter may be increased by the availability of Hansi Mueller, an immense influence in midfield who has been unfit so far but should at least be on the bench this evening. He will probably be joined there by Rummenigge, who wears his distinction of being European Footballer of the Year twice almost as casually as if it were a boilersuit. What he did as a substitute in extra-time against France must have reminded Italy that they are opposed by a special category of men.

Of course, in the area of technical ability, the Italians are even more exceptional. They are, without doubt, the more richly endowed football team of the two. They defend magnificently and with Conte running damagingly in the wide spaces, Antognoni recovered from injury to reinforce him and the superb Rossi (unbelievably sharp after the two years' suspension imposed following a bribes scandal) again exhibiting the full range of his fluid control and the deadly relevance of his positioning, Italy could win this final in style. That would make it easy to echo the thoughts of Ron Greenwood, back at home in Brighton: 'I'd love it to happen for Enzo. He's such a warm, sympathetic, human individual and he has fought so hard to lift the Italian game away from its grimmer attitudes. A good man will win if he does.'

And yet I cannot ignore the words of an eight-year-old who was sitting at my elbow as we watched the semi-final. 'Kick it somewhere good,' she shouted. Whatever the technical merits of the case, I suspect that West Germany may kick it somewhere better, or at any rate more profitable, than their opponents.

Italy, and that good man, did win.

Uruguay threatened with expulsion

(*The Observer*, 15 June 1986)

THE INSULTS, threats and molestation inflicted by Uruguayans on Joel Quiniou, the Frenchman who refereed the bitter match in which the South Americans knocked Scotland out of the World Cup on Friday, brought swift punishment yesterday from FIFA, the supreme governing body of football.

Hermann Neuberger, chairman of the World Cup Organising Committee, announced in Mexico City that the Uruguayan Federation have been cautioned, fined 25,000 Swiss francs and warned that any repetition of their offences will carry the risk of expulsion from the competition. Their coach, Omar Borras, having been found guilty of uttering 'uncouth' remarks about M. Quiniou (he called the official a 'murderer') has been banned from his team's bench for tomorrow's game with Argentina in Puebla and given a stern warning.

Mr Neuberger revealed at a crowded press conference that before their meeting with Scotland the Uruguayans had been reprimanded by letter because of unsporting behaviour by players and coaching staff on the bench during their very first match of the tournament, against West Germany at Queretaro on 4 June. He did not mention the ordering-off of one of their players, Bossio, during their second appearance in the first phase just completed (perhaps FIFA felt that Denmark's 6–1 battering of the Uruguayans was the ideal retribution in that case), but went on to report something that many of us in the room had witnessed at first hand – the fact that 'the situation was even more serious' at the match with Scotland. 'There was unfair and ungentlemanly behaviour on the bench and on the part of players,' he said. 'Worst of all, the referee was molested and even threatened. Moreover, the coach of the Uruguayan delegation, Mr Borras, used uncouth language and insulted the referee.'

What all of this emphasises is that the genius of the Scots for turning the World Cup finals into a torture chamber for themselves has found the most malevolent of allies here in Mexico City, where the footballers of Uruguay have provided yet another necessary reminder that no amount of technical brilliance can either excuse or obscure a set of attitudes so squalid that they go far beyond any question of poor sportsmanship and suggest a basic lack of decency in the playing of the game. Given their tiny population of around three million, the Uruguayans' achievement in producing so many players of high talent is perhaps the most extra-ordinary phenomenon in international football. They won the in-augural world championship in 1930 and took the title again in Brazil's own Maracana stadium in 1950 and the men they sent out at Neza, on the ugly, cruelly impoverished edge of Mexico City in the middle of Friday, have the skills, athleticism and tactical assurance to alarm the very best teams in these finals. But appreciation of their thrilling abilities is too often turned to bile by their contemptuous disregard not only for the laws of the game and the limbs of their opponents but for any remotely civilised code of conduct.

Alex Ferguson, the manager of Scotland, was understandably emotional at the end of the miserably frustrating goalless draw that dumped his own squad out of the competition but all around him in the acrimonious turmoil of the post-match press conference was evidence to support his assertion that the Uruguayan footballers – and the officials and camp followers who constantly exhort them to further excesses – have 'no respect for other people's dignity'. Nearby, Bobby Charlton, whose bearing throughout one of the truly great careers gives him an unignorable voice at such times, was making a quiet declaration. 'We just shouldn't play these people again,' he said, and it obviously did not matter much whether the 'we' meant British teams or embraced all who try to uphold reasonable standards. 'It's simply not worth it,' added Charlton. 'The way they go on has nothing to do with football, nothing to do with sport.'

Some of the deeply resentful utterances made at the Neza stadium in the hour or so after Scotland and Uruguay returned to the dressing-ooms will reverberate for months or years and a few may have official repercussions. Omar Borras said that there had been a murder on the field and the murderer was the referee, which was his poetically outrageous condemnation of the decision by Joel Quiniou to dismiss Jose Batista for a cruel foul on Gordon Strachan inside the first minutes of action.

Alex Ferguson in turn accused Borras of 'lying and cheating' but perhaps the remark calculated to stir the most serious reaction was that in which Ernie Walker, the Secretary of the Scottish Football Association, branded the Uruguayans 'the scum' of the world game. The words brought unavoidable echoes of the prolonged controversy that descended on Alf Ramsey in 1966 when, in circumstances somewhat similar to Friday's (but with the vital difference that England won a match riddled with hostility and went on to take the World Cup), he berated the Argentines for behaving like animals.

FIFA would have been unforgivably lax if Uruguay's disfiguring contribution here had not been the subject of a prompt and formal inquiry and it is not wild to ask if expulsion from the competition might already be appropriate punishment. There is, however, a clear possibility that one or two of those who have reacted from the sidelines of the horror show will be in trouble, too. Ernie Walker is an intelligent as well as a strong-natured man and he will realise that his brief outburst may come back to haunt him.

There is no doubt that Scotland's failure to grasp the unique opportunity granted by being allowed to compete against 10 men for virtually an hour and a half at Neza, the chance of at last lifting themselves beyond the first phase of the World Cup finals, is likely to haunt them forever. When all allowances have been made for the grossly unsettling effect of encountering cynicism as unrelenting as that displayed by Uruguay, and every adage about the difficulties of overcoming 10 men has been accommodated, the inescapable truth is that the Scots were a dreadful disappointment to themselves and the many millions of Mexicans and others around the globe who were desperate for them to win.

They just did not have the fundamental talent, the wit or imagination to do the job. Even more worrying for some of their most ardent supporters was the suspicion that the team suffered a weird loss of nerve. These are not the sort of players who could ever be mistaken for cowards but they appeared to be shell-shocked rather than invigorated by the removal of Batista and played most of the rest of the match as if their minds and spirits had been chilled by dread of the monumental embarrassment implicit in failing when events, for once, seemed to be conspiring to see them through. Of course, Uruguay, in the midst of all their villainy, paraded wonderful ball skills and a capacity for organisation that almost always gave them strength in numbers where it was most needed. Scottish claims that the South Americans merely blocked the way to their goal with an implacable, wholly negative barrier of bodies just won't wash.

It is true that Francescoli was asked to keep the entire Scots back-line occupied on his own for much of the time and the fact that he did so quite readily is a tribute to a level of close control and brilliant screening of the ball such as only two or three footballers now active could hope to equal. But Ramos did superb running in the first half, Barrios, Santin and Cabrera were all liable to become positive in isolated flourishes and, over the 90 minutes, Uruguay came at least as close to scoring as opponents who needed a goal when they did not — as one splendid reflex save by Leighton testified.

Barrios, the tall midfielder who is their captain, exemplified the baffling compound of the admirable and the deplorable that makes his countrymen worse than aggravating on the football field. When he was concentrating on the ball he was excitingly adroit but much of his afternoon was spent provoking the opposition and inflicting persistent interference on the referee. In the latter role he was an infuriating pest and a potentially crooked influence on the game.

It is presumably unfair to speculate, as many observers did, that Joel Quiniou meant to bring out the yellow card to Batista after 53 seconds, produced the red one instead and had to brazen out the consequences, but his courageous initial gesture definitely rendered him reluctant to deal harshly with the Uruguayans later. So the provocations, posturings, sneak fouls far from the ball and all the basic tools of their dirty trickery drew only mild rebukes. They really are an astonishing bunch and there should be a prize for anyone who can enlighten us about their national psyche. Does their conduct betray a deadly combination of a small nation's chip on the shoulder and Latin machismo, or is the grim mixture of poverty and political repression in the country the source? Talk of paranoid psychopathic tendencies may be too strong but when 11 of them pull on football shirts the result is not endearing.

The best response to their nastiness would have been a good hiding but Scotland never threatened to deliver it. We knew that they did not have the gifted individuals to approach emulation of Denmark's glorious exploitation of the same numerical advantage. Ferguson says that essential factors such as diet and the absence of a genuine sports-orientated upbringing preclude the production of athletes like the electric Michael Laudrup. But the trundling predictability of Scotland's endeavour, the slow-witted ineptitude of their attempt to find creative spaces for the extra man, were disastrously exacerbated by the pathetic quality of their crosses when they did penetrate to the byeline and a criminal inaccuracy with straightforward passes in other areas of the field.

This is not the moment to be hard on individuals, though quite a few were brutally exposed as labourers in a craftsman's world. Alex Ferguson may have made some imperfect decisions against Uruguay but he has the equipment of a great manager and now that he has returned 'to begin the rebuilding of Aberdeen' he might easily lay healthy foundations for the national team, too.

Back at the battlefield, England know that if they beat Paraguay on Wednesday they face Argentina or Uruguay. Wishing Bobby Robson luck is not just a matter of politeness.

England find the right philosophy

(*The Observer*, 15 June 1986)

THE FIRST TIME Dave Sexton saw the national football team of Paraguay they had a midfield player who wore a black beret on the field and were notable for a collective obsession with acrobatic bicycle kicks that put opponents in frequent danger of decapitation.

Sexton himself might have seemed fairly eccentric in those distant days, since he was studying the World Cup of 1958 from a tent pitched in the Swedish countryside while subsisting on what he had been able to scrape together from the unspectacular wages paid to a hard-working forward by Brighton and Hove Albion, the newly crowned champions of the English Third Division. Now, after a long career in club management that brought extremes of satisfaction and heartache at Leyton Orient, Chelsea, Manchester United, Coventry and Queens Park Rangers, he is still a student of the World Cup in general and Paraguay in particular and here in Mexico City his reports may be a vital factor in helping Bobby Robson and England to overcome the South Americans at the Aztec Stadium next Wednesday and move on into the quarter-finals of football's greatest competition.

Just as tents have been replaced by expensive hotels in Sexton's life, so the Paraguayans have thrown aside the quaint headgear and extravagant flourishes of technique that bemused him nearly 30 years ago. He and his fellow observer, Howard Wilkinson, the manager of Sheffield Wednesday, will provide Robson with a detailed picture of a young, spirited team whose skilful and excitingly direct attacking play is capable of compensating for some serious weaknesses in defence.

Facing Paraguay – who have impressed as quick, brave, inventive and refreshingly free of the cynicism that often mars the talent of more celebrated representatives of their continent – would have been a daunting prospect for the England who scuffled so unconvincingly against Portugal and Morocco in the draining heat of Monterrey. But the improvement in organisation and effectiveness was so dramatic in the slaughter of Poland last Wednesday afternoon that there need be no more than a normal, healthy nervousness about encountering Latin skills at the demanding altitude of Mexico City. England have been tempered in the furnace in more ways than one. Surviving the sweaty nightmare of conditions they believe to be as debilitating as those experienced at any location in these finals is likely to persuade them that climbing from Monterrey's 1,765 feet to Mexico City, which stands at well over 7,000, will be a bearable hardship so long as overcast skies continue to keep the capital relatively cool. There is unquestionably a growing conviction among foreign players and their mentors that heat, not altitude, could turn out to be the deadliest natural enemy here.

Yet even escaping from the climatic ordeals of Monterrey obviously holds far less significance for England than their emergence from the tactical confusion and morale-sapping dissension which, until this last week, threatened to fragment their World Cup challenge and leave them to drift home at the end of the first phase in a cloud of rancorous disappointment. Many outside the camp will feel that there was only the faintest trace of glory in finishing runners-up to Morocco in Group F, whose early fumblings sometimes made it look like the tournament's equivalent of a remedial reading group. However, considering what had gone before, the performance against Poland was a genuine and thrilling triumph. And there can be no doubt that it owed a great deal to the positive repercussions of the frequently vehement debate stirred by the deep dissatisfaction some members of the squad expressed over the playing methods employed in the 1–0 defeat by Portugal and the goalless draw with Morocco.

Bobby Robson is entitled to insist that England did enough to beat Portugal before an epidemic of late blunders cost them both points (and might well have resulted in more than the single goal they lost) and ending level with Morocco was a worthwhile achievement after Bryan Robson's dislocated shoulder and Ray Wilkins's expulsion had deprived their side of two captains just short of the interval and obliged 10 men to salvage what they could.

But such extenuating circumstances were never going to obscure the fundamental shortcomings of the team's work in those matches or quell the bitter complaints of defenders who felt they had suffered most from the overall dishevelment. The worst disagreements stemmed from the crippling absence of compactness in midfield produced by a tactical looseness particularly identified with the use of Waddle as a roving attacker in wide positions and a standing invitation to the full-backs to flood forward through a formation insufficiently balanced or disciplined to cover the spaces they were vacating.

Anyone who tries to play down the seriousness of the disputes that arose around these issues is either ignorant of what went on behind the closed doors of the training quarters or intent on hiding the truth. Fortunately, the manager was ready to come to terms with the realities in time to send the right 11 footballers on to the field against Poland and to deploy them to such practical, rational effect that qualification for a place in the last 16 was scarcely in question from the kick-off.

Boniek might have scored before Lineker offered the first of his three splendid goals but I cannot accept that even such an early blow would have altered the outcome. With Trevor Steven and Steve Hodge, operating with sustained energy on the flanks in midfield, Hoddle freed to exploit his talent for penetrative distribution from a position in the middle of that line rather than having his vision cramped by being out on the right, and Reid co-ordinating everything with old-fashioned cunning and tireless competitiveness, England were instantly possessed of shape and purpose.

The back four, in which Fenwick and the admirable Butcher were able to stay in sufficiently close contact to provide mutual compensation for the lack of pace that can make them vulnerable, was suddenly a unit at ease with itself and the full-backs could attempt surging breaks without feeling as insecure as high-wire artists in a gale. At the front, the brisk mobility and intelligent economy of Beardsley had supplanted the muscular lunges and hopeful leaps of Hateley and amid the swirl of relevant movement Lineker rediscovered the inspired subtlety of positioning and swift simplicity of execution that make him a great finisher.

Two of England's first-half goals were memorably brilliant in their creation and completion and if the third originated in an outrageous error by the Polish goalkeeper, Lineker's punishing stroke was again a declaration of class. By the interval the Poles were dead, the spectre of a humiliating exit had receded and Robson's men were heading towards the next challenge with their spirits and their reputations almost miraculously restored.

Some will argue, with more than a hint of legitimacy, that the restructuring of his team was imposed on Bobby Robson by the disablement of his best player, Bryan Robson, and the suspension of Wilkins. They will maintain their criticism of the manager by insisting that necessity was the mother of rationalisation, that fruitful decisions were forced on him by a dilemma. Does that matter? Should it worry us any more than the recognition that the way England played in destroying Poland – with a solid midfield line of four footballers bright and flexible enough to be compact in front of the back four when needed and aggressively creative when granted the opportunity – was essentially the method applied by Alf Ramsey here in 1970? Surely the answer is no, for the important point is that England now know what they are doing, now acknowledge that the conditions and opponents to be coped with in this competition call for something very different from the optimistic and haphazard belligerence with which they launched their campaign.

The 4–4–2 formation will be retained for the collision with Paraguay (with Fenwick's two yellow cards and automatic suspension bringing Martin of West Ham into the back line as the only change to the team that beat the Poles) and anyone who still doubts its validity would be ill-advised to utter such scepticism in front of Peter Reid. That tough, unfailingly honest little man, whose Everton alliance with Steven, Stevens and Lineker did so much to generate happiness in mid-week, was sipping a drink to help put back the six pounds he had shed at Estadio Universitario as he talked around midnight at Saltillo about the rewarding agonies of a few hours before.

'After 10 minutes I was knackered,' he said. 'I thought "I'll never get through this." But I got a second wind and lasted out all right. It makes a hell of a difference when you play nice and tight with the kind of well-balanced midfield we had. You know that if you get in trouble it doesn't have to be disastrous because you won't be isolated, there will always be somebody close at hand to help you out.

'If you're all stretched out as you can be with a looser, less disciplined system, you can be running your guts out and never getting to the ball. Then, in that terrible heat, your problem isn't just physical. It's mental too and when your mind goes it's good night. We could keep going because we knew that every effort had some purpose. With all the movement we got up front from Peter Beardsley and Gary Lineker we always had plenty of options when parting with the ball and we were well enough organised to hit more confident, more ambitious passes. The whole thing worked really well.'

Will Lineker show the same assassin's certainty when Paraguay are on the hit-list? Dave Sexton, having seen the Paraguayans draw with Mexico and Belgium, thinks he will at least have chances to do so. 'We had a 2–2 draw with their youth side at the world championships in Russia last August and their seniors play much the same way,' says Sexton. 'They are refreshingly direct, not piddling around at the back for minutes at a time but preferring to get on with the game in your half of the field. Although they are not big fellas they will hold on to the ball, invite you to challenge, resist your challenge and press on and they are bloody quick. They combine the usual South American foot skill with directness in the last third of the park.

'They have plenty of ability to work the ball through the midfield, where Nunez has been doing an excellent job for them and Canete is even better. Canete is the main link between the defence and the forwards and good at getting himself into the box as well. He has fine dribbling skills, holds the ball well under pressure and redirects their attack, which is pretty lively with three men up front – Ferreira wide on the right, Cabanas in the middle and Mendoza on the left. They believe in whipping in plenty of crosses, hitting the spaces with their centres and relying on people to attack the ball really bravely.

'So they can cause problems going forward and there's an extra threat from Mendoza's shooting, especially at free kicks. But they are not very disciplined in defence, where they use the big number three, Zabala, as sweeper or free man in the back four. There is plenty of space for their opponents to attack. Defence is the weakest part of their team and England should have some joy there. Paraguay's goalie isn't bad, mind you, although he's a bit reckless.

'It should be a good game. The Paraguayans will foul you but that's not the first thing in their minds. They are not as cynical as some South American sides. There should be no silliness.'

The biggest name in Paraguay's team, and indeed one of the biggest in South America, is Julio Romero, who plays with Fluminense in Brazil, but he has not taken the eye in the matches the England scouts have watched. However, Dave Sexton, whose World Cup duties have been interspersed with studies for the Open University degree he hopes to take quite soon, is too thoughtful a man to underrate Romero or anyone else. The theme of his course is Reason and Experience and it involves him with such formidable players as Spinoza, Descartes and Locke.

Bobby Robson's England might have trouble taking the ball away from that lot but with their new, persuasive 4–4–2 they may well leave Paraguay's argument in tatters.

At the mercy of the Prima Maradona

(*The Observer*, 22 June 1986)

SET DIEGO MARADONA alongside Pele, George Best, Johan Cruyff or most of the other truly great goalscoring attackers in the history of football and at first glance he might seem to be a Jeep among racing cars.

Standing barely five foot six inches tall and weighing several pounds more than 11 stone, he is so stocky as to be almost squat and no one unaware of what he has done could possibly associate such a physique with sinuous infiltration of the crowded penalty areas of the modern game. But his is a Formula One machine all right, a phenomenon capable of reducing the best and swiftest defenders to impotent pursuit, of leaving them as miserable stragglers baffled by astonishing surges of acceleration and the most remarkable power steering in sport. Maradona's changes of direction are so devastatingly sudden and extreme that they must impose a huge strain on his lower body. Surely there has not been such a pelvis since Elvis Presley was in his prime.

The English players who wait to face the Argentine master today in what promises to be an electrifying quarter-final of the World Cup would not be human if they were not haunted by the suspicion that in the heat of a Mexico City noon they will (if I may again pilfer Pat Crerand's tribute to his team-mate Best) be 'left with twisted blood'.

It would, of course, be an idiotic oversimplification to present such a match as essentially a confrontation between two men. Yet when all its thousand complexities – from tactical permutations to the form of the 20 other individuals on the field at the Aztec Stadium to the psychological residue of the Falklands conflict of four years ago – have been stripped away, the most vital struggle may well be that involving Maradona and Peter Shilton in the England goal.

Shilton has always been one of the two outstandingly important members of Bobby Robson's squad and, since the sad but inevitable undermining by injury of Bryan Robson's significance, optimism about the English team's prospects has become increasingly inseparable from the goalkeeper's performances.

Predictably, he has let no one down. A characteristic save from Boniek prevented an early swelling of Polish confidence before England had scored in Monterrey 10 days ago and again on Wednesday he intervened dramatically to deny Paraguay a lead that might have encouraged those overwhelmingly naïve but intermittently skilful South Americans to prove awkward.

In both cases England emerged from initial nervousness and disorganisation, quickly found a convincing rhythm and, inspired by the superb natural finishing of Lineker, swept to thoroughly satisfying 3–0 victories. 'That is the beauty of having the big man in goal,' says Ron Greenwood, who managed the national squad through their thwarted World Cup challenge in Spain in 1982 and is following this one from the stands as an analyst for BBC Radio. 'And now he is skipper he is even more determined that he won't let anything go past him.'

The statistics Shilton has accumulated so far over nine matches in the World Cup finals have indeed hinted at resistance bordering on invincibility. Although England were eliminated in Spain at the stage roughly equivalent to today's quarter-final, he was beaten only once in five games and the single goal he has surrendered in the six hours played here was attributable not to any error of his but to an extraordinary chain of blunders put together against Portugal by all four men in the back line of his defence.

Losing two goals in those nine matches is amazing enough but the mere figures cannot fully convey the extent of his achievement or the importance of his presence. He is 11 years older than Maradona, who is 25, but a couple of decades as a professional have not dulled his dedication or his brilliance and the barrier he constantly makes of his large and muscular frame (six foot and often nearly 14 stone) could provide an immense problem for even the most penetrative improviser football now possesses.

Naturally, Bobby Robson will want to ensure that Maradona runs into plenty of cunning and spirited hindrance long before he comes within effective range of the world's finest goalkeeper and it is depressingly unfortunate that the manager must cope with the probable removal of Reid from his options by a serious recurrence of the right ankle injury which has been troubling the Everton midfielder for weeks.

There can be little doubt that, given the ease and frequency with which Bryan Robson's right shoulder dislocates itself and thus makes selection of that marvellous player an apparently unacceptable risk, the strongest line-up currently at England's disposal is the 4–4–2 formation that demolished Poland and Paraguay. In that team Reid's battling qualities and unfailing practicality, his willingness to submerge his ego in the role of reliable fetcher and carrier, have been basic to the considerable success of the middle four. With him always reassuringly on hand, and those young lions Hodge and Steven steaming enterprisingly but sensibly up and down the flanks, Hoddle has been granted the freedom to blossom at last as the creative influence his technical virtuosity has long entitled him to be.

The Tottenham star's most informed admirers still worry about his stamina and the strange flaw in otherwise rich instincts for the game that prevents him from making himself available for the ball as readily as he uses it once it has been given to him. But his recent work has been sufficiently distinguished (especially the sustained excellence that did so much to dismantle Paraguay) to prompt no less an observer than 'San Diego' himself to say: 'I'm worried about Hoddle because everything comes from him. He is a good rival.' Maradona also singled out Lineker for the kind of praise that quiet destroyer might wear like a medal: 'He's a great surprise – beautiful. It is a pleasure to watch him move.'

It is true that Lineker – in whom fierce pace and positional flair are married to the sort of economy and commonsense that have persuaded him to side-foot away all but one of the five goals that have already made him a leading scorer in this competition – has been crucial to the improvement England have shown in their past two matches. So, unmistakably, has Beardsley. The introduction of this little hero's tirelessly inventive running and crisp control and distribution in place of the lumberingly limited contributions of Hateley has transformed the attack, not least by diminishing the temptation among his team-mates to pump unimaginative high balls into the opposition's box.

However, before pleasure in England's rising standards becomes excessive, a cold douche of realism should be applied by remembering precisely what they have accomplished up until now. They have reached the last eight in this World Cup on the strength of two good wins over palpably moderate opponents.

Meanwhile the fearsomely positive Russians, creators of chances by the hatful, were engulfed by ill-luck, their own defensive peculiarities and the stubborn resilience of Belgium, and regrettably bundled out; the formidable talents of Italy were humiliatingly outclassed by the splendidly complementary gifts of Michel Platini's France and left with only Enzo Bearzot's wonderful dignity to alleviate their pain; and Denmark's swashbuckling marauders lost a stunningly amateur equaliser to Spain and continued to perform so amateurishly thereafter that the intelligently deployed, hungrily competitive Spaniards buried them like paupers. To find England still around after such mayhem may be a surprise, but here they are ready to take issue with Argentina and the most dangerous forward of his generation.

The Argentines proved in the course of ushering Uruguay, everybody's favourite villains, from the stage that regarding them as a one-man band would be disastrously stupid. Their defence, in which Brown (whose Irish great-grandfather carried the name across the Atlantic) is an authoritative sweeper and Batista an exceptionally determined marker, is impressively organised. And they crowd the midfield with technically sophisticated, highly mobile players, of whom Burruchaga is usually the most eager to press forward in support of an attack that has Valdano and Pasculli as aggressive, flexible allies for the floating, unchartable menace of Maradona.

Dave Sexton, who watched the defeat of Uruguay on behalf of England, describes Argentina as a very fine side with a good, athletic, quick and strong defence to protect whatever rewards Maradona and his accomplices can plunder at the other end. 'Our front-runners will have to work much harder than they did in beating Paraguay, who are an infinitely more naïve team than Argentina,' Sexton said in the week. It was understandable that he should counsel against making the stopping of Maradona the be-all and end-all of England's tactics and go on to suggest that Argentina might be hurt down the flanks, where there is more vulnerability than is to be found through the middle.

Yet concentrating on Maradona is not a sign of paranoia, just a recognition of the facts. Out on the sun-warmed playing fields of the Club America on Thursday, when the Argentines opened the doors of their training quarters in a suburb of Mexico City for a morning of interviews, Jorge Valdano (the tall Real Madrid striker who is himself a deadly weapon for the South Americans) became almost lyrical when he assessed Maradona's relevance to his country's World Cup ambitions. 'He is the soul of our team,' said Valdano. 'He is our great offensive key. Diego can make a balanced team into world champions. Without him we would have to change our whole tactical scheme, perhaps have to find new players, to make up for the attacking possibilities Diego provides just by his presence.'

When Valdano was asked how he would try to deal with Maradona if faced with the genius as an opponent, his strong face gave way to a wide smile and he said: 'I would mark the man.' But will that approach make sense for England? Ron Greenwood, who sent out a team to beat Argentina 3–1 in a friendly at Wembley in 1980, does not think so. Greenwood takes pains to stress that the Maradona his men met in that match was not nearly the force he is here. 'He has grown up a lot since then. He was just a baby at that time, in fact he was still a baby when he played in the World Cup finals in Spain, where he reacted badly to things he just shrugs off now. That is his Barcelona experience, his Napoli experience showing through.

'Here he looks a mature man and a very strong man. When we played him in 1980 he had just come on the scene but I knew even then that if you tried to mark Maradona one-for-one he would murder you – isolate you and leave you stranded. I told our fellas that what he wouldn't be used to was people coming at him from all sides. So I said that we wouldn't designate a one-to-one marker but everybody who was near him should attack his possession, creating the effect of coming at him from all angles. We had players closing in from the sides and chasing after him from the back. The lads did it very well and we restricted his space and he didn't cause us anything like as much trouble as he might have done, although I remember one run into the box that left four of our lot struggling and nearly produced a goal.

'But he's a different player now. I was really impressed by his display against Uruguay, I thought it was masterful. He seemed to be in everything, and made at least two chances that should definitely have led to goals. He was hampered, he was pushed but he didn't retaliate, he just got on with his job. I thought, "Full marks to you, old son".'

Bobby Robson's reflections are bound to be less philosophical as he wrestles with the seemingly unavoidable dilemma of how to replace Reid in midfield. There is speculation that Bryan Robson will return to the fray, harness and all, but the Argentines could not be expected to ignore the invitation of his tortured shoulder. Wilkins, who is out from under his suspension (as is Fenwick), might come back if he could be persuaded to duplicate Reid's humble attitude and let Hoddle go on running the show. But perhaps the best bet would be Gary Stevens of Tottenham, who has pace and physical assertiveness to compensate for the defensive slackness that can afflict his play.

The England manager may be wishing he could legitimately summon the services of the callous crush of photographers who almost barged Maradona to the ground on Thursday morning. Whatever personnel or strategy he opts for, Robson won't be encouraged by the simple words the great footballer offered in the midst of that open-air bedlam. 'The English are big and strong in defence,' he said, 'but their movements are sluggish and we are going to try and take advantage of this with short bursts of speed to pass them.'

If anything weighs more heavily on English spirits than that ominous utterance, it can only be the thought of the crowd trouble that could be nourished on both sides by memories of the win over Argentina in a bitter World Cup quarter-final at Wembley 20 years ago and by the more momentous defeat inflicted in the South Atlantic in 1982. Let's hope spectators and players behave like honest, unmalevolent rivals today.

Victory at the Aztec Stadium would certainly give more cause for undiluted celebration than there ever was when the injunction 'Rejoice' was intoned around Downing Street four years ago. And losing would surely be tolerable, for defeat in sport is only a little death. It is one I fear England will suffer this afternoon.

They did.

The genius who is too hot to handle

(*The Observer*, 29 June 1986)

IF THERE IS AN effective way of killing off the threat of Diego Maradona by marking him, it probably involves putting a white cross over his heart and tethering him to a stake in front of a firing squad. Even then there would be the fear that he might suddenly dip his shoulder and cause the riflemen to start shooting one another.

Never before in more than half a century of World Cups has the talent of a single footballer loomed so pervasively over everybody's thinking about the final. Maradona's impact goes far beyond the simple realisation that he is indisputably the best and most exciting player now at work in the game. It is inseparable from the potent sense of declaration inherent in almost everything he has done on the field here in Mexico, from his vast public's conviction that he has chosen the Aztec Stadium as the setting for the definitive statement of his genius.

All the brilliant performances he has packed into a glittering career since his emergence as a boy wonder in Buenos Aires seem to have been mere rehearsal for what he is seeking to do now as a 25-year-old at the height of his powers. A global television audience estimated at two billion will watch this afternoon as he attempts to lead Argentina to victory over West Germany in the last decisive contest of the 1986 world championship and surely all but a tiny Teutonic minority are going to will him to succeed. For a non-German to do otherwise would be some kind of betrayal of the old universal craving to see inspired excellence get its due.

Yet there are grounds for dreading an anti-climax, for no footballers anywhere are more impressively equipped in terms of temperament or track-record to frustrate Maradona and the gifted men around him than are the opponents they will face today. The strength of West Germany's challenge is starkly conveyed by the fact that this is their fifth World Cup final and should they win it, and thus equal the three championships of Brazil and Italy, they will establish themselves as the most consistently successful competitors of all.

Those statistics do not, however, represent the heart of their menace to Argentina. That is to be found in their capacity for winning the Cup at the expense of teams recognised as the most talented in the tournament. In 1954 everyone knew that Hungary were the masters of the game, but the

Germans refused to bow to the obvious and finished as champions. Twenty years later Johan Cruyff and Holland were the victims of a similar assault on the form-book and the dreams of a multitude of idealists.

Such historic upsets can hardly be dismissed as the products of freakish good fortune. There were great players in those winning teams of 1954 and 1974 (Franz Beckenbauer, who will be at the Aztec Stadium as manager, was magnificent in that latter year) and even the more ordinary members had good technical habits, an aptitude for tactical organisation and superb morale. The same qualities are increasingly in evidence here, though West Germany have made a flawed and stumbling advance on the final. Once again they are demonstrating an intimidating knack of extracting the maximum from the abilities at their disposal, of claiming more than the going rate for their skills, and it was ominous that the most convincing football they have played so far should have been inflicted on France in the semi-final.

Admittedly, the French had been conspicuously wearied by their epic quarter-final with Brazil and Platini in particular looked like a star in the process of burning out. But anyone who saw the way the Germans out-thought and outran them had to make a shuddering acknowledgment that the horrors suffered by Hungary and Holland might be lying in wait for Argentina. Certainly Beckenbauer's troops will not be automatically unnerved by the prospect of confronting Maradona and the clutch of other outstanding players – notably Enrique, Burruchaga and Valdano as attackers and Batista, Ruggieri and Brown, the imposing sweeper, in defence – who entitle the Argentine coach, Carlos Bilardo, to the ire he displays when crassly accused of fielding a one-man band.

The German manager believes that these efforts of earlier opponents, including England, to deal with Maradona without assigning any individual to mark him one-on-one were foredoomed and he is almost sure to adopt a strategy that involves close personal harassment of the game's deadliest predator. Unlike Bobby Robson, his English counter-part, Beckenbauer is at least lucky enough to have players with the specific skills and experience required to justify even a hope that such marking will go well. Briegel has used his physical power and athletic running to good effect against Maradona when Verona have faced Napoli in the Italian League and one or two others, especially Eder, might undertake the final's least coveted role without total pessimism.

But it is no surprise to learn that the probable choice for the policing job is Lothar Matthaus, a midfielder who was first seen by this reporter early in 1982 when, in the space of one week and as a novice internationalist who had barely reached the age of 21, he was asked to mark Zico in Rio and Maradona in Buenos Aires. He performed splendidly in both matches, giving ample promise of the distinguished career in the national colours that has since given him 40-odd caps.

Matthaus's regular contribution to the West German team these days is as a free-running, hard-shooting attacker from midfield, but it may well make sense this afternoon to revert to applying his combative vitality, intelligence and nerve more negatively. Whether the switch, if it comes, will bring anything but misery to young Lothar is another matter.

Bobby Moore, who may know as much about the eternal verities of defending as any man ever did, says quietly that he cannot think of a player in this World Cup who would be a decent even-money bet to subdue Maradona on a one-to-one basis. Moore was, of course, the captain of England when they overcame a young Beckenbauer and his mates at Wembley in the final of 1966. Though he still looks trim enough to be pulling a strip over his head, he is quite glad to be merely watching the conclusive stages here. The Argentina-Belgium semi-final gave him his first view of Maradona in the flesh and he was as thrilled as the rest of us in the stands by the sustained brilliance with which the Belgians were undone.

Moore's pleasure was deepened by a keen appreciation of how calculatingly Maradona's most unforgettable flourishes were deployed. 'Obviously in the four years between two World Cups he has found the maturity that enables him to cope with a competition like this. In Spain in 1982 he was under great pressure to live up to the reputation he had been given. He was very young and some of his reactions were stupid. It was a hell of a responsibility for somebody as young as that to be saddled with being called the greatest player in the world, the new Pele and all that stuff. His response was a bit crazy.

'Now he has really grown up as a player. What impresses me particularly about him here is that he has a profound knowledge of what is required of him. He doesn't get carried away with the idea of trying to do it all on his own. If he finds himself in a situation where he is being held up, he's quite content to play simple passes, he'll just lay the ball off to somebody and stand still. Apart from what he can do on the ball, his wonderful first-time touch, the perfect weight of his passing, those terrific surges, he has marvellous vision. And nowadays he is always looking to stay on his feet, to use his incredible strength to resist challenges and carry on with the run.'

Moore feels that the very greatest of footballers should not be graded, just celebrated. But, understandably, his old adversary, Pele, is supreme in his experience. 'Pele was the most complete player I have ever seen, capable of everything. He could have played in just about any position on the field. Maradona wouldn't be his equal in the air, for instance. If I had to make a comparison between Maradona and another of the really great players, the closest to him for me was Cruyff, a guy who could destroy you from nothing and had the same fluency on the ball.'

When asked how he would try to stop Maradona, Moore smiled and admitted that he was happy to keep the issue hypothetical. 'If you had the problem it would take some working out,' he said. 'To mark man to man you would need an exceptionally, almost an impossibly quick guy to deal with him. On the other hand if you try to wait for him he will use the other Argentinian players as a screen to get on the blind side as he did when scoring the first of his two goals against Belgium. Because he is so left-footed you would try to force him on to his right foot. The Belgians did that on the first goal but he twisted and sent the ball in with a firm flick of his left.

'You could change your mind six times a day about how to deal with him. But if any team can come up with some formula it's likely to be the Germans. They've got quick-tackling defenders and traditionally they're the best scufflers in the world.'

There was an element of highly honourable scuffling in the way England came through a period of alarming Argentina supremacy in last Sunday's quarter-final to offer a late and thrilling retaliatory surge that brought one goal and might have added an equaliser. Suggesting that such equality would have been just is, however, as unrealistic as seeing the penetrative runs of Barnes in the last 20 minutes as proof that the winger should have been on the pitch from the start, rather than drafted in as a substitute.

It should be remembered that England could not force themselves into the match until Argentina sought to be passively protective towards a two-goal lead. While the South Americans were in their more aggressive mood, any attempt by Bobby Robson to deviate from the 4–4–2 that had emerged as easily his best formation would have courted calamity.

England deserve substantial credit for their spirited showing against the Argentines, though the theory that they would have stood a fifty-fifty chance of making the semi-finals had Maradona not used a hand to steer the first goal past an unbelievably lax Shilton is an exercise in self-delusion. Obviously, even if we leave aside the question of whether the British papers that denounced Maradona as a cheat would have observed the same propriety if England had gone through in similar circumstances, the great man was definitely out of order. Yet I cannot help thinking that reactions to what he did have been harsh, and not simply because he is of a generation conditioned to exploit such illicit good fortune.

Of course, he could have set a noble example to the youth of the world, lit a small torch against the corruption so sickeningly prevalent in sport. He would have been an international hero. But would his team-mates have seen him in that light? They should have done, but would they? Or would they have regarded such a glorious admission of guilt as outrageous vanity, the act of someone who wanted to play George Washington at their expense? Considering the emotional intensity of the bond that links Maradona to the team he leads and inspires, it would not be astonishing if he preferred to risk condemnation from the rest of us rather than invite their resentment and disapproval.

In any case, I must confess that, whatever his minor sins along the way, I am glad he will be out there on the wide expanse of the Aztec Stadium's field. West Germany, with formidable competitors like Berthold, Jakobs and the marking Matthaus in defence, Magath, Klaus Allofs and Voeller in attack and the prodigious Briegel in a hundred hurtful places, will battle fiercely.

But I hope Diego tears them apart. Where genius is concerned some of us are unashamedly prejudiced.

Jewels in a dung-heap

(*The Observer*, 6 July 1986)

FOOTBALL MUST be an even greater game than we thought it was. How else could it continue to thrill half the population of the planet with its grace and fluency and simply communicated excitements as presented in the World Cup finals while the competition itself is in constantly increasing danger of being suffocated under the dung-heap of hypocrisy, money-grabbing expediency and shameless manipulation piled upon it by FIFA and that overblown organisation's egregious president, Joao Havelange.

Havelange, who is to moral leadership what General George Custer was to military prudence, has developed a public blandness in justifying the unjustifiable, an affected aloofness to criticism that seeks to dismiss the most serious accusations about the excesses of his regime and basic questions about his personal finances as unworthy of response. His is a powerful nature in which unmistakable vanity is usually kept so skilfully under control that its principal expression is the soft-voiced, slightly exasperated manner he employed at press conferences in Mexico to brush aside perfectly legitimate enquiries as if they were the irrelevant rantings of an eccentric trouble-maker who had wandered in off the street.

Given the unendearing character of FIFA – it seems to sprawl across the globe as a vast and indulgent international club with a complicated hierarchy of perks and privileges, blazers, badges and expense accounts – Havelange will be hard to shift from the top. No one in his position has ever been as energetic or adroit in marshalling voting support, especially among the obscure new members of FIFA who keep coming over the hill in droves. He undoubtedly makes the extreme implications of FIFA democracy work for him. His cadaverous, faintly sinister presence is not the kind that would have instant appeal on the open hustings but clearly the Brazilian is an expert lobbyist in those other, shadowy areas where the whispered deals are made.

The inner convolutions of the arrangements that took the World Cup to Mexico are certainly not likely to be discussed out loud. Though most of us who visited that troubled country for the football carried away memories fragrant with the warmth and generosity of the Mexican people, nothing can dispel the odour of mercenary convenience, of favours done and paid for, that surrounded the decision to put the biggest sports show on earth on such a currently unsuitable stage.

The sense that the most intrinsically attractive of team games is being relentlessly exploited to boost egos and bank balances can only be made more depressing by the self-serving rationalisations that have emanated from Mexico City since the ball stopped rolling. In particular, the attempts of Havelange to refute fundamental criticisms of the 1986 finals by accusing competing teams of professional incompetence are offensive in their absurdity.

When he makes claims of perfection on behalf of the playing regulations applied in Mexico – refusing to acknowledge blatant examples of grossly inadequate refereeing, the bloated, ill-conceived shape of the competition or the intolerable arbitrariness of having penalty shoot-outs settle three of the four quarter-finals – he simply emphasises how far he is prepared to go in ramming his own grotesquely subjective view of what is good for football down the world's throat. Unless he is deposed quickly, the threat to the sport's integrity can only grow and, since such an abrupt removal seems about as probable as the impeachment of Ronald Reagan, the considerable pleasures provided on the other side of the Atlantic during June were bound to be tainted by uneasy suspicions of being at a dubiously subsidised party.

But such misgivings should not diminish our appreciation of entertainment whose general standards were conspicuously higher than the equivalent offering in Spain four years ago and may have featured a wider range of excitingly gifted teams than the World Cup finals have contained since they were previously played in Mexico 16 years ago.

Last Sunday's climax will be recalled as fairly muted, mainly because the greatest of contemporary footballers, Diego Maradona, did not reproduce the form with which he had earlier seen off England and Belgium. But credit should be given to the marking by Lothar Matthaus and Karl-Heinz Foerster and to the spirit, organisation and comprehensive football intelligence of the West German team who, emphatically, did not betray the traditions of a nation making a record fifth appearance in the final.

In any case, Maradona's beautiful talent had rather more than a marginal impact on the course of a match that produced the right result and had other substantial satisfactions, not least the proof offered by Argentina, and by Jorge Valdano especially, that the genius was in worthy company. Valdano subdued his habitually aggressive inclinations to deploy his extraordinary strength as a runner in positions where he could create a barrier to the surging forays of Briegel along the German left. His would have been the performance of the afternoon even if he had not galloped diagonally the length of the field before coolly sliding in Argentina's second goal. It must be said that Valdano's composure in thrusting home the sword was scarcely threatened by the contribution of Schumacher. The German goalkeeper had a quiet nightmare of a final.

Maradona's absence from the score-sheet last Sunday left Gary Lineker as the leading marksman in the tournament, a status that serves to stress the genuine quality of the young Midlander's gifts as a finisher. Lineker's prodigious sharpness did a lot to ensure that England made a pretty respectable showing after emerging from their miserable first-phase stumblings. A place in the last eight was just about what they deserved and getting there removed any need to feel regret about their endeavours or resentment over their dismissal.

If any of the hundreds of footballers who went home as losers were entitled to resentment, they were surely the thrilling representatives of Brazil, who in any logical retrospective assessment must be reckoned the most potent collection of talents let loose upon the competition. Even the excellence of France should have been buried by the exhilarating pace, variety and imagination of Brazil's superb attacking in that unforgettable Guadalajara quarter-final long before the cruelty of the penalty shoot-out intervened. The Brazilians could be installed now as legitimate favourites for the finals of 1990 in Italy. They have established a permanent organisational context within which their national squad can develop, and what a squad it promises to be. Zico, Junior, Socrates and Falcao are past tense but, of the men who so impressed in Mexico, Julio Cesar, Josimar, Branco, Elzo, Alemao, Careca, Muller and Paulo Silas are all 25 or under. Knowing Brazil's capacity for discovering new stars between World Cups, betting against their chances in four years' time calls for a strong mixture of rashness and European prejudice.

Remembering what they did in Guadalajara stirs the blood almost as much as the images burned into the brain by journeys endured behind the gloriously macho drivers appointed to hurtle press buses to and from the World Cup arenas last month. Peering through their windscreens as if through a gunsight, they gave the impression of being failed kamikaze pilots who had flunked because of excessive impetuosity. Some of the best took the run between the middle of Mexico City and Neza, the squalid, heart-breakingly impoverished suburb whose incongruously modern and well-appointed stadium housed two of Scotland's three matches. The road to Neza is the sort of thoroughfare where you are tempted to lift a manhole cover in search of a breath of air, except that in those parts there is the fear that manholes might contain men.

The drivers who took us in a blaring blur through those streets regarded everything in their way, living or inanimate, as a target. Dogs were particularly appealing and there were plenty of them. Some of the hairiest and most memorably unkempt dogs in existence were forever to be seen lying around in the dust like the discarded heads of lavatory cleaners' mops.

As one whose experience of their lurching dramatics was made even more interesting by having three cracked ribs, I can say that those mad

virtuosos will remain almost as vivid as Maradona in my recollection of
June 1986. Wherever they are now, I wish them well and hope they will
live a while longer to indulge their conviction that the Highway Code
should be left to cryptographers.

*Brazil did not develop into the force I hoped they would be in Italy,
though they were unlucky to be eliminated by an unattractive Argentine
team who finished as beaten finalists in a dismally disappointing
tournament.*

Assassination by the paper bullet

(*The Observer*, 27 May 1990)

THE RUBBISH hurled at Bobby Robson's head over the past few days reminds us that some of the worst of our country's hooliganism has nothing to do with tattoos, beer bellies or Union Jack singlets.

Its practitioners concentrate on vandalising the reputations and feelings of individuals and they were sure to have a spree at the England manager's expense after he and others mishandled the release of the news that he will return to club football with PSV Eindhoven, of Holland, at the conclusion of the World Cup finals. But nothing could have prepared Robson for the lunatic viciousness that has characterised the bitterest condemnations of his actions.

He is standing up remarkably well to a reviling onslaught which, as the representative of the *News of the World* observed, 'might be just about the worst the English have aimed at anybody since Lord Haw Haw'. At a press conference in the gardens of the team's seaside hotel 40 kilometres outside Cagliari yesterday, he permitted his middle-aged good looks to crumple occasionally into an expression of tortured gloom. But he is capable of doing that when the subject under discussion is nothing more calamitous than a forward's groin strain. He is obviously strengthened by the knowledge that the real blame for the current mess belongs elsewhere.

Those who feared that the English would pollute these finals have been proved right before the appearance of a single rampaging fan. The contamination has come with the arrival in Sardinia of a parcel of values so phoney and malodorous that they should have been delivered in a garbage truck. Of course, the rest of the world is not likely to pay much attention to the chauvinist hypocrisies and absurd moral posturings of the crudest journalistic assaults on Robson. But we are obliged to wonder what has happened to the perspectives and sense of balance of our society when *Today* newspaper, having branded him a liar, a cheat and traitor, a 'pathetic shambles of a man', continues an editorial comment by saying: 'In previous centuries, a man who commited such treachery would have been sent to the Tower.'

In any century, someone who thinks that is a legitimate allusion in a piece about a football manager changing his job should be sent to a padded room.

And that, when all the disingenuous emotionalism of his persecutors has been stripped away, is what is happening here – Robson is moving from a job many of those detractors insist he shouldn't have to join new employers who covet him sufficiently to provide a two-year contract worth £500,000. Such a definition of the episode is an over-simplification but a far more honest and reasonable one than that forming the basis for all the pseudo-patriotic humbug and puritanical homilies emanating from some unlikely pillars of rectitude.

Apart from raking over sexual exploits from a past that has been, to say the least, carnally complicated, the main concern of the assassins has been to convey the impression that Robson is running out on his players and the nation on the eve of the World Cup. Of the extra-marital sex, it must be said that the deceits associated with it can never be endearing or increase respect for those involved. But aside from acknowledging that men with rather more momentous responsibilities than the England manager's (John F. Kennedy and David Lloyd George, to name everybody's favourite examples) have fornicated enthusiastically without being abused as he is, it is worth mentioning that so many stones are being thrown from within glass houses that we may be deafened by a great crashing and splintering any minute now.

In any case, the big revelations about his infidelities occurred a year ago. As any sane person would have guessed, they had zero effect on the morale of the national team, though one of the tabloids might have been tempted to argue that stories of their leader's potency had encouraged the lads to run up the sequence of 17 matches without defeat which only ended against Uruguay last Tuesday.

So, in spite of the kiss-and-tell (more properly bed-and-blab) tales being sold by a former lover, there isn't enough fuel left in the sex scandal to power the juggernaut of vituperation that has been rolling over Robson. It has relied heavily on the allegations that he is guilty of treasonable defection for personal gain. These are outrageously serious charges to base on what seems to be essentially a case of ill-timed negotiations about his professional future presented in a desperately bad light by the leaking of the story before his colleagues on the England coaching staff and the players in his squad could be informed of the facts.

To say that the decision to move on after the World Cup (he never thought of going before it) is itself unforgivable treachery is farcical, especially when so many of those saying it have been trying so hard to bundle him on to his bike. There is a long tradition of national team managers arranging to take other jobs at the end of major tournaments and it is being maintained at these finals by Franz Beckenbauer of West Germany and Sebastiao Lazaroni of Brazil, who is contracted to take over Fiorentina. While Rinus Michels was guiding Holland to triumph in the European Championship of 1988, everyone knew that he would move immediately afterwards to the German club Bayer Leverkusen. No one suggested that his success in the championship was tainted by that intention.

The timing of Robson's acceptance of the offer from PSV Eindhoven was far from ideal but neither that nor the further year remaining on his contract with the Football Association can remotely justify the accusations of heinous betrayal. Claims that he should have refused to entertain the Dutch club's approach, that he should have chased them away with declarations that he couldn't allow any thought other than the challenge for the World Cup to enter his mind at this time, are scarcely realistic. Whether he was right to interpret a meeting about two weeks ago with Bert Millichip, the chairman of the FA Council, as clearly indicating that the Association meant to part with him when the present agreement expired, or Mr Millichip's more noncommittal version of the exchange is seen as accurate, the simple truth is that anything short of a glittering performance in this tournament would have been unlikely to save him. Considering the battering he has already suffered through much of his eight years as manager, could he be blamed, at 57, for deciding that it was time to tip-toe through the tulips towards his exit?

Having witnessed the way Robson has been hounded, Graham Taylor, of Aston Villa, who is such an odds-on favourite to succeed him that insiders believe there is no longer any contest, might be excused for asking himself if the attractions of the post can ever compensate for the risk of degradation. Robson is particularly aggrieved over being labelled a money-grabber. 'I took a fairly heavy cut in pay when I stopped being manager of Ipswich to take the England job and I have remained on a relatively modest salary for eight years while others with comparable credentials in the club game have spiralled far above me,' he said yesterday. 'I have never chased money.'

His salary of slightly more than £80,000 a year is indeed a fraction of the sums commanded by such as Kenny Dalglish at Liverpool and, although his habit of having a regular deal with a newspaper has always appeared a questionable arrangement for a national manager, the word is that the connection which has existed with the *Mail on Sunday* for the past four years pays him appreciably less than his previous contract with the *Sunday Mirror*. Inevitably, the Sardinian air was laden yesterday with propositions guaranteeing him bucketfuls of tabloid gold. It is to be hoped that he resists. There are plenty of reasons for criticising Bobby Robson as a manager but as a man he certainly does not deserve the merciless abuse inflicted on him. There is already a tide of sympathy rising in his favour. If he keeps his dignity, it may swell to a flood.

When the spoils fall to the spoilers

(*The Observer*, 17 June 1990)

THERE ARE PEOPLE around this World Cup who believe that the best way to solve the problems of British football is to jail the hooligans and take the ball into protective custody.

Even an inanimate object, they will tell you, should be saved from the abusive treatment habitually inflicted by the footballers who represent England, Ireland and Scotland. As for neutral spectators, the torture administered to them in Cagliari a few nights ago was almost a violation of the Geneva Convention. Unless the teams sent out by Bobby Robson and Jack Charlton use this weekend to provide an antidote to the contaminating effects of their crude collision, the rest of the world will start to see the Football League as a serious menace to the worthwhile values of the game. Of course, by the time you read this, the Saturday late show with the Dutch at the Sant'Elia Stadium may have restored some English prestige and if, in Palermo today, the Republic can force the Egyptians to accept that they are here to behave like outsiders then criticism of Big Jack and his methods will be drowned in celebration.

But a couple of satisfactory scorelines, or even a clutch of them, will not necessarily disperse the deep uneasiness stirred in many of us every time our football is paraded alongside the more exciting and graceful version offered by other countries. It may seem that a Scotsman needs outrageous cheek to question the neighbours' aesthetics after a display against Costa Rica which, when the intervention of a little ill-luck has been duly recognised, remains a monument to ponderous inadequacy. However, the Scottish squad can reasonably be left out on the edge of the debate, since they were identified before leaving home as by far the weakest their nation had ever dispatched to the World Cup and merely confirmed that diagnosis in their laborious loss to the Costa Ricans. Their standards in that match were exemplified by their trundling attempts to break from the midfield, moving at a pace that might have been bettered by a woman pushing a pram.

Somewhat more was expected of England and Ireland but, even if both progress beyond the first phase of the tournament, they are obviously going to have difficulty in capturing the affection and admiration of anyone outside their own armies of nationalistic supporters. Does that matter? Isn't winning all that counts? In war maybe, but in sport a few eccentrics still cling to different, cornier priorities, like the old-fashioned pursuit of style and even glory.

What has been produced elsewhere in this World Cup has not always been stylish or glorious. The reigning champions, Argentina, are as yet unconvincing and Maradona himself shows signs of developing mortal feet, though referees continue to overlook fouls as if he had the hand of God. The Brazilians, if we except the splendours of Careca's front play, seem as eager to appear workmanlike as brilliant, the Italians' fluent advances founder around the penalty area in a way which reminds us that the best finishers in their league are foreigners, and the Dutch side who drew with Egypt betrayed a lack of motivation all the more depressing because it showed most glaringly in two of the greatest players alive, Rijkaard and Van Basten.

But, whatever their blemishes, Brazil and Italy gave us flourishes of thrilling creative football and the West Germans – whose game is informed by ethnic and traditional factors not vastly dissimilar to our own – buried the Yugoslavs with surges of adventurous, skilful attacking. Add to all that the exuberant contempt for reputations brought out of Africa by Cameroon and Egypt and it will be seen immediately that England–Ireland was a shameful insult to its context.

Wind and rain made conditions horribly awkward in Cagliari last Monday but if the match had taken place on an ice floe at the height of a tornado its ugliness would hardly have been excusable. Pigeon races have been won in less flying time than the ball had that night.

Our football made its entrance to the World Cup like someone arriving at a symphony concert on a skateboard with a ghetto-blaster turned up to full volume. This was, as somebody said, yob football, the kind that made you feel the players should have been wearing tattoos instead of strips. It wasn't dirty, in the sense that the men involved weren't malevolent towards one another, but they were cruel enough to the uncommitted in the crowd. That the problem can be traced back to the miserable shortcomings of the current First Division is undeniable. A league blighted by so much poverty of ambition, imagination and technique is not going to export enlightenment and artistry and managers of national teams obliged to recruit from it must be perennially handicapped.

Nevertheless, it is fair to ask such managers to show an inclination to rage against the dying of the light in our domestic game. And it is here that a provocative irony occurs in any honest analysis of the impact England and Ireland are having on football's supreme tournament. It boils down to the simple fact that Jack Charlton, because of the potency of his leadership and the astonishing scale of his accomplishments, may have more to answer for at the end of the day than the less influential Bobby Robson.

Charlton has transformed Irish football, given the Republic's players and supporters, indeed the entire population, years of excitement and a status in the sport they could previously only dream about. He has done all of this with a playing method that achieves results and demands absolute respect. But, even for someone as pro-Irish and as fond of Charlton as I am, loving the way his teams play is an impossibility. I don't expect Jack, or the multitude who are ready to canonise him, to give a damn about an outsider's reaction. They must realise, however, that if he persists obsessively (as he surely will) with his smothering accentuation of the negative on the field, the claim that his success comes from mixing English grit with Irish wit will be blatantly untenable. His team are cast unmistakably in his pragmatic English mould.

Perhaps such considerations are meaningless compared with all the pleasure the recent achievements of the Republic's footballers have spread through their countrymen. Perhaps, too, we should remember when witnessing the scuffling nature of many of those achievements that there is a genuine form of glory, a hint of nobility almost, to be gained in sport from making courage and sweat and determination triumph over superior talent. Yet a playing philosophy that ruthlessly submerges creativity in the interests of effective spoiling has to be worrying. It is the lopsidedness of Charlton's creed, his refusal to attempt a true balance between legitimate, hustling disruption of the opposition and assertion of his own side's skills, that generates misgivings about his long-term influence. Sometimes English football, with its simplistic physicality, appears to be digging a hole and trying to drag the rest of the world into it – and Jack has long arms.

England may be due most of the blame for Monday's shambles, since they are supposed to be a power in the competition, equipped with outstandingly gifted individuals, and were therefore disgraced by their failure to suggest they would ever find a solution to Ireland's harrying. But Charlton must acknowledge that his approach virtually guarantees such turmoil, that he in fact seeks it to a considerable extent, betting on his men's capacity to establish and exploit second-phase possession of the ball. There is nothing remotely immoral about that (and the Republic are conspicuously fair battlers) but it does not often make for an enthralling spectacle, unless you are heavily prejudiced by birth.

Even being a patriotic Irishman is not always sufficient to make the Republic's performances uplifting. John Giles, who was the principal creator in the Leeds team with whom Charlton made his name and who was subsequently manager of the national squad, conveys as much as he comments expertly on the World Cup in the Dublin studios of Irish Television. There is no taint of envy in Giles, who is a strong enough nature to be instantly believed when he says that Jack is bringing all the unifying joy to the nation that was his own consuming objective in the job, but as a master practitioner of the game and superb interpreter of its refinements the Dubliner cannot stifle his profound concern about his old team-mate's priorities.

'Much of what Jack is doing is magnificent,' Giles said when we talked on the telephone on Friday. 'The spirit and organisation and the success he has brought to the team are all wonderful. But to say I regularly enjoy watching them play would be dishonest. He has been absolutely brilliant in making the players aware of the importance of what they do when they don't have the ball. No other country in the World Cup can compete with them in that vital aspect of the game and it is a huge professional achievement. But that is where Jack puts the emphasis all the time, and so his major strength is also a weakness. There is no real emphasis on what would be regarded as the traditional beauty of the game – what you do when you *have* the ball.

'When you do have the ball it is your duty to use it as constructively as you can. Sometimes that may mean the centre-half hoofing it into the stands, because there is no reasonable alternative, but in the main you must have a structure which allows your skilful players to deliver the goods. Jack had no room for the likes of Liam Brady. He prefers a Townsend. Yet on the park, as everywhere else, you must speculate to accumulate. If you invest in real skill you will get real returns.

'With Jack there's hardly any structure at all for using the ball when his team are in possession. If a full-back gets it and there is a constructive pass on to someone in midfield the fella will know that's not what Jack wants, and he'll knock the ball up the line into space. It doesn't thrill me too much. But what we are seeing from Jack may be the new reality of football. If he gets through the first phase and in among the other survivors in the knock-out stages, he could do big, big damage.'

John Giles was talking about damage to the opposition. But – since he had earlier wondered seriously if Jack Charlton might have preferred the defensive attributes of Mick McCarthy to those of Bobby Moore – perhaps a few purists would take a different meaning from his words.

The poverty of this world

(*The Observer*, 8 July 1990)

JUST WHEN THEY were helping to raise the tone of a disappointing World Cup party, England were callously tossed out along with the empties.

They had not even committed the offence of losing a football match. But neither had the hosts and they, too, found themselves sitting on the kerb holding their heads – and wondering how the hell they ever stood for such house rules in their own house.

Everybody accepts that even World Cup semi-finals cannot be allowed to drag on endlessly but there is widespread agreement that the penalty shoot-out has too many flaws to be a tolerable means of accelerating a settlement. Since its worst defect is that it distorts a team game into an ordeal for individuals in isolation, a far better compromise in the event of a draw at the end of 90 minutes would be to remove two or three players from each side and then play on until a goal is scored. Considering that space on the field has been drastically shrunk by the rising level of athleticism, there is already a case for reducing the number of players forming a team from 11 to 10. Cutting it further to, say, eight at the start of sudden-death extra time would probably produce a result soon enough to suit even the peremptory demands of television. Sixteen men would play something very different from (and no doubt inferior to) the traditional game. But it would retain more of the true essence than a penalty shoot-out ever can. Defeat would remain the collective experience it is meant to be, not the kind of concentrated personal misery it became for Stuart Pearce and Chris Waddle in Turin on Wednesday night.

'You obviously do what you can to make the lads feel better but nothing you say means very much,' said Gary Lineker, who had struck his own penalty against West Germany as effectively as the two with which he completed the unjust execution of Cameroon in Naples the previous Sunday. 'A miss like that is going to stay with you for a long time, maybe forever.'

It would be scant consolation for Waddle to know that the wild slash of his left leg which seemed in more danger of sending the ball out of the Delle Alpi Stadium than into the net was almost certainly an irrelevance. Pearce had already failed and the instinct that enabled Peter Shilton to

dive the right way for all the four penalties taken by the Germans had
done him no good against the quality of their striking. He was scarcely
favourite to do any better with a fifth kick had it been needed. Shilton,
who went into last night's third-place decider with Italy in Bari as the
most impressive goalkeeper in the tournament, would find it hard to keep
a smile off his 40-year-old face if he heard some of the fancy tributes to his
23-year-old German counterpart, Bodo Illgner, that were occasioned by
the saving of Pearce's penalty. According to the eulogists, that stop was
testimony to young Bodo's iron nerve and owed much to a brief but
intense study he had made of the demeanour of the English kickers while
they were waiting to have a go at him.

From where I was sitting, what happened was that Bodo dived
sideways but left his legs behind long enough to block a shot which
Pearce, predictably going for power rather than direction, had struck
more or less straight at the middle of the goal. The more romantic version
is worrying only because it suggests that some people are willing to see the
shoot-out as a serious extension of the game, to be dignified by detailed
analysis. In fact, it is first cousin to a roll of the dice and should be done
away with without delay.

Bobby Robson coped well with the pain of its consequences on
Thursday morning as he talked at relaxed length in the sunlit garden of
his team's attractive country hotel near Asti, where plentiful birdsong
held its own with the noise of traffic from a distant autostrada and the
roar of an occasional plane heading into Milan or Turin. Naturally, pride
and disappointment mingled in most of what he said. But the lack of
agitation in his features and the easy coherence of his reflections on the
night before and the entire eight years of his England managership
showed that he recognised it as a coup to be going out on a high.

His right to feel good is based on how his men performed in their semi-
final rather than the achievement of reaching that stage of a World Cup
whose dubious standards can be accurately inferred from the presence of
Argentina in the final. On the road to this evening's showdown with
Germany in the Olympic Stadium in Rome, the Argentines have won only
two matches outright and one of those, the 1–0 defeat of Brazil, was such
a case of larceny that they should have been playing in prison denim.

The format of the competition (those accursed penalties again) and the
depressing inadequacy of other challengers have permitted Argentina to
scuffle and stumble their way through. Sporadic flourishes of Maradona's
severely diminished but still magical talent have only served to remind us
of how miserably this World Cup compares with the more memorable of
its predecessors. There were more undeniably great players performing at
their peak in the Brazil team who won in Mexico in 1970 than have been
paraded by all the 24 countries that started out here. And in addition to
the Brazil of Pele, Gerson, Tostao, Rivelino, Carlos Alberto, Jairzinho

and Clodoaldo, that World Cup had the best England team I have ever watched – with the towering gifts of Moore and Bobby Charlton superbly supported in almost every position – as well as a West Germany squad containing Beckenbauer, Overath and Muller.

If the 1970 World Cup finals were the finest of the seven series this reporter has covered since 1966, these have been very much the poorest. Don Howe, England's coach, while heaping praise on the players he works with for building up to the excellence of Wednesday night, concurs with my low rating of the overall quality, citing the extreme shortage of outstanding forward play as especially disappointing. England–West Germany in Turin was not one of the epics of the game. But it was a splendid collision of two good and positive teams, a rousing, skilful contest fought out in an uncompromising but thoroughly sporting spirit.

The Germans have done most to push back the tide of mediocrity in Italia '90. Yet their manager, Franz Beckenbauer, is justified in asserting that the Italians when on song in the earlier stages (notably against Czechoslovakia) looked capable of keeping the Cup at home.

Maybe Italy became acquainted with their own vulnerability during exposure to the determination of the Republic of Ireland, who rose to new heights in the Olympic Stadium last weekend, punctuating their usual spirited hustling with sufficient smooth passing to make it obvious that just a little more pace and sharpness in the box might have brought historic victory. Any hope that Italy would rediscover their swagger in time to deal with Argentina in the semi-final was reduced by Azeglio Vicini's decision to restore the strangely bland Vialli to his attack and, with Argentina at last finding form and frequently breaking forward on confident runs, the hosts were soon sliding towards death by penalties.

They are salvaging less from the wreckage of their challenge than are their opponents in last night's third-place match. England were often a dreary sight before last week but – apart from knowing that the struggle with Germany was as evenly balanced as any football game can be, that losing was more a technicality than a reality – they can be reassured by the extent to which these two hours confirmed the emergence of a new nucleus of high-calibre players.

There are at least five in their early to mid-twenties around whom the successor to Bobby Robson as manager (presumably Graham Taylor of Aston Villa) may be able to construct a fairly formidable unit. At Asti Robson was musing on the irony of leaving the job when his support in the country is probably stronger than it has ever been and the resources at his disposal perhaps the most promising he has had. But he has to admit that some of the most remarkable contributions on Wednesday came from men who might have been involved prominently in his plans sooner than they were. That is conspicuously true of Gascoigne, defined by the manager as 'probably the best young player in the tournament . . . one of the finest to emerge in Britain in a number of years', a 23-year-old 'on the threshold of something that is quite unique'.

Platt is another about to make himself indispensable. It is too early to suggest that he can be a Bryan Robson but Platt's rate of development hardens the likelihood that the great captain's international career is over. No such elegiac thoughts are in order about John Barnes but he is undoubtedly the saddest figure in the England party at this moment. All the glories of his club form have stubbornly refused yet again to translate into successful performances for his country.

Even Pearce and Waddle are not sure to feel more troubled than he will on the journey home.

End of the world

(*The Sunday Times*, 3 July 1994)

IT WAS the grubby tumult of an unscheduled press conference in Dallas on Thursday evening that most effectively conveyed the sadness seeping through the squalor of Diego Maradona's expulsion from the World Cup. As a mass of hands holding microphones closed around him like a carnivorous plant, the drawn, slightly hunted look on his Spanish-Indian face said more about the nature and origins of his predicament than the predictable words of denial and complaint that came from his mouth.

The evidence that he had been using forbidden drugs to lose weight at an unnatural rate partly explained that look. But another form of loss, an imminent and perhaps permanent separation from the game that has been the steadiest theme of his dishevelled life, showed there too.

Since Maradona was in his teens, his has been the most resonant name in the world's most popular sport. But its capacity to evoke images of skills as dazzling as any ever seen on the football field has been swamped in recent years by recurring scandal. When that drug test proved positive there was less justification for shock than for sorrow.

This is only the third time since these finals were first played 64 years ago that a player has been expelled for drug use. Nobody was betting on coincidence when it emerged that the individual condemned by his urine sample was a 33-year-old whose addiction to cocaine previously caused him to be banned from football for 15 months and put him at odds with the law in Italy and (after he fled Europe to escape charges that are still outstanding) in his native Argentina. Such precedents ensured sceptical resistance to initial reports that this latest offence was simply a case of innocent medication that went wrong.

The apologist argument seemed to gain some weight when the proscribed substance traced to Maradona was identified as ephedrine, which is so far from being a heavy among pharmaceutical villains that it can be found in medicines on sale in chemists' shops to relieve the symptoms of asthma and nasal congestion. FIFA, football's governing body, killed that defence at birth by announcing that Maradona's sample had, in fact, betrayed an improbable cocktail of five drugs which were all ephedrine-related but would never be present as a combination in anything sold over the counter. Soon the Argentine football authorities – anxious to distance themselves from the wrongdoing and minimise the possibility of losing the three World Cup points their team earned in the 2–1 defeat of Nigeria that led to the fateful drug test – sought to pre-empt official action by declaring their captain and soiled icon persona non grata.

FIFA stepped in anyway, imposing an interim ban that will prevent Maradona from playing as a professional anywhere in the world between now and the conclusive decision on his future due to be taken after the World Cup ends on 17 July. Thus the stage was set for that unedifying press conference in Dallas.

Maradona's statements were mainly concerned with denying he had taken drugs or let down the people who love him. There were also pious, if not particularly humble, expressions of hope that his team-mates (whose demoralised reaction to his melodramatic removal from their midst had just been demonstrated in a 2–0 loss to Bulgaria) would show 'that Argentina goes on living without Maradona'.

Of the FIFA ban, he said: 'They beat me over the head without any compunction. It hurts me so badly … my soul is broken.' When one sentence was translated as a declaration that he did not want 'another revenge', it had to be deduced that revenge meant comeback.

It has been easy to read in his tortured features at moments of stress in the past two or three weeks the cost of the unnatural demands he made on himself physically and psychologically to further the World Cup comeback that has ended so disastrously. His reasons for taking an ephedrine cocktail have no apparent connection with the eagerness he has shown in the past to snort cocaine. But the actions could be linked nevertheless.

Cocaine abuse was the manifestation of a self-destructive lifestyle and a personality lurching out of control. One of the most blatant indications that Maradona was letting himself go was always the rapid accumulation of fat on his stocky, almost squat physique and it seems likely that it was when he felt the need of chemical assistance in the periodic blitzes on his surplus weight that ephedrine came into the picture.

If ephedrine is taken in concentrated doses it can act as an adrenaline-like stimulant, with the effect of increasing energy and helping the taker to lose weight. Since Maradona is credited with twice gaining and shedding nearly two stones during the past year, it is legitimate to guess that the cocktail hour may have assumed a special importance in his routine.

His constant battles with crazily fluctuating weight and his insistence on surrounding himself with a sycophantic entourage are not the only respects in which Maradona behaves more like some wayward boxers of his generation than the majority of footballers. That is not surprising. The suddenness of his elevation from the direst poverty in the Buenos Aires slum of Villa Fiorito, where he was the fifth of eight children his parents raised in a two-roomed shanty on a mud street, to all the self-indulgence a tidal wave of money can buy, is a phenomenon more common to the fight business than football.

But the fawning, clamorously personal adulation that flooded in on Maradona wherever he went in the early days of his career is something to which no fighter, not even Muhammad Ali, has been subjected. Nor has any other footballer experienced it on the same scale. Pele, the Brazilian whose achievements probably confirmed him as the greatest player the game has ever seen, was an obvious candidate. But he had a personality that enabled him to take the benefits of celebrity without allowing it to derail his own sense of himself. Maybe a disciplined upbringing in a small town in the interior of Minas Gerais state in south-eastern Brazil was a help.

Coming from the hard streets on the edge of a big city, using the smartness acquired there to compensate for the curtailment of his formal education at the age of 13, Maradona might have been expected to have an equal, if different, talent for survival. But for years he has been courting doom.

Whether because of the core elements in his own nature or his exposure as a child-prodigy to the powerful example of cynical adults, he has been encouraged by success to become increasingly volatile, vain and selfishly capricious. Inevitably, he discovered that the public could be even more capricious than he was and when his reputation among the Italian fans went sour it did so to such a spectacular extent that in 1990 he was voted the most hated man in Italy.

He started learning the perils and advantages of being a household name as a nine-year-old when his prodigious ability to juggle a ball with his feet made him a television entertainer. But, though the advantages predominated for a long time after he made his first-division debut with Argentinos Juniors 10 days short of his 16th birthday, the perils always threatened to get him in the end.

Now that they have, many are inclined to shrug and tell us that what we are seeing is merely the comeuppance of an incorrigible low-life. In support of this condemnation, there is an indictment that lists Maradona's drug troubles of three years ago, together with his admitted appetite for prostitutes and a prolonged police investigation into alleged links with the Camorra, the Neapolitan mafia, not to mention the odd paternity suit, plus a catalogue of more minor incidents stretching into this year and the occasion in February when he discouraged besieging reporters with a barrage of airgun pellets. FIFA's application of the boot has, suggest the bitterest voices, rid the World Cup of a squalid embarrassment.

George Vecsey, a *New York Times* columnist whose credentials include not only values that are usually sane and humane but a genuine

fondness for football that is rare among his brethren, did not hold back
when he put the case for the prosecution on Friday.

'Diego Armando,' wrote Vecsey, with an unaffectionate inclusion of
Maradona's middle name, 'is a raging one-man cornucopia of menace,
anger, suspicion, swagger, callousness and contempt. He materialised in
Argentina's first two games, scoring a goal in one, still with a master's
passing touch, but visually he was a creepy, blustering gangster. He
would take a flop on the earth and when he saw it was doing him no good,
he would arise with this arrogant smirk and make bad-actor's gestures
that said, "Well, you can't blame a guy for trying".

'He could still play. Give him that. But he knew he was putting one
over on us. He had beaten the odds. He had come back from the
graveyard of the socially unacceptable to prance around on somebody
else's lawn. He's been out of control for years, an international monster,
created by adoring publics in Argentina and Italy, with too much money
and too little discipline and no respect for anybody.'

Vecsey's uncharacteristic lack of compassion and the merciless
extravagance of his criticism render his reaction unacceptable. He makes
it sound as if he would have found the sight of Hitler as centre-forward
for Germany preferable to that of Maradona in the Argentine midfield.
The truth is that, for many of us, neither Maradona's antisocial conduct
off the field nor the cheap strokes he occasionally seeks to pull on it could
ever be enough to diminish the pleasure we took in finding him such an
effective influence on his fourth world championship.

None of the other players on duty in the United States could hope to
match his inspired touch on the ball or the tactical cunning he has
amassed in 21 World Cup appearances dating from 1982. Had he been
permitted to turn out for a 22nd time, he would have been the only player
ever to do so.

Admirers believe he should have collected the record long ago, that his
participation in the World Cup should have begun in 1978, the year
Argentina won the trophy on their own soil. His extreme youth and
inexperience persuaded Cesar Menotti, the Argentine manager, that
Maradona was not ready for glory in 1978. But before he was out of his
teens he was being recognised as a player who could be mentioned in the
same breath as Pele.

When I first saw him at work with the ball he was practising under the
supervision of Menotti at a sports complex near Buenos Aires. He was
totally absorbed in repeatedly sprinting along a touchline and crossing
the ball in full stride, an exercise that is not elaborate but calls for high
skill if the centres are to be varied in trajectory and consistently precise.
Maradona's were. Already he had a compelling presence, an aura of the
exceptional, and he drew every pair of eyes in the place.

It has not always been to his advantage that he has continued to have that effect as he has moved from Boca Juniors to Barcelona, to Napoli, to Sevilla and then, in September of 1993, back to Argentine club football with the unfashionable Newell's Old Boys. The Old Boys, like so many of his previous employers, found him playing the old soldier and sacked him for missing training in February of this year.

As recently as late March, when he was a fat spectator on the bench as Argentina were beaten 2–0 by Brazil in Recife, it seemed inconceivable he could be a factor in the World Cup finals. But he and his entourage duly turned up in America to form a team within a team at the Argentine camp in Massachusetts. What happened in the privacy of that group is now stirring bad blood among the members.

The sad slimmer who was the centre of all this is no longer to be seen. He is said to have sought comfort with his wife and two daughters. The memories he carries from the 1994 World Cup will be even grimmer than those he took away from Spain in 1982, when he exploded wildly after being severely battered, and suffered the disgrace of being ordered off. His recollections of Italy in 1990 must be mixed at best. In spite of a serious ankle problem, he did lead Argentina as far as the final, where they lost a dismal match to West Germany, but the team under his command were of a brutish disposition.

For him, and everyone who ever thrilled to the impossible reach of his virtuosity, the one memory that will never dim is Mexico in 1986. The prejudiced will maintain that even there he blemished his towering domination of the event unforgivably with the 'Hand of God' goal against England. But, while acknowledging that he was wrong to let Argentina profit from a goal turned in by his hand and wrong again when he joked about the incident afterwards, I have always wondered if the British papers that denounced Maradona as a cheat would have fumed as convincingly had England gone through to the semi-finals in similar circumstances.

In any case, we need look no further than the same quarter-final to see the other side of the man's contribution to football. His second goal – climax to an incredibly sustained and dramatic surge in which the deft touches of his left foot and innumerable shifts of balance and direction left a clutch of England defenders mesmerised and trailing – was as great as any scored in the World Cup since its inception in 1930.

As he braces himself to cope with the loss of the irreplaceable, maybe we should try to remember Diego Maradona at his finest. We should also admit that, however nasty he has been at times, he is not quite Satan – though he could play like the devil.

America looks towards a new horizon

(*The Sunday Times*, 10 July 1994)

WHETHER THE consequences of America's creditable showing in this World Cup turn out to be important or trivial, lasting or fleeting, here and now there is an obligation to recognise the admirable qualities of the players who produced it. The natural tendency is to lunge into predictions about the impact their achievements will have on the future of professional football in the USA. But, since such forecasts are invalidated by the scarcity of reliable evidence, it makes sense to remember that sport has less to do with expansionist dreams and commercial projections than with the celebration of the moment.

It was certainly quite a moment, prolonged and exhilarating, that the US team created. If they had accomplished no more than the silencing of a lot of smart mouths from coast to coast, the marginalising of all those tiresome, insular cynics who sought to portray football as a pastime for adolescent girls that might contaminate the manhood of the nation, they would deserve widespread gratitude. But what they did out on the field had a much more positive dimension. They played with such honesty and seriousness of purpose, with such a strong and integrated spirit, that ultimately their efforts were not merely impressive but enough to evoke an emotional warmth – and not only from their countrymen.

Perhaps the unprecedented enthusiasm for the planet's favourite game that has been generated among Americans by the World Cup, and their own footballers' exciting contribution to it, will obliterate all the lessons of recent history and lay the foundation of a mass conversion. Packed stadiums and astonishing television ratings (golf and baseball have been hammered in fair combat) must give Alan Rothenberg, principal organiser of the tournament, plenty of credibility as he seeks sponsorship and TV deals for the national league, involving 12 cities, that is due to be launched in April 1995.

Yet Major League Soccer will have to overcome intimidating problems, not least the difficulty of assembling enough indigenous players of talent to make good the promise that only a strictly limited quota of foreigners will be permitted at each club. Given the warlike noises emanating from the existing American Professional Soccer League, who have many of the likeliest players under contract but have been denied the Division One status granted by FIFA to MLS, that issue alone could be a nightmare. And there will be others.

So Rothenberg will have need of the resilience that was one of the most attractive attributes of the USA's World Cup contenders. Their success owed much to a hard core of optimism, the can-do factor, the conviction that bucking the odds is part of the American way. There was nothing offensively brash or damagingly naive about their self-belief. When confronted by the greater sophistication of Romania, Colombia and Switzerland, even when asked to cope with Brazil, they did not react like the outmatched boxer who closes his eyes and starts swinging, gambling that if he is knocked out he will at least be given credit for going down bravely. They responded to the sometimes enigmatic methods of their coach, Bora Milutinovic, who was born in Yugoslavia but has spent many of his 49 years as a nomad in a tracksuit, acquiring considerable worldliness and a fractured version of several languages. Milutinovic distinguished himself at previous World Cups with the unformidable squads of Mexico (1986) and Costa Rica (1990) and, although some of the US players found him a puzzling, almost mystical figure, he again proved remarkably effective at inculcating the right habits and attitudes.

By the time they qualified to face Brazil in the second round, his men were neither awed nor cocky, just ready to do themselves justice in front of a huge and festive Fourth of July crowd at Stanford Stadium. Of course, justice in that instance meant losing. Brazil were galvanised rather than weakened after being reduced to 10 men a minute before the interval, when a blow from Leonardo's elbow broke a bone behind Tab Ramos's left ear – sending the victim to hospital and putting the perpetrator's thrilling skills on the sidelines for the rest of the competition. Once bone struck bone, a nasty injury and an ordering-off were inevitable, but this was a case where the results were out of all proportion to the motives of the offender. Ramos had been fouling Leonardo, clinging to him with an aggravating persistence that earned the American a yellow card before he was felled. Television replays support the contrite Brazilian's claim that all he intended to do was break free of the pestering attentions from behind, that he never imagined Ramos's head was in the path of his elbow. Leonardo handled himself with dignity in the days following the incident and the regret he expressed when he visited Ramos in hospital came across as sincere. But, even if the only charge that could be made against him was that he acted recklessly, that was more than sufficient to damn him. Brazil's efforts to have his sentence lightened had little chance of succeeding.

The blow itself was frightening. 'I heard this noise in my head that was like a train going through, and all I thought was Oh my God, I'm going to die right here,' Ramos reported afterwards. It was not testimony to make FIFA lenient with Leonardo.

The US, already deprived by suspension of the vital services of John Harkes on the left side of midfield, had no semblance of creative thrust after the confident, inventive Ramos was removed from the right side. As pressure mounted, the wholehearted defiance offered by Marcelo Balboa and Alexi Lalas in central defence could not be expected to hold out against the increasingly urgent probings of Romario and Bebeto, and it didn't. Lalas, who reminds some of us of a young Billy Connolly but impressed *Sports Illustrated* as resembling the love-child of Rasputin and Phyllis Diller, gave himself and his game further nationwide exposure later in the week when he fooled around with David Letterman, host of America's most talked-about talk show. As Letterman trimmed Lalas's straggly red beard, and both booted balls into the audience, outsiders struggled to remember when Americans last made such an affectionate fuss about losers.

A change of heart was justified. The US team have a player called Tom Dooley, but they don't have the slightest cause to hang down their heads and cry.

Highs and lows of Hagi

(*The Sunday Times*, 10 July 1994)

SHOULD GHEORGHE HAGI become just a fraction more clinical in slicing open the opposition, he may have to play the rest of the World Cup in a mask and gown. There could well be better teams than Romania left in these finals, and there are definitely several who are conspicuously more athletic, but nowhere else is there the outright reliance on incisive technique that characterises the counter-attacking method within which Hagi excels.

That the Romanians take the good wishes of a multitude of neutrals into their quarter-final against Sweden today is further confirmation that the aesthetic approach still carries some clout in modern football. Such reassurance has been available in welcome profusion throughout this competition, but there has been an element of almost intellectual calculation in Romania's play that has set them apart, even in the company of notably skilful squads. Their game is a celebration of cleverness, an insistent, faintly provocative declaration of faith in their own wit, perceptiveness and rich capacity to make hurtful use of the ball.

At times they seem to be of another age, of an era when footballers (and fighters) were unlikely to be seen prancing on their toes or regularly sprinting into attacks, when they preferred to jockey and shuffle deviously in search of openings before darting in with killer blows. Maybe a slightly dated form of unarmed combat, ju-jitsu, provides the best analogy for their skill in making opponents' aggression self-destructive. However, once the adversary is off-balance, they are merciless, applying finishes that are as liable to be thunderous as refined.

Hagi exemplifies that ability to alternate between treating the ball with caressing subtlety and blasting it with controlled violence. His left foot has the much more extravagant gamut of functions and is his weapon of choice, as he showed when he used it against Argentina for two passes of breathtaking delicacy from the right wing that had the effect of picking the outer and inner locks of the Argentine defence and setting up an insouciant final thrust by Dumitrescu at the near post.

But his confidence in his right was demonstrated later in the same match by the unhesitating thump with which he turned an adroitly measured pass from Dumitrescu into the third Romanian goal that was to prove fatal to South American challengers weakened by the removal of Maradona and the truncated rest period they were given after losing to Bulgaria. It is hard to believe that a more searing shot will be struck in the World Cup.

By putting himself at the centre of such dramatic moments Hagi has persuaded many that his is the outstanding contribution to the tournament so far. That is scarcely a judgment to draw angry objections, for his play is constantly alive with thrilling possibilities and enough of them have been realised here to electrify the vast crowds that have become standard across America. His devastating interventions are so unmistakably touched with greatness, so representative of the highest arts the game can offer, that the listing of his name on the team-sheet quickens the heartbeat.

But if his brilliance is undeniable, it is also undeniably sporadic. Whether he is assessed on the basis of any one match or his entire career to the age of 29, sustained effectiveness has never been his currency. His talent has always been a recurring comet rather than a bright and steady star. The consensus among professional football men in Western Europe has been that he lacked the commitment and consistency to guarantee the proper exploitation of his exceptional gifts. That is why there was far more scepticism than envy among the managers of English clubs gathered at the World Cup when word came through that Tottenham Hotspur were trying to secure his transfer from Brescia in Italy.

They pointed to the poor return gained by Real Madrid when they signed Hagi after Italia '90. He managed only three goals in 29 matches during his first season. His haul improved to 12 in 1991–92, but neither his experience in Spain nor what he has done with Brescia (his initial season, 1992–93, brought relegation from Serie A but they recovered swiftly and have just been promoted), convinces the English doubters that Spurs and Barcelona, their most publicised rivals for Hagi's contract, are reading the evidence accurately. Even his performances in the USA are seen by some as, at best, blurring rather than dispelling the fundamental questions about his value as a club player.

John Giles, whose small, compact physique, balanced movement and guileful ways while in his prime with Leeds United and Ireland are instantly brought to mind by the sight of Hagi, has not allowed the comparison to discourage him from criticising the Romanian hero sharply on Irish television. Giles is as appreciative as anybody of his flourishes of class but condemns his failure to be persistently involved, his willingness to be a bystander for long spells while others are obliged to compensate for his remoteness.

If Hagi can ignore such distant rebukes, the same cannot be said of the criticism he has received from Romania's coach, Anghel Iordanescu, who confirmed at a Los Angeles press conference in midweek that he diluted the tide of adulation with a few home truths after his travel-worn team were beaten 4–1 in Detroit by Switzerland in the first phase. All players, he said, must submit to the same tactical discipline. But Iordanescu, who scored 26 goals in 64 appearances for his country, recognises Hagi as a uniquely inspirational figure in Romanian football and is obviously delighted he has shed the rolls of fat that were encumbering him only a few months ago.

His will, too, has apparently been honed for a determined challenge in America and though he is sensitive about suggestions that he has undersold his abilities in the past, there are signs that he senses the need to show the world his worth before it is too late. We must assume that the application of his genius will always be sporadic, that the pattern is ineradicable, but he seems in the mood to make his spectacular intrusions on the field more telling than ever.

. Perhaps he is encouraged as never before by the emergence in time for this championship of a remarkably talented crop of Romanian players. There are impressive defenders, such as the resolute Prodan and Belodedici, a composed, intelligent sweeper. The midfielders have functioned well around the anchoring presence of Popescu and, when the renowned counter-assaults are launched, Hagi is by no means sure to monopolise the glory. Raducioiu, at 24, is a striker of exciting quality, and Dumitrescu, often attacking from wide on the left, has been extraordinary. Dumitrescu has pace and excellent feet and he homes in on goal with a natural predator's certainty. He, rather than Hagi, may be the man the likes of Spurs should be coveting. But Hagi gives the impression that being surrounded by a cast of such gifted kinsmen might inspire him to dominate centre stage in professional sport's greatest theatre. His dark eyes were wary through most of that press conference in the week but he brightened when talking about his relationship with the squad. 'It is important that at my age I am together with such a group of players,' he said. 'It is good to have the chance to be in this generation of Romanian footballers.'

He is convincing when he says the players feel they have a heavy obligation to the hundreds of thousands who poured into the streets of Bucharest to acclaim their win over Argentina and are hailing the World Cup run as the most joyous uplifting of their daily lives since the Ceausescu dictatorship was overthrown. A son of Ceausescu has travelled with the squad, but everything that is said around the camp about the current success tends to come back to the way the spirit of Romanian football was liberated after the revolution.

'Our country has always possessed very talented players,' Iordanescu said, 'but in the past, because of the political system, they could not cultivate their own image, their personality in terms of showing the people what they could offer, what they could give. After the revolution the players were able to sign contracts with professional teams where they could show their true ability and true value.'

Hagi spoke specifically of the revolution's impact on the working life of footballers: 'For those of us who are playing overseas, the vital effect is obviously a broadening of experience. But for the players who stayed at home there is something more basic. They have come to understand that sport is competition, that even if someone is your best friend it is not wrong to want to be better than he is.'

Now Hagi and his friends mean to force us to admit that they are better than the footballers of every other nation on earth. Just getting past Sweden will be enough of a problem. But I confess to hoping that they manage it.

The hand of immortality beckons the Brazilians

(*The Sunday Times*, 17 July 1994)

NOBODY AT this World Cup final will better understand what it means to the Brazilian players, how the good or bad after-shocks of one Californian afternoon are going to ripple through the rest of their lives, than Dr Eduardo Gonçalves.

In another place, another time, Dr Gonçalves had another name. He was Tostão, one of the greatest footballers even Brazil has ever produced, a member of the elite within an elite who shaped the World Cup triumph in Mexico 24 years ago that may have represented the highest point of beauty and sophistication the game is destined to reach.

Now, as the parching effects of two and a half decades without the championship create a fever of expectancy among their countrymen, spreading a nervous heat to the players being asked to end the drought, a number of the men who won the Cup with unforgettable élan in the Aztec Stadium have gathered in Los Angeles. Pele, Gerson, Carlos Alberto and Rivelino are all here. But the most interesting presence is that of Dr Gonçalves, alias Tostão, not least because of the efforts he made over 20 years to separate those identities.

The obsessive concern with football in Brazil, the tendency to invest it with an importance that Bill Shankly might have found excessive, was always likely to be a problem for a man as serious as Tostão. On the field, in every fluent movement of his slight, well-balanced figure there was evidence of cerebration. Such signs can be misleading, for many men who play like intellectuals give the impression of suffering an instant shrinking of the brain whenever they step off the park. But for Tostão, the focus of coherence in that sublime 1970 attack, the difficulty was forcing others to accept how much his interests widened after he stopped kicking the ball.

He saw the narrow existence of an icon as a form of doom. His retirement had been advanced by eye trouble that would have denied him glory in Mexico but for brilliant surgery performed in Houston, Texas, and once he stopped playing to concentrate on his medical career in his home city of Belo Horizonte, he took elaborate pains to distance himself from football. He never went near matches, much less the Brazilian radio and television programmes that purvey endless talk about them. Tostão (it is the term for a tiny coin and was a nickname earned by his slightness as a youth) disappeared inside the rather portly persona of Dr Gonçalves.

That the former self has re-emerged here as a television commentator strikes some romantics as talismanic.

At a more practical level, Tostão has aided the cause with supportive comments about the policies of Brazil's coach, Carlos Alberto Parreira. That might seem natural, since Parreira's approach draws heavily on the unique experience of Mario Zagalo, who helped to win the trophy as a player in 1958 and 1962 and managed the successful challenge in 1970. But others from Zagalo's Mexican brigade, notably Pele and Gerson, have been bitterly critical of the present regime, castigating Parreira as a betrayer of the lyrical soul of Brazilian football.

Tostão understands their nostalgia but endorses the coach's assertion that worldwide developments, especially improved athleticism and increasing attention to tactical organisation, enforced compromise. The case made by Parreira, both verbally and through the performances of his players, is essentially convincing and it is hard to dismiss the suspicion that some of the condemnations coming down from the gods' gallery are nourished by the fact that he did not have a professional career as a player.

His CV as a coach includes a Brazilian club championship with Fluminense, a previous brief spell in control of the national team and appearances in the World Cup finals of 1982 and 1990 with Kuwait and the United Arab Emirates. He is intelligent and articulate and, in partnership with Zagalo, he makes effective statements on the field, too.

Having lost three key central defenders (Ricardo Gomes, Ricardo Rocha and Mozer) as a result of injury, and the exciting Leonardo from left-back because of suspension, his achievements since recalling Branco at full-back and drafting Aldair and Marcio Santos into the middle of the defence must impress any objective witness. If competence far outweighs inspiration in his midfield, that does not reflect conservatism so much as the conspicuous absence of a Gerson, a Rivelino or a Falcão from Brazil's current resources.

At least they have Bebeto and Romario (the forward Tostão rates unequivocally as 'the best in the world') and Parreira can scarcely be accused of failing to exploit their talents. Yet unfair allegations of dull pragmatism persist. 'Do you expect me to win the World Cup with a disorganised Brazil?' he asked in exasperation the other day. 'We still apply the main principles of the Brazilian way, with a flat back four, zonal marking and the emphasis on possession of the ball.'

The intensity of the pressure crowding in on the 51-year-old coach and the squad he will take to the Rose Bowl today is not readily comprehended by people from other nations – even those, like our own, with powerful sports traditions. Few races are more passionate about football than the Italians and no country's media could sustain a more vindictive scrutiny than Arrigo Sacchi and his players will have to endure if they are deemed to have let their public down. But, obviously, the game cannot pervade an old, culturally rich society like Italy's as totally as it does the younger, rawer society of Brazil.

Nor is there a comparable phenomenon elsewhere in South America. The grimmest event associated with this World Cup, the murder in Medellin of Andres Escobar, the defender who scored an own goal in Colombia's defeat by the United States, presumably had more to do with drugs and gambling than demented nationalism. Football is huge in Colombia but not quite as central to everyday experience as it has long been in the vast neighbour to the south.

There have, admittedly, been signs for years now that the Brazilian passion for the game was being steadily diluted. Newer sports have laid claim to the allegiance of large sections of a population that has nearly doubled (90 million to 155 million) in the past quarter of a century. Volleyball, at which Brazil leads the world, has an immense following and, of course, the dramatic feats in motor racing of such as Emerson Fittipaldi, Nelson Piquet and, above all, the late Ayrton Senna have hypnotised the nation. The days when crowds of 150,000 were regularly attracted to Maracana in Rio have long gone.

A considerable percentage of today's Brazilians were unborn when Carlos Alberto, having imperiously driven in the last of the four goals that swamped Italy in that 1970 final, held the Jules Rimet Trophy up in a captain's salute to the acres of yellow-and-green flags and banners that danced around the Aztec Stadium. As the average attendances at club matches continued to slide downwards, it was natural to conclude that at last the old spell was broken and the most remarkable hold any sport ever exerted on the emotions of an entire race was loosening. Maybe, if you take the long-term view, it is. But neither Rio nor the Rose Bowl will be the place to look for confirmation today. For the moment at least, the love affair is as torrid as ever.

Brazil is awash with social and economic problems and last month the worst cold snap in almost 20 years did terrible damage to the coffee fields. It will take a lot more than a decent crop of footballers to compensate for all that hardship. But a repeat of the 1970 annihilation of Italy would provide a cheering respite.

Romario: a hitman from the streets

(*The Sunday Times*, 17 July 1994)

WHEREVER HE goes, on or off the football field, Romario carries with him a sense of big-city streets. His game, like his personality, reflects an upbringing in a Rio slum where it was advisable to take before being taken.

He has the quickness of mind and body to thrive in crowds, especially crowds of defenders in the penalty box. While other forwards seek the comfort of open spaces, he is inclined to head into jostling concentrations of opponents, confident his pickpocket's deftness will leave them embarrassed and give him the scoring chances that are the spoils of such calculated hustling. The Brazilian coach, Carlos Alberto Parreira, described him simply as a killer in front of goal, and the range of his finishing techniques is ample justification.

Of course, no striker's method is infallible and Romario's surging, jinking penetrations – his close-quarters exploitation of a swirl of intricate feints and a touch on the ball that seems too delicate to be associated with his short and sturdy legs – never materialised when his club, Barcelona, were slaughtered by the rampant brilliance of Milan in the European Cup final two months ago. But that was a collective, not an individual, disaster, and one in which only a fevered imagination will discern omens for Brazil's meeting with Italy in today's final. Romario's menace was snuffed out in Athens like a candle in a whirlwind, but it could always be expected to reassert itself within the stimulating company of his national team here.

No one was less shocked than he was when the goal that belatedly killed off the outclassed Swedes in Wednesday's semi-final at the Pasadena Rose Bowl left him well placed to claim the golden boot awarded to the top scorer in the tournament. Having struck for the fifth time in this World Cup, by hoisting his stocky, 5ft 6in frame to an improbable altitude for the kind of hammering downward header he acknowledges is a rarity in his arsenal, he made it plain that he thinks both he and his team are exactly where they deserve to be.

Yet there is nothing offensive or irritating about the self-belief that comes off him in waves. His capacity to upset a variety of managers at both club and international level, from Bobby Robson at PSV Eindhoven (his base before Barcelona) to Sebastião Lazaroni, who was in charge of the Brazil squad for Italia '90, must be accepted as proof that his subjective interpretation of his responsibilities often makes his behaviour hard to tolerate. However, the impression he has given in interviews here is not of an arrogant brat but of an intelligent, irreverently witty 28-year-old whose outspoken independence can be charming, even if the determination to avoid taking rubbish from anyone probably spills over too frequently into troublesome awkwardness.

Reluctance to curb his tongue has cost him many caps. He has 59, compared with the 88 gained by Bebeto, the lithe, smoothly destructive forward from La Coruña who is his main rival in the goalscoring charts of the Spanish League but has formed a thrillingly productive partnership with him in the past month. Bebeto is two years older but there would be less of a discrepancy in the caps totals had Romario not angered Mario Zagalo, one of the giant figures of Brazilian football and currently the highly influential assistant to Parreira, with yet another unloading of provocative opinions after being left out of a friendly match with Germany in Porto Alegre in December, 1992. Leaving him out became a habit until Brazil's worrying form in the qualifying series for the World Cup forced his recall for the last of those games, against Uruguay.

Scoring the two goals that guaranteed a passage to the USA was not likely to quieten him, and sure enough he arrived in America amid stories that he had refused to sit beside Bebeto on the flight north. In fact, the bother originated with the Woolworth psychology of an official who sought to promote camaraderie by seating him between Bebeto and a third forward, Muller, who happens to be someone Romario really doesn't like.

Suggestions of deep animosity between himself and Bebeto were difficult to credit as they shared a press conference in the week. They exchanged a string of compliments and Romario gave his more shy and sensitive 'friend' one boisterous cuddle. 'Bebeto knows how much I like and respect him,' he said. 'But we are very different people. The only thing we have in common is that we both score goals. Bebeto off the field is more the type who stays at home. I'm a street cat.'

There is a continuing connection with the streets of his past in the neighbourhood bar he bought for his father in Vila da Penha in northern Rio. Romario, who is a cafuso, of mixed black and Indian blood, has always been close to his father and the bond became even stronger early in May when the older man suffered the ordeal of being held for several days by kidnappers, who then released him without securing a ransom.

Though he enjoys life in Spain with his wife Monica and their two children, Romario's heart remains in the city where he was so much of a prodigy that he signed for Vasco da Gama at 14. Football lifted him out of Favela do Jacarezinho. But today the entire Brazilian nation may have cause to be grateful that nothing could ever take the favela out of his football.

It was not Romario's finishing but a penalty shoot-out that enabled Brazil to beat Italy in the World Cup final and claim the unique distinction of being champions for a fourth time.